Digging for Words

Archaeolinguistic case studies from the
XV Nordic TAG Conference held at the
University of Copenhagen, 16–18 April 2015

Edited by

Rune Iversen
Guus Kroonen

BAR International Series 2888

2018

Published in 2018 by
BAR Publishing, Oxford

BAR International Series 2888

Digging for Words

ISBN 978 1 4073 1642 0

© The editors and contributors severally 2018

COVER IMAGE *Map of the distribution of languages across the world. Image created by 'Lazar Taxon', and used under a GNU Free Documentation License.*

The Authors' moral rights under the 1988 UK Copyright,
Designs and Patents Act are hereby expressly asserted.

All rights reserved. No part of this work may be copied, reproduced, stored,
sold, distributed, scanned, saved in any form of digital format or transmitted
in any form digitally, without the written permission of the Publisher.

Printed in England

PUBLISHING

BAR titles are available from:

          BAR Publishing
          122 Banbury Rd, Oxford, OX2 7BP, UK
EMAIL info@barpublishing.com
PHONE +44 (0)1865 310431
FAX +44 (0)1865 316916
          www.barpublishing.com

Contents

List of Maps and Illustrations iv

List of Tables iv

List of Contributors v

Session Programme vi

Preface vii
Rune Iversen and Guus Kroonen

Investigating Interaction between South America and West Mexico through the Lexicon of Metallurgy 1
Kate Bellamy

(Re)considering the Archaeolinguistics of Mesoamerica 20
Kathryn M. Hudson and John S. Henderson

Re-examining the Linguistic Prehistory of Aleut 31
Anna Berge

An Archaeology of Air 39
Jeff Benjamin

Maritime Helsinki – Two Case Studies Combining Archaeology and Linguistics in the Helsinki Archipelago 46
Annukka Debenjak, Marika Luhtala and Paula Kouki

Vectors of Language Spread at the Central Steppe Periphery: Finno-Ugric as a Catalyst Language 58
Johanna Nichols and Richard A. Rhodes

Notes on the Indo-European Vocabulary of Sheep, Wool and Textile Production 69
Birgit Anette Olsen

Ancient Witches and Modern Folktales in the Archaeological Records of Northern Italy 78
Debora Moretti

List of Maps and Illustrations

Location of languages in West Mexico 5
Location of languages in the Isthmo-Colombian Area 5
Location of languages in the Andes and neighbouring regions 6
Distribution of terms for 'gold' in the Andes 7
Distribution of Jicatuyo and Choloma ceramic supersystems 26
Magdalena Red-painted olla (Jicatuyo supersystem) 26
Conejo Bichrome bowl (Choloma supersystem) 26
Distribution of Lenca varieties 26
The Helsinki archipelago 46
GIS models of sea level change for Villinki and Vallisaari 47
Archaeological sites by type and period in the Helsinki area 49
Villinki on Samuel Broterus' map from 1697 51
Villinki in 1798 52
Vallisaari ("Aleksanders ön") and the surrounding islands 54
The Uralic range 62

List of Tables

Prehistoric loanwords between Aleut and non-Eskimo languages 34
Neolithic to Bronze Age on the western and central steppes 58
PU and PIE lexical sharings 64
Total PU and PIR matches 65

List of Contributors

Kate Bellamy, Leiden University Centre for Linguistics, Leiden University

Jeff Benjamin, Department of Anthropology, Columbia University in the City of New York

Anna Berge, Alaska Native Language Center, University of Alaska Fairbanks

Annukka Debenjak, Archaeology Department, University of Helsinki

Rune Iversen, SAXO-Institute - Archaeology, Ethnology, Greek & Latin, History, University of Copenhagen

Guus Kroonen, Department of Nordic Studies and Linguistics, University of Copenhagen

John S. Henderson, Department of Anthropology, Cornell University

Kathryn M. Hudson, Department of Anthropology and Department of Linguistics, University at Buffalo

Marika Luhtala, Department of Finnish, Finno-Ugrian and Scandinavian Studies, University of Helsinki

Debora Moretti, Department of History, Bristol University

Johanna Nichols, Department of Slavic Languages and Literatures, University of California (Berkeley)

Paula Kouki, Archaeology Department, University of Helsinki

Birgit Anette Olsen, Department of Nordic Studies and Linguistics, University of Copenhagen

Richard A. Rhodes, Department of Linguistics, University of California (Berkeley)

Session Programme

Day one, April 17

Laura Wright (University of Cambridge): On the house-name *Sunnyside* in England and Scotland.

Michael Lerche Nielsen (University of Copenhagen): Place-names and archaeology.

Klavs Randsborg (University of Copenhagen): "Latin & Lies" – Readings of early literary sources on the North.

Marika Mägi (University of Tallin): Languages in action: Two modes in overseas communication in the Viking Age eastern Baltic.

Ulrika Rosendahl (University of Helsinki): Medieval encounter – language and settlement during the Swedish colonization of Southern Finland.

Paula Kouki, Annukka Debenjak, Marika Luhtala, Terhi Ainiala, Mika Lavento (University of Helsinki): Maritime Helsinki - reconstructing the settlement history of Helsinki archipelago by means of toponomastic and archaeological research.

Gerd Carling (University of Lund): Cultural vocabularies in relation to cultural artifacts and practices. An excursion in Indo-European linguistics and archaeology from the viewpoint of subsistence system taxonomy

Debora Moretti (Bristol University): Ancient Witches and Modern Folktales in the Archaeological Records of Northern Italy.

Mark Clendon (University of Adelaide): Hierarchy and architecture in Old Europe.

Jeff Benjamin (Columbia University): An Archaeology of Air.

Anna Berge (University of Alaska): Reexamining the linguistic prehistory of Aleut.

Day two, April 18

Rosa-Maria Worm Danbo (University of Copenhagen): A Study of the Major Sound Changes in the Greater-Ch'olan-Tzeltalan Branch of the Mayan Language Family and Their Applications to Maya Epigraphy.

Kathryn M. Hudson (University at Buffalo) & John S. Henderson (Cornell University): (Re)Considering the Archaeolinguistics of Southeastern Mesoamerica.

Kate Bellamy (Leiden University): Investigating interactions between West Mexico and the Andes using the lexicon of metallurgy.

Koen Bostoen, Bernard Clist, Pierre de Maret, Gilles-Maurice de Schryver (University of Ghent): Linguistic and archaeological perspectives on population dynamics in the Lower Congo: Matches and mismatches.

George van Driem (University of Berne): Archaeology, Linguistics and Genetics: Rice and People in the Eastern Himalayan Corridor.

Johanna Nichols (University of California, Berkeley): Domestication and language spreads in early northern Eurasia.

Birgit Anette Olsen (University of Copenhagen): The Indo-European Vocabulary of Sheep, Wool and Textile Production.

Wolfgang Haak (Max Planck Institute for the Science of Human History), Iosif Lazaridis, Nick Patterson, Johannes Krause, David Anthony, Alan Cooper, Kurt Werner Alt and David Reich: Late Neolithic migration from the steppe as a likely source for Indo-European languages in Europe.

Hans-Jürgen Bandelt (University of Hamburg): Early spread of Indo-European languages through interdemic socioeconomic networks: a cautionary note.

Bjarne Simmelkjær Sandgaard Hansen (University of Copenhagen): Teaching Archaeolinguistics.

Guus Kroonen & Rune Iversen (University of Copenhagen): Summing-up.

Preface

In this volume of British Archaeological Reports (BAR), we offer a selection of case studies on the interface between linguistics and archaeology. These case studies were presented at the session 'Archaeology and Language – the Future of Archaeo-Linguistic Studies' at the XV Nordic Theoretical Archaeology Group (Nordic TAG) hosted by the Departments of Archaeology and Near Eastern Archaeology at the University of Copenhagen in April 2015.

The concept leading to this session was conceived following a rather serendipitous cooperation between the two session organisers that had begun at Copenhagen University several years earlier (Iversen & Kroonen, 2015, 2017). Although being active in different fields, archaeology and linguistics, we found that the chronological and geographic scope of our independent research projects showed a considerable overlap, notably in the isolation and interpretation of the evidence for contact between hypothesized cultural and linguistic groups in Late Neolithic and Early Bronze Age Denmark (see Iversen and Kroonen 2015, 2017. It was the ensuing dialogue between our disciplines that inspired us to organize this meeting.

The main goal of the session was to present new and ongoing studies that combine aspects of archaeology and linguistics, theoretical perspectives on the field of archaeolinguistics and to encourage more new, worthwhile studies on archaeology and language. The questions we raised in this session focussed on the future of archaeolinguistic research, namely: What can we learn from each other? And what kind of research questions are particularly suitable for future integrated studies?

We, as the organisers of the session, were very happy with the great interest it attracted. It was the largest session at that year's Nordic TAG with contributions covering large parts of the world and spanning many different time periods and topics (see below). In particular, we would like to thank the linguists and archaeologists who contributed to this volume, but we also like to thank the rest of the participants who presented their papers, as well as all of those who attended our session and participated in the discussions.

The session resulted in a number of contributions, which we have ordered according to geographic location. We set off in the Americas, following the metallurgical links between South America and West Mexico as studied by Kate Bellamy. We remain here to enjoy John S. Henderson and Kathryn M. Hudson's study of the archaeolinguistics of Mesoamerica, then move on to North America with Anna Berge's re-examination of the linguistic pre-history of the Aleut languages. Somewhere along the heavily urbanized Atlantic coast of the United States, we take off with Jeff Benjamin's archaeology of air, landing in Europe to engage in an archaeolinguistic survey of the Helsinki archipelago. From here Johanna Nichols guides us to the east, tracing the spread of the Uralic languages along the ancient Fur Road. Finally, we turn back to Europe with Birgit Olsen's inroads into the Indo-European terminology for wool and textiles in Italic. Here, we conclude our journey with Debora Moretti's archaeolinguistic study of the North-Italian folklore concerning witchcraft.

Thanks are due to the staff at BAR Publishing, in particular Jane Burkowski and Chris Myers, for their help in producing this volume. We also thank the anonymous peer reviewers, both those involved in the initial assessment of the individual papers and those who reviewed the volume in its entirety at a later stage. The scholars behind these two rounds of reviews were enormously helpful at raising the quality of this publication, for which we are highly grateful. Finally, we thank Anthony Jakob, who assisted enormously in proofing and correcting the language of the final draft of this volume.

Rune Iversen (University of Copenhagen)
Guus Kroonen (Universities of Leiden and Copenhagen)

References

Iversen, R. and G. Kroonen (2015), "Arkæolingvistik - kan vi bruge sprogvidenskaben til noget?", *Arkæologisk Forum*, 33, 3-7.

—— (2017), "Talking Neolithic: Linguistic and Archaeological Perspectives on How Indo-European Was Implemented in Southern Scandinavia", *American Journal of Archaeology*, 121 (4), 511-25.

Investigating Interaction between South America and West Mexico through the Lexicon of Metallurgy

Kate Bellamy[1], Leiden University Centre for Linguistics

1. Introduction

Scholars in several disciplines have suggested the existence of long-distance interaction between peoples in the Andean region of South America and West Mexico[2] from the Formative period to the Late Postclassic[3]. In archaeology, the evidence for this contact includes similarities in weaving techniques and clothing styles (Anawalt, 1992), shaft tombs and their funerary offerings (Albiez-Wieck, 2011: 405), certain pottery styles (Coe & Koontz, 2008: 48), and metallurgical techniques and objects (Hosler, 2009, 1994; Gorenstein & Pollard, 1983). Recent findings in genetics (Brucato et al., 2015) indicate the presence of a small but significant Andean component in certain Mesoamerican populations, also suggesting contact between the two regions. In linguistics, Swadesh's (1967) proposed genealogical link between Purépecha in West Mexico and Quechua in the Andes has been largely discredited (Campbell, 1997), but does continue to hold sway in some, less mainstream, circles (e.g. Sánchez Diaz, 1999).

Of the different types of evidence offered for this long-distance interaction, metallurgy is the most convincing. While the origins of extractive metallurgy continue to be debated, it is clear that it evolved independently in more than one place worldwide (Radivojević et al. 2010: 2775), with the Americas providing a particularly compelling example (Mapunda, 2013) outside of the Old World. However, metallurgy as a complex multi-stage technology was present prehistorically in only three regions of the Americas: (i) the Peruvian/Andean area, (ii) Colombia-Lower Central America, and (iii) West Mexico (Maldonado, 2012; West, 1994). The two phases of metalworking identified for West Mexico (Hosler, 1994: 45) both display remarkable influence from South America, notably Colombia in Phase One (roughly from 700-1100 CE) and the Andean/Pacific coast regions in Phase Two (from around 1100 CE onwards), in terms of both the techniques used and objects produced. Even more convincing is the notable lack of technological evolution in West Mexico, suggesting a direct import rather than a local development (Hosler, 1994: ch. 6).

The presence of prototype artefacts and South American-style technological information in West Mexico points to the presence of South American metalworkers. Traders from the south may have imparted some knowledge of metallurgy, but in order for a complete transfer to take place, and in the absence of continuous overland diffusion, metalworkers must have come to West Mexico (Hosler, 1994: 185). It seems reasonable, therefore, to postulate that interaction took place for the steps involved in this complex process to be transmitted. In this paper, I investigate this proposed interaction through the lexicon of metallurgy, seeking to identify lexical borrowing as evidence of interaction between peoples from the two regions. Minimally, one could expect the transfer of key lexical elements related to processes and objects, elements that may survive in a language beyond the lifespan of the contact event. However, I find no evidence of such language contact between the two regions in metallurgy-related vocabulary. This result contradicts certain findings from archaeology and genetics, but can be explained in terms of the largely non-verbal nature of the transmission of technical knowledge, as well as the cultural continuity of technology.

The rest of this paper is structured as follows: Section two offers an overview of the evidence for the proposed interaction between the two regions from archaeology, genetics and linguistics. Section three outlines the linguistic material and samples used, while section four presents the key results. I offer a discussion of the results in section five and conclude the paper in section six.

2. Background
In this section, I provide an overview of the evidence for interaction between South America and West Mexico from archaeology (2.1), genetics (2.2) and linguistics (2.3).

2.1 Archaeology
Interaction between the Andean and northwest Pacific coast regions of South America (notably Ecuador and northern Peru) and West Mexico has been posited for periods from the Early Formative to the Late Postclassic. Early statements lacked stratigraphic support and so relied solely on surface similarities: consider Reichel-Dolmatoff's pronouncement that there was "something vaguely familiar" about the Capacha material (Kelly, 1980: 35). Borhegyi (1961: 143-144) more systematically assembled a list of eight groups of parallel traits found in the two regions: settlement patterns, ceramics, techniques, figurines, miscellaneous pottery objects, stonework, metallurgy and miscellaneous traits, although many of them now seem too general to be diagnostic of interaction. Nonetheless, the largely unidirectional south to north nature of the transfer (but see the

---

[1] I would like to thank Willem Adelaar, Alex Geurds, Hans Roskamp, Matthias Pache and an anonymous reviewer for their comments on this paper. The research leading to these results has received funding from the European Research Council under the European Union's Seventh Framework Programme (FP7/2007-2013) / ERC Grant Agreement No. 295918.

[2] West Mexico is defined as encompassing the modern-day states of Michoacán, Jalisco, Nayarit, Colima and Sinaloa (Weaver, 1972) and perhaps also Durango, Guanajuato and Zacatecas (Adams, 1977). The area can be considered a cultural area, whose core comprises Michoacán, Nayarit, Jalisco and Guerrero.

[3] Following Coe & Koontz (2008: 236), the chronological periods cited for Mexico refer to the following: Formative/Preclassic (1800 BCE-150 CE), Classic (150-650 CE), Epiclassic (650-900 CE), Postclassic (900-1521 CE). Central Andean periods (or horizons) cited follow Lechtman (2014: 15): Archaic (pre-2000BCE), Initial period (2000 BCE-800 BCE), Early Horizon (800 BCE-0), Early Intermediate Period (0-650 CE), Middle Horizon (6550 CE-1000 CE), Late Intermediate Period (1000 CE-1450 CE), Late Horizon (1450 CE-1532 CE).

discussion of shaft tombs below), as well as the lack of these features in Central America, points to a long distance, long-term maritime interaction scenario (see, e.g., Callaghan, 2003). Furthermore, the topography of Central America between these two regions – mainly mangroves and steep slopes – makes overland travel an unlikely possibility (A. Geurds, p.c. 28/10/2015). Therefore, it is unlikely that these traits diffused gradually between groups by overland routes.

The earliest indication of interaction is provided by the Capacha cultural complex of West Mexico, dated to around 1450 BCE (Williams, 2004). Among the four types of pottery vessels associated with this horizon, the stirrup-spout pot displays affinities with similar items in archaeological contexts related to the Formative in the Andes, as well as in other parts of modern-day Mexico[4]. An example of the dichrome (red-on-cream slipping) decorative style from a similar period found in the Machalilla seacoast culture of Ecuador indicates a further possible connection with Capacha (Kelly, 1974). The later shaft tomb tradition (a possible successor of the El Opeño culture found in northwest Michoacán, also culturally linked to the Capacha complex (Williams, 2004)) of the West Mexican states of Jalisco, Colima and Nayarit also displays functional and morphological similarities with tombs located in Colombia, Ecuador, Peru, western Venezuela and Pacific Panama (Smith, 1978: 186-189). The earliest of these southern shaft tombs dates to 555 BCE at San Agustín, Colombia (Smith, 1978: 188), while the West Mexican tradition dates to the Late Formative and Early Classic periods. Moreover, we can note a similarity in type of cranial deformation known as *tabula erecta* found in Machalilla (Ecuador) and Capacha, as well as at the El Opeño and Tlatilco sites of West Mexico (Kelly, 1980: 35).

At the Chorrera-phase site of Chacras in Ecuador (c. 1500-300 BCE), hollow figurines were found that depict females wearing short skirts and mini-mantles. Very similar costumes can be observed on ceramic figurines from the West Mexican shaft tomb site of Ixtlán del Río (400 BCE-400 CE), which also display multiple earrings and geometric polychrome motifs on their clothing. The *Relación de Michoacán* (de Alcalá, 1988), a sixteenth century ethnohistory of the Tarascan[5] people, indicates that these garments were being worn in the protohistoric and early colonial periods in Michoacán.

Anawalt (1992) notes that Tarascan clothing styles differed considerably from those of other Mesoamerican groups (Anawalt, 1992: 115-116), possibly indicating outside influence. Loom-woven textile fragments found in Ecuador and West Mexico (as well as in the southwestern USA) made using the supplementary-weft and alternating-warp float weave weaving techniques (Anawalt, 1992: 124–126) are also held up as evidence of interaction.

Some of the strongest evidence for contact lies in the domain of metallurgy. Extractive metallurgy developed relatively late in the Americas, several millennia after the Near East and Europe, emerging in the central Andean region between 1800 and 200 BCE (Maldonado, 2012), although small hammered pieces of gold and native copper have been found from the Terminal Archaic (2155–1936 BCE; Lechtman, 2014: 15). By the time of the Spanish conquest, three main metalworking areas existed in the New World: (i) Peruvian/Andean area; (ii) Colombia-Lower Central America[6], which can be divided into the Altiplano cultures and the Muisca, Quimbaya, Sinú and Tairona cultures of central/northern Columbia (Shimada, 1994); and (iii) West Mexico (Maldonado, 2012; West, 1994). These areas are not considered to be loci of independent innovation (but see de Grinberg, 1990: 21); rather many scholars propose that metallurgical techniques spread northward from South America to West Mexico via a maritime route (e.g. Arsandaux & Rivet, 1921; Edwards 1960, 1965; Hosler, 1994, 2009). Previous accounts claiming an Asian influence on metallurgy in South America particularly (e.g. Heine-Geldern, 1954) have been universally discounted.

Hosler (1994, 2009) identifies two periods in West Mexican metallurgy: (i) Period I, 700-1100 CE, which originates in Central and South America (notably Colombia), and (ii) Period II, 1100 CE to Spanish contact, stemming from the Andean and Ecuadorian coastal regions of South America. During Period I, the lost wax casting method was common in West Mexico, reflecting techniques employed in Columbia, especially amongst the Quimbaya (Shimada, 1994). Both the Tarascan and Andean cultures made intentional use of bronze and copper-arsenic alloys, seemingly for their physical and sonic properties (Hosler, 1994). In Period II, bronze[7] was also used to make practical objects such as needles, fishhooks, tweezers, axe heads, awls and possibly also agricultural *coa* blades, although the lack of weapons in both periods is notable. The colour of these alloyed

---

[4] Kelly (1980) claims, however, that this style cannot be defined as either wholly Mesoamerican or South American. This reluctance to link the two styles is also supported by the lack of stylistic similarities in the figurines found in the two regions in the same period, as well as disagreement over the tomb chronology in northwest South America (see Kelly, 1980: 36), which stretches from 1500 BCE to 500 CE. As such, the Mexican shaft tombs have temporal priority over their South American counterparts, rendering a south-to-north direction of influence harder to support.

[5] I use the term Tarascan to refer to the ancestors of the modern-day Purépecha, notably in the prehispanic and early colonial period, in line with general usage. For the modern language and people, I use the more accepted autodenomination Purépecha (see, e.g. Warren, 1991: ix-x).

[6] Some scholars (e.g. Sauer, 1966; Helms, 1979, cited in Cooke and Bray, 1985:35) contend that the evidence in Central America suggests a trade rather than production scenario. This position is countered by, for example, West (1994) and Cook and Bray (1985), mainly on the basis of descriptions found in contact-period chronicles.

[7] A curious anomaly can easily be observed, however: alloys were being produced and used in South America when metalworking was first introduced into West Mexico, but it is only after 1100 CE that alloying began to be used in the latter region. The gap in transmission is curious and has not yet been adequately explained in the literature.

objects was their most important property in this later phase, with Hosler (1994: 138-139) claiming that West Mexican metalworkers purposefully over-alloyed their bronzes in order to create objects that displayed a brilliance and radiance akin to gold and silver (see also Roskamp, 2010).

The presence of prototype artefacts and particular processing techniques certainly suggests the presence of South American metalworkers in West Mexico. Traders from the south may have imparted some metallurgical knowledge, but metalworkers proper must have come to West Mexico to transfer the technology (Hosler, 1994: 185). Indeed "[t]he physical presence of Andean artisans in West Mexico is the most plausible way to explain the transmission of smelting, smithing and casting techniques" (Hosler, 1994: 186). Hosler claims that "[s]ome elements of Period 2 metallurgy were introduced via the same maritime exchange system[8] operating off the coast of Ecuador that had earlier transmitted the technical know-how and prototype objects of Period 1. [...][9]" (Hosler, 1994: 184). Indeed, merchant groups in Ecuador and Peru had balsawood rafts and dugout canoes with sails; the former were used for shorter haul trips, e.g. to central Peru, while the larger canoes were used to travel to West Mexico (Edwards, 1960). These merchants probably travelled to West Mexico in search of the highly prized *Spondylus princeps* shells (e.g. Marcos, 1977/78). Andean demand for *Spondylus* shells could not always be met from the Ecuadorian coast alone, so merchants from this region travelled further north in search of the prized bivalve, which grows in warm waters of the Pacific Ocean in discontinuous pockets from the Gulf of Guayaquil in Ecuador to the Gulf of California (Mexico). In exchange for *Spondylus*, merchants received obsidian and copper, prized materials found further inland. It is of note that most metalworking sites in West Mexico are located along the coastal plain or have riverine access to it, i.e. where the bivalves were harvested. Hosler, Lechtman & Holm (1990) and Horcasitas (1980) also cite the appearance of so-called axe-monies dating to between 500 and 1500 CE in coastal Ecuador and Peru, as well as West Mexico and Oaxaca, as additional support for this maritime diffusion theory.

In a letter to the Spanish king (Charles V) in 1525, the chronicler Rodrigo de Albornoz wrote that Indians in Zacatula (modern-day Zacatotlán, West Mexico), at the mouth of the Río Balsas, claimed that their fathers and grandfathers spoke of the periodic appearance of other Indians from certain "islands" who came to the coast from the south in large dugout canoes (García Icazbalceta, 2010). They brought with them "exquisite" trade items and took back other local goods. If the sea was high, these traders stayed for five to six months, until the sea calmed and they could return. In contrast, the *Lienzo de Jucutacato*, a pictorial account from 1565 regarding the origins of the people of Jicalán (Michoacán), their settlement and first offices, claims that Nahuatl-speaking Toltec groups with metalworking skills arrived from Veracruz in gulf southeast Mexico, passing through Central Mexico and settling in a number of locations in Michoacán (see Roskamp 1998, 2005). This native account constitutes a sacred history, combining both historic and mythical elements to support the authors' claims to the ownership of mines and natural resources (Roskamp, 2013). It also contradicts the South American introduction of metallurgy favoured by Hosler and predecessors, while also highlighting similarities in cosmovision between central and western Mexican groups, notably the Nahuas and Tarascans.

Indeed, it should be emphasised that these essentially diffusionist accounts are not universally supported. Schulze (2008: 214-218) draws attention to relevant issues in West Mexico, notably problems in identifying the provenance of certain isotopes, as well as the lack of a complete typology of, for instance, copper bells. Furthermore, some metal artefacts, such as those found at Tzintzuntzan, Michoacán (a former capital of the Tarascan Empire), display closer similarities to others in southern Mexico and the Mayan region, suggesting a closer connection to those regions (cf. the migration scenario described in the *Lienzo de Jucutacato*, above). Moreover, since the publication of Hosler (1994), very little new material has emerged in support (or otherwise) of the South America-West Mexico connection, reflecting the difficulties associated with conducting fieldwork in much of West Mexico, but also mirroring the move away from macro-level approaches in the discipline.

2.2 Genetics

No full genetic studies have addressed the question of interaction between South America and West Mexico, although Brucato et al. (2015) offer some initial suggestive results. In this study based on a genome-wide database of 62 Native American populations, a clear 'Andean' component is identified mainly, as expected, in individuals from Andean populations. However, this Andean component is also significantly present – albeit as a very small proportion – in the genome of four Mesoamerican populations, namely the Kaqchikel, Mixtec, Maya and Purépecha. Its presence in Mesoamerica is not correlated with the presence of other South American components, thus ruling out the possibility that it was brought by contacts via the Caribbean islands. It is also virtually absent

---

[8] The more southerly arm of the Andean maritime exchange system, linking Ecuador and southern Peru, referred to here is the Chincha Kingdom of Peru, a supposedly powerful coastal state and key trading port that emerged around 1100 CE. Within this system, copper was used as an exchange commodity, and exchange rates for both gold and silver were fixed (Nigra et al., 2014: 43). So-called *mindalaes*, or merchant Indians, also bartered exotics including gold and silver from their base in Quito (Ecuador), paying tribute in, *inter alia*, gold to local lords from whose service they were exempt (Salomon, 1986: 105).

[9] Hosler also claims that "some lower Central American and Colombian components of the technology, such as buttons, may have diffused overland [...]" (Hosler, 1994: 184). I will not discuss the possibility of an overland introduction in this paper as the evidence for it is much scarcer.

in Central America, suggesting that it also was not introduced via overland routes.

We know that the Purépecha and Mixtec were renowned prehispanic metalworkers (see, e.g., Hosler, 1994; McEwan, 2000), while recurrent bat motifs on bells found in a huge cache in Honduras in the early twentieth century point to links in iconography and cosmovision with the Kaqchikel and other Mayan groups (Blackiston, 1910). Copper bells were also produced and traded in the Yucatan Peninsula, even though the metal does not occur there naturally (Paris, 2008). As such, Brucato et al. (2015) calculated the shortest distance separating each Mesoamerican group from an archaeological site with evidence of metalworking. This distance proved to be significantly correlated with the percentage of the 'Andean' component in the populations, indicating that its presence in Mesoamerica might partly be mediated by the transmission of metallurgy. While these findings are certainly suggestive of some kind of long-distance interaction, the lack of chronology – i.e. when this 'Andean' component arrived in Mesoamerica – limits their influence.

2.3 Linguistics
The linguistic evidence for a connection between South America and West Mexico is probably the least convincing, and most controversial, of the three types presented in this paper. Moreover, the connections proposed relate to genealogical rather than contact relationships, indicating a potentially different type of connection. In short, two main linguistic relationships have been proposed. The first claims a deep-time (around 46 minimum centuries) link between two language isolates: Purépecha in West Mexico and Quechua in the Andes (Swadesh, 1956, 1967). The second posits a sub-group of the Chibchan group, encompassing languages from Mesoamerica (including Purépecha), Central America and the Isthmo-Colombian area[10] (Greenberg, 1987).

The genealogical relationship proposed in Swadesh (1967) has been cited in some archaeological papers (e.g. Anawalt, 1992), somewhat problematically, as both accepted fact in linguistics and as support for a contact relationship. Campbell claims, however, that a Purépecha-Quechua relation is "out of the question" (1997: 325-326), but concedes that his decision is based on scarce linguistic evidence, since Swadesh's study was small and, tellingly, supports much archaeological evidence (see 2.1). McClaran (1976: 154) supports this view, while conceding that that linguistic relations between Mesoamerica and South America definitely exist but are "vacuously postulated in the absence of reconstructions and rules for deriving the attested languages […] from the reconstructions" (McClaran, 1976: 154).

In short, the comparative linguistic data do not currently support an argument for relatedness between languages of the two regions. But the lack of a proven genealogical connection should not rule out the possibility of finding evidence for language contact, which would support the archaeological and genetic arguments (see 2.1 and 2.2). The weight of archaeological evidence in metallurgy particularly motivates an argument for contact between people, likely artisans, of South America and West Mexico from the Late Classic onwards. Interaction generally implies some form of communication, and in both short-term and long-term scenarios, linguistic material can be transferred (see, e.g., Thomason, 2001). Through the use of two languages, lexical items can be transferred, especially in the case of culturally-specific vocabulary, often in order to fill a lexical gap. In other words, "[i]f there has been diffusion of any sort, there is every reason to suppose that some loanwords must also exist" (Swadesh, 1964: 538). This article thus explores the interaction theories put forward in archaeology and genetics through the lens of language contact.

3. Sample
Two key elements were compiled for this study: the language sample and the metallurgy vocabulary wordlist. In order to select a language sample, I first delimited the regions where metalworking is known to have occurred in the prehispanic period (from the Formative to Spanish invasion), namely: (i) Andean region, (ii) Colombia/Lower Central America (also known as the Isthmo-Colombian area)[11], and (iii) West Mexico (or, more precisely, the West Mexican Metalworking Zone (Hosler, 2009)). On the basis of known modern language distributions (e.g. Lewis et al., 2015; Kaufman, 2007), as well as colonial language surveys (e.g. Gerhard, 1993), I compiled a list of languages in the regions, totalling 104. Included were modern and sixteenth-century variants of the same language, where available (e.g. Purépecha, Nahuatl, Quechua), modern and pre-modern (but not sixteenth-century) variants (e.g. Otomí), only modern variants (e.g. Cora and Huichol, Uto-Aztecan languages spoken at the northern edge of West Mexico), or only the variant available for now extinct languages (e.g. Cuitlatec, an isolate spoken in Guerrero, Mexico until the 1940s). I also included languages of the cultures mentioned in Hosler (1994) and Horcasitas (1981) as being spoken by societies that had metallurgy, as well as a number of neighbouring languages for comparative purposes (see Figures 1-3, and Appendix A) especially relevant in cases of widespread diffusion.

---

[10] This Chibchan group comprises the following languages: Antioquia, Aruak, Chibcha, Cuitlatec, Cuna, Guaymi, Lenca, Malibu, Misumalpan, Motilon, Paya, Rama, Tlamanca, Tarascan, Xinca and Yanoama (Greenberg, 1987).

[11] The Isthmo-Colombian area, also known previously in the literature as the Intermediate Area or Chibchan Sphere, stretches from eastern Honduras in the north to Colombia and Venezuela in the south through the core of Panama and Costa Rica. For a discussion of the defining features and limits of the area, as well of the nomenclature, see Hoopes and Fonseca (2003).

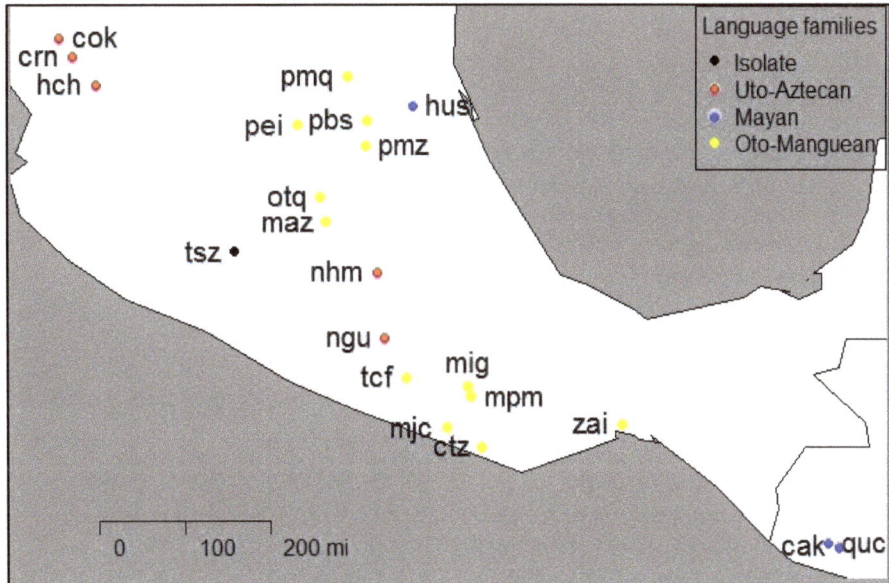

Fig. 1: Location of languages in West Mexico used in this study.

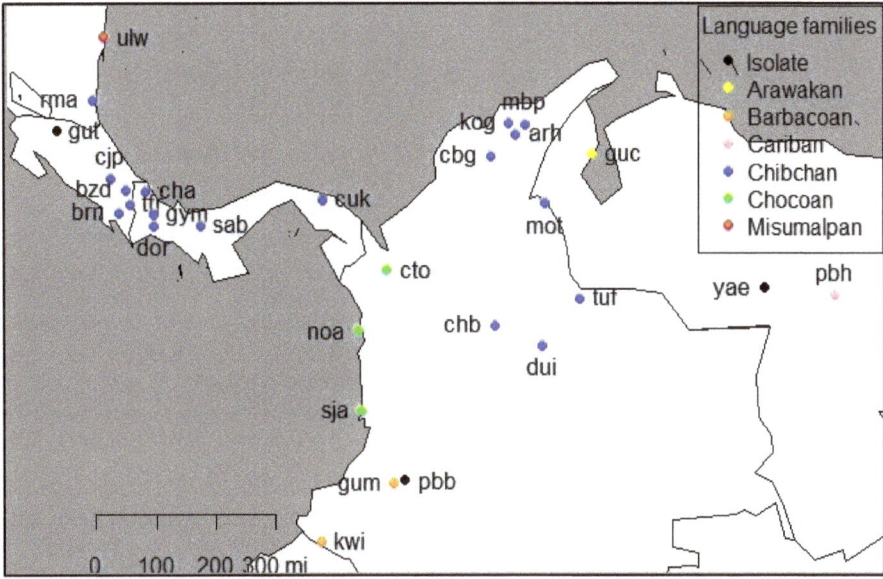

Fig. 2: Location of languages in the Isthmo-Colombian Area used in this study.

Comparative lexical studies take as their point of departure a standardised wordlist, which is completed for every language in the sample. Basic vocabulary is often collected on the basis of the so-called Swadesh (1971) or Leipzig-Jakarta lists of cross-culturally valid meanings (Haspelmath & Tadmor, 2009). Vocabulary related to more specific semantic domains may be found in, for example, the Intercontinental Dictionary Series (Key & Comrie, 2007) or Numeral Systems of the World's Languages (Chan, 2016). Given the absence of a readily available list of terms for the domain of metallurgy, I compiled a novel one comprising 123 items (see Appendix B), whose terms cover metals (e.g. copper, gold, silver), processes (e.g. to extend, polish, solder, shape), tools (e.g. file, [sledge]hammer, pliers), objects produced (e.g. bells, rattles, rings, tweezers), occupations (e.g. copper-worker, ironmonger) and the workplace (e.g. bellows, fire, pit, workshop). Key sources for this compilation were a trilingual Purépecha-Spanish-English dictionary of metalworking terms relevant to the hammered copper tradition of Santa Clara del Cobre, Michoacán (Pérez Pamatz & Lucas, 2004), and archaeological works on West Mexico (Hosler 1994, 2009) and the Andes (Shimada, 1994).

The division into categories – tools, processes, etc. – is reminiscent of the five related components that Lemonnier (1992: 5-6) claims every technology comprises, namely: (i) matter, i.e. the material on which a technique acts, (ii) energy, the forces which move objects and transfer matter, (iii) objects, often called artefacts, tools, or means of work, (iv) gestures, which move the objects involved in a technological action, and which may be organized in sequences, and (v) specific knowledge, which may be conscious or unconscious and not necessarily expressed by the actors, and constitute 'know-how' or manual skills.[12]

4. Findings

The most striking finding is the lack of clear loanwords from South America in any of the West Mexican languages in the sample. Possible explanations for this absence are discussed in Section 5. Nonetheless, a number of observations can still be made regarding loans on a smaller scale, as well as shared naming strategies between the regions for metals (Section 4.1) and metal objects (4.2).

4.1 Metal naming strategies

In the absence of any notable instances of loanwords between the areas under analysis, shared naming strategies become the most worthwhile locus of study. For terms referring to specific metals, as well as for the generic term, six naming strategies have been identified that cross-cut the three metalworking regions in the sample, namely the use of: (i) colour terms, generally compounded, (ii) other physical properties, also generally compounded, (iii) terms for excretions of different types, (iv) borrowings, (v) processes, and (vi) extensions to the environment, i.e. toponyms and hydronyms.

Let us begin with naming strategies based on colour terms. Copper is most frequently considered a red metal, named as such in Purépecha (isolate) *tiyamu charapeti* 'metal/iron red', Coastal Mixtec (Oto-Manguean) *xùhùn cuaahá* 'copper money, copper' (lit. 'money red'), Classical and Modern Huastec (Mayan) *tzacpatal* 'red iron/metal', K'iche' (Core K'iche'an) *kiäq puaq* 'red money/silver', Lengua (Lengua-Mascoy) *yan-sowu ik-yithwase* 'like red iron', and Cofán (isolate) *kiʔa yošaβa* 'red metal'. However Chiriguano (Tupían) and Wichí (Matacoan), both in South America, use terms including an element meaning 'yellow' to label their copper, viz Chiriguano *korepoti ijuag^{w}e* 'lit. mine.excrement-yellow', and Wichí *la-činah-'tʔoh kaʔteʔ* 'copper, bronze' (lit. 'poss.-iron (its) skin yellow'). Highland Mixtec, in contrast to its Coastal counterpart, displays *kaa kuaan* 'metal, iron, steel yellow' to refer to both copper and gold, while Classical Otomí also combines the terms for yellow and iron in *xancaxtii bueca* 'copper'. K'iche' (Core K'iche'an) uses a different colour again in the compound *räx ch'ich'* 'iron; steel' (lit. 'blue, green metal'). Moreover, the four colours of copper (blue, green, yellow and red, found in its various forms pre- and post-processing) can all be discerned on the insect known as the *tepuzchapule* or *chapulín del cobre* 'copper-grasshopper' in Nahuatl (Uto-Aztecan) and Spanish respectively, found in Guerrero, West Mexico (Hendrichs, 1944).

Compounds with 'money, metal' and 'white' predominate in terms for silver, for example, Coastal Mixtec (Oto-Manguean) *xùhùn cuitsín* 'money white', Mazahua

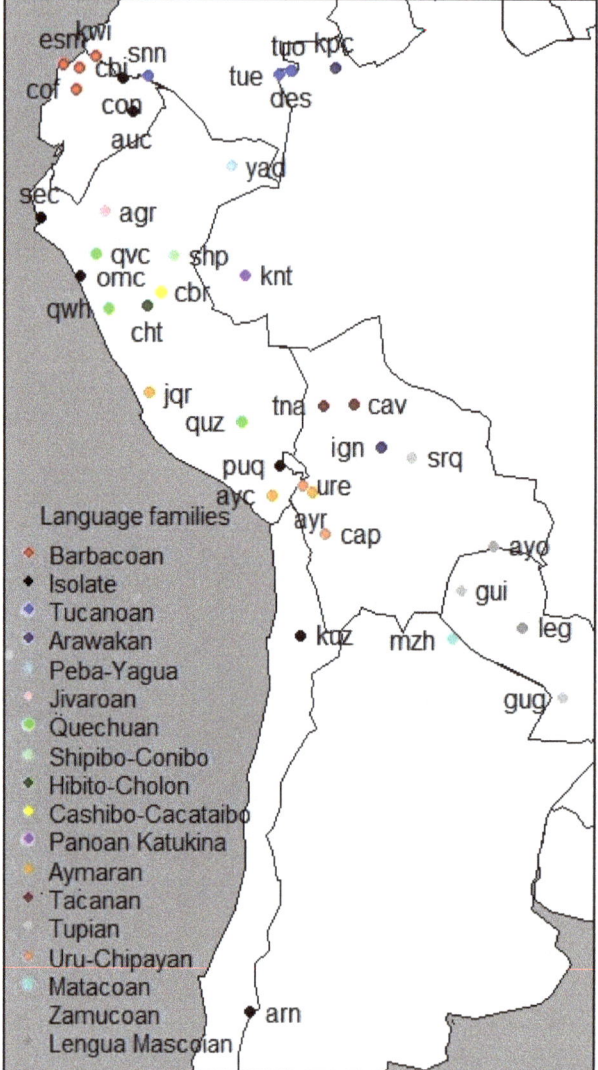

Fig. 3: Location of languages in the Andes and neighbouring regions used in this study.

(Oto-Pamean) *tʔɔxʉ* 'white', Otomí *nataxii* 'white' (the latter two forms may be related), Kaqchikel (Core K'iche'an) *saka mero* 'white money', Paez (isolate) *gueyóchime* 'white metal', Chiriguano (Tupían) *korepoti-tĩi* '(arse)hole.excrement-white', Lengua (Lengua-Mascoy) *yan-sowu ik-mopaiya* 'like white iron', and Teribe (Chibchan) *dëburr frubrunë* 'money white'.

Gold is described as yellow in Classical and Modern Purépecha (isolate) *tiripeti*, from the root *tirí-* 'dull yellow', Classical and Modern Huastec (Mayan) *taquimanul* 'yellow metal', Classical and Modern Kaqchikel (Core K'iche'an) *ʒana puvak, q'anapuwäq* 'yellow silver/money', K'iche' (Core K'iche'an) *q'än puaq* 'yellow silver, money; also copper', Coastal Mixtec (Oto-Manguean) *xùhùn cuàan* 'money yellow', Bribri *inúkür xiká skirirí* 'money material yellow' and Teribe (both Chibchan) *dëburr xoñõró* 'money yellow', Chiriguano *korepoti-ǰu* and Guaraní *kuarepoti-ǰu* (both Tupían) 'mine.excrement-yellow', Lengua (Lengua-Mascoy) *yan-sowu ik-yatiktama* 'like yellow iron', Tsafiki (Barbacoan) *laske kala* 'yellow silver'. The term for 'gold' in Miskito (Misumalpan) is synonymous with that for 'yellow' - *lalahni* – but with no compounding. Paez (isolate), on the

---
[12] An anonymous reviewer notes that Lemonnier's categorisation lacks the products of the metalworking process. While the match between the two categorisations is clearly not exact, the broad parallels are worth mentioning, especially in light of the discussion regarding the anthropology of technology and the nature of knowledge transmission in Section 5.

other hand has a term for gold including 'red' and not 'yellow': *ßyuu beh* lit. 'money red'. Ayoreo (Zamucoan) far to the south of the Andean region has *ge'beeke naaŋana-'taai* lit. 'metal that shines', although the element *naaŋana-* seems to be related to *naaŋana-'taai; naaŋana-taa-'ge* 'blue'. This relation reminds us of the Cha'palaa (Barbacoan) term *lushi* 'money', which is also related to the term for 'blue'. The colour term probably derives from the word for silver rather than vice versa; in order to construct the colour term additional morphology must be added, e.g. *lushkatata* 'blue, green' (Wiebe & Wiebe, 2015), *lushishi* 'sky blue'. The latter term demonstrates how the final syllable must be reduplicated for a special ideophone-like class of words for qualities (Floyd, p.c. 27/09/2015).

The Ayoreo 'shiny metal' example could also be included under the second naming strategy, namely that based on the physical properties of the metals. Ulwa (Misumalpan) and Guambiano (Barbacoan) emphasise the shininess of precious metals by using the terms *kî yaringka* 'gold' (lit. 'stone shiny') and *pilapik* 'gold, silver', related to the term for 'shiny' (Floyd, p.c. 27/09/2015), respectively. Aymara possesses the term *isayawri* 'very hard copper', reflecting the stronger, less brittle properties of bronze as compared with copper once heated and worked. In line with the known geographic distribution of alloying knowledge in the Andean region, we also find *kisu* 'another type of copper which the Indians used like steel because when mixed with another metal it becomes harder' in Classical Aymara (Aymaran).[13] Kallawaya (mixed language) displays *jichcha jiri* 'bronze, lit. false stone' and *llalle jiri* 'iron, copper; lit. good stone', while Uru (Uru-Chipayan) gives *čok-kxā* 'copper; lit fat silver'. In Ngäbere (Chibchan) we find *jä tuäre* 'stone beautiful' for 'gold', reminiscent of these Kallawaya compounds including a familiar material. Sonic properties are also present in the sample, but only in West Mexico with Matlaltzinca (Oto-Pamean) *inmahathi* 'silver, lit. that which rings/sounds'.

The third strategy identified is naming according to various types of excretions. In Chiriguano and Guaraní (both Tupían), we find *korepoti ijuagʷe* and *kuarepoti-ǰu* 'copper' (lit. mine.excrement-yellow); Chiriguano (Tupían) *korepoti-tĩi* 'silver' (lit. (arse)hole.excrement-white), Chiriguano *korepoti* and Guaraní *kuarepoti-ǰu* 'gold' (lit. sun=defecate-yellow, 'yellow sun faeces'). The circumlocution for copper is apparently a "Jesuitic depreciative creation" (Dietrich, 2015 [2007]), reflecting native ideas regarding the origin of metals. However, Roskamp (2010: 70) notes that two prehispanic Mesoamerican cultures also possessed conceptions related to excrement of the main celestial bodies: Nahuas, from the central valleys of Mexico, referred to gold as *teocuitlatl* 'holy shit' or *tonatiuh icuitl* 'excrement of the sun'. The Tarascans of Michoacán also believed gold to represent the sun's excrement, and silver that of the moon, but did not encode this lexically (idem.).

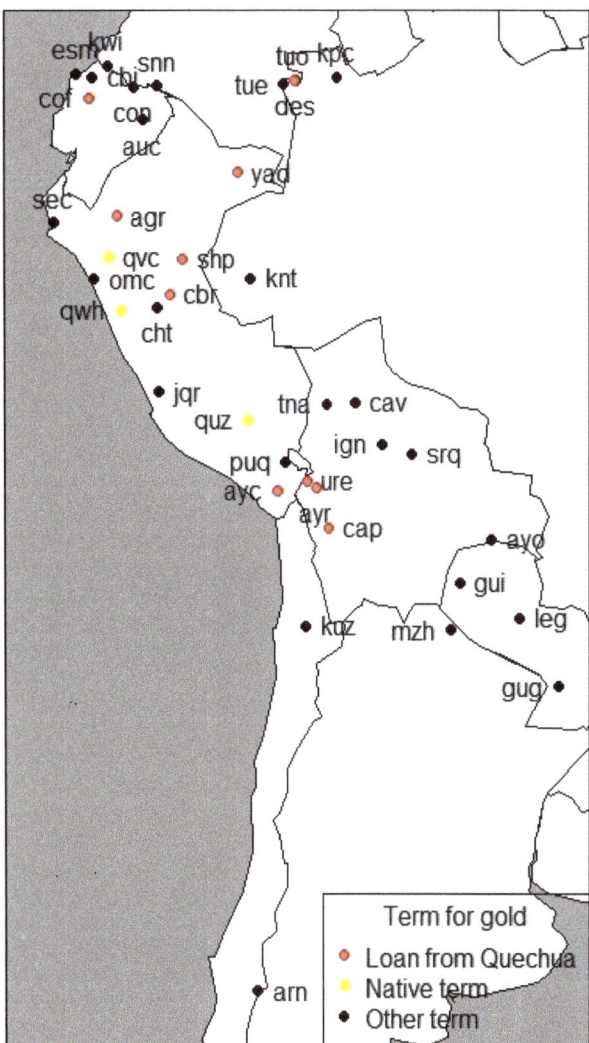

Fig. 4: Distribution of terms for 'gold' in the Andes.

As indicated in the introduction, no long-distance lexical borrowing has been identified in this study. However, borrowing at a more local level can be observed, especially in the case of Quechua *qori* 'gold' (see Figure 4). The term has been borrowed into various other languages across the Andes and Amazon regions, often with the same meaning and little phonological adaptation, viz: *qori* (Aymara, Aymaran), *qori* (also 'tin, tinplate', Chipaya, Uru-Chipayan), *qori* (Uru, Uru-Chipayan), choa-*curi* lit. 'earth gold' (Tukano, Tucanoan), *kuri* (Aguaruna, Jivaroan), *kuri* (Cashibo, Panoan), *kori* (Cofán), *kori* (Shipibo-Conibo, Panoan). A related case is *kuruki/kuriki* (Yagua, Peba-Yaguan), which is borrowed from Quechua *qullqi* 'money' despite its surface similarity to *qori*. The variation in the medial vowel reflects the lowering of the original Quechua /u/ to /o/ in a uvular environment (/q/).

No such examples of diffusion can be found in unrelated languages in Mesoamerica or the Isthmo-Colombian Area. However, it is also worth noting the case of Taíno *wanĩ* 'low grade of gold', which gives us the Modern Spanish *guanín* 'idem'. Moreover the Galibi (Cariban) term for copper, *karakuli* lit. 'money-gold', emerges as a loan in Warao (isolate) *karakori/corucuri* (also 'tool blade'), and *kalakuli* (also 'silver') in Wayampi (Tupían).

---

[13] We also find *kis* in the Chumulu dialect of Dorasque (Chibchan), which may be a loan from Classical Aymara.

Note the parallel here with Quechua *qara qori* lit. 'bare/naked gold'.

Ironsmithing only emerged in these original metalworking areas with the arrival of the Spanish, who brought their own techniques from Europe. Until that point, native technologies had focussed on copper, gold, silver and alloys thereof, notably arsenic and tin bronzes. As such, we might expect fewer native terms for 'iron', i.e. a higher proportion of loanwords from Spanish. In fact, there are no more loans from the Spanish *fierro, hierro* 'iron' in the sample than for other terms: *firru, fyerru, jirru, jyerru* (Cajamarca Quechua), *firru* (Jacaru, Aymaran), *hiru* (Chipaya, Uru-Chipayan), *hiórro* (Emberá, Chocoan), *ɸe'ro, he'ro* (Tsafiki, Barbacoan), *jeru* (Cha'palaa, Barbacoan), and *hihu* (Aguaruna, Jivaroan), a total of seven (the same as for copper), all in the Andean region.

A number of other localised borrowings are also observable: (i) Cajamarca and Classical Quechua (Quechuan) *qquillay* 'iron; silver, money' appears as *quellaya yauri* 'iron, copper, needle' in Classical Aymara; (ii) Cusco, Cajamarca and Ancash Quechua (Quechuan) *chay-anta* 'iron, metal, tin' (lit. 'shine-copper') emerges as *chunta-chay* in Uru (Uru-Chipayan) and possibly also *c'haj* in Mochica (isolate); (iii) the terms *saanzen, saanzén, santsən* 'iron' in Guambiano (Barbacoan) and *satsám, cam* 'iron, metal' in Paez (isolate) also bear a suggestive resemblance; (iv) the term *carimbo* 'iron for marking/branding Caribbean Indians and black Africans' is loaned from the Kimbundu (Angola; Central-Western Bantu) *kirimbu* (da Silva Maia, 1959) into Island Carib and from there to Taíno (Arawakan). *Carimbo* is used in modern-day Brazilian Portuguese as 'stamp', while *calimba* still exists in Cuban Spanish, but now refers to 'iron with which one brands animals' (RAE, 2014); (v) Miskito (Misumalpan) of Honduras and Nicaragua has borrowed *silak* 'steel' from the Rama (Chibchan) *shílak, sílak* 'iron'. This example demonstrates how a society with no known prehispanic metalworking has borrowed and extended a term from a neighbouring, unrelated language to fill a conceptual gap.

The fifth, but not very widespread, strategy is the use of processes used in metalworking to name the metals themselves. Siona (Tucanoan) possesses a compound that refers to the process of gathering placer gold, namely *sʔoa kut'i* lit. wash money'. Classical Quechua *hičʰay* 'to pour into mould, smelt' now refers only to the more generic verb 'to pour'. Purépecha (isolate) recalls the shaping phases of the process in *tayacata* 'silver' from the root *taya-* 'to give blows'. Shipibo-Conibo (Panoan) *yami βoi* lit. 'metal beeswax[14]' also seems to reflect an aspect of the lost-wax casting process.

Finally, terms for metals also emerge in toponyms and hydronyms in both the Isthmo-Colombian and West Mexican regions. Kuna (Chibchan) incorporates *or* 'gold' (likely not a borrowing from Spanish, cf. Cabécar (Chibchan) *oloi* 'shine') into a hydronym, *Tiórti* 'gold river'. Ngäbere (Chibchan) displays the toponym *Pocri* in Los Santos department (Panama), meaning 'place of the lance/spear' (Pinart, 1897). *Bugaba* (Dorasque, Chibchan) has the same meaning. In West Mexico copper prevails over gold in toponyms, e.g. *Tepoztlán* 'place where copper abounds' (Nahuatl, Southern Uto-Aztecan), whence *tepuztecatl* 'native of Tepoztlán'.

4.2 Naming strategies for metal objects

In the same vein as the metal naming strategies, metal objects in the sample display certain similarities in naming strategies, namely: (i) Use of metal terms (polysemy), (ii) natural world predecessors, (iii) loans (largely from Spanish), and (iv) sound symbolism, which is possibly also related to the natural world predecessors.

A large amount of polysemy is also observable in the terms for metal objects in the sample wordlist. For example in Huastec (Mayan), *patal* means 'bell' and 'lance' as well as 'metal', a pattern also partially reflected in Cuitlatec (isolate) *pihpɨ* 'bell; metal, iron'. In Awa-Pit (Barbacoan), *pyalmiŋ* 'axe' is also 'silver, money', a pattern reminiscent of the so-called axe-monies that were used as a type of currency in long-distance trade between South America and West Mexico (see, e.g. Hosler et al., 1990). Note also Quechua *tumi* 'sacrificial axe', which can also refer to these axe-monies. Miskito (Misumalpan) possesses *ayan* 'iron; plancha', Bribri (Chibchan) *ta-be* 'iron, knife, anything made of iron', Mazahua (Oto-Manguean) *tʔëzi* 'iron; machine, tractor'. Cashibo (Panoan) also classifies *mani* as 'metal axe and things of foreign origin', the Classical Huastec *lencodpatal* is literally analysed as 'fishhook-metal', while Nahuatl (Southern Uto-Aztecan) *tepuz(tli)* conflates 'pin' and 'copper'. An even broader meaning can be found in Classical Aymara (Aymaran), where *juch'usa* refers to a 'round thing such as a stick, pole, pin'.

A further example of polysemy, as well as a clear case of borrowing, is the Quechua *yawrina* 'fishhook' and Cusco Quechua *yawri* 'needle', from Aymara *yawri* 'copper, iron'. Another clear case of borrowing in the Andes is found in Classical Quechua (Quechuan) *ttipqui ttopo* 'pin', Cusco/Cajamarca/Ancash Quechua (Quechuan) *tupu* 'pin, brooch' which emerges in Puquina (Puquinan) *tupu* 'pin, needle', Classical Mapudungun *tupú* 'pin' and Chipaya (Uru-Chipayan) *tupu* 'pin'. In Mapudungun we also find *tirana* 'tweezers', borrowed from (here) Cusco Quechua *t'irana* (< *t'ira-* 'to pluck' and *-na* instrumental nominalizer) 'idem'.

Yet it is clear that new metal objects did not necessarily require a new label, especially in areas where metallurgy emerged later. Some objects that came to be made of metal had predecessors (and thus labels) in the natural world or as part of lithic or wooden technology. Examples include 'arrow', which in Damana/Malayo (Chibchan) is *bi-ngʉla* 'maguey arrow/spine', Classical Aymara (Aymaran) *piqacha, phichaqa, pichaqa* 'long needle of thorn, copper or iron that can be used for sewing'. Taíno

---
[14] The term 'wax' reconstructs to Proto-Panoan *βoičo. See also *yami with related meanings 'iron, machete, metal' (IDS, 2007), found in modern reflexes such as Amahuaca *yamí* 'metal axe', Capanahua *yami* 'axe'.

(Arawakan) had the term *manaya* 'stone knife, axe made of planks of royal palm'. We also find Guatuso (Chibchan) *zafára* 'wooden knife', Sirionó (Tupían) *yvyra raimbe* 'wooden sword' (Cadogan, 1992); Huichol (U-A) *oparu* 'stick in the form of a sword'. Chimila (Chibchan) has extended the meaning of *kaŋʔraʔ* 'arrow shaft' to 'gun' on the basis of similarities in shape or use[15]. It is also worth noting a parallel in terms for precious stones and gems, which may come to refer to new materials, as in the Quechua *qispi* 'crystal, glass', where the former term is likely the original meaning (Adelaar, p.c. 23/10/2015).

Two major Spanish loans can be noted in the terms for 'coin, money'. The first is *tumín* in various West Mexican languages: *tuminu* (Purépecha, isolate), *tamèiŋ* (Pame, Oto-Pamean), *tumino* (Cuitlatec, isolate), *tomin* (Nahuatl), *túmiin* (Cora); *tumini* (Huichol; all three Southern Uto-Aztecan), *tumin* (Huastec, Mayan); *tomim* (Classical Huastec, Mayan), *tomines* (Classical Zapotec; Oto-Manguean). *Tumino* must be a relatively early loan into Mesoamerican languages since it appears, albeit not as the simple translational equivalent for 'money', but as part of phrases containing this meaning, in the Classical Purépecha *Diccionario Grande* which, while undated, is thought to date from before or around 1587 (Warren, 1991: xix). The term also occurs in other ethnohistorical documents, such as those from Zinapecuaro (Michoacán) dating to 1566, indicating an even earlier appearance. The second major loan from Spanish is *plata* 'silver, money', found in a smaller number of only South American languages: *burata* (Warao, isolate), *parata thórro, parata* (Emberá, Chocoan), *pʰaratʰa* (Epena, Chocoan), *arata* (Panare, Cariban), *podata* (Waorani, isolate). A third and more minor loan derives from the Spanish *dinero* 'money', being found in *nnehrrü* (Guajiro, Arawakan) and *niyeruse* (Desana, Tucanoan).

Finally, there are a number of examples of apparent sound symbolism, e.g. terms for 'blowtube' or 'to blow' begin with /p-/ or /ph-/ in Quechua, Aymara, Puquina, Mochica, Kunza, Mapuche, Tsafiki, Atacame, Chipaya, Paez, Desana, Tukano, Chimila, Waunana (all South America). The Classical and Modern Quechua terms *taca taca* 'silver- or coppersmith hammerer' and *takana* 'to hammer' respectively may also fall into this category. Also note the reduplicated forms, Guatuso *kuːtʃ-kuːtʃ* 'hammer' and Warao *jurujurú* 'to file', which may reflect the repetitive action or motion both associated with the tool or process in question.

5. Discussion

We saw in Section 4 that there is little evidence of direct lexical borrowing between the Andean region and West Mexico in the domain of metalworking, despite support from archaeology and genetics for interaction in this, and other, domains. The only evidence of widespread borrowing was from Quechua to other unrelated languages in the Andes; Mesoamerica and the Intermediate Area displayed a small amount of borrowing within their own boundaries but no evidence of longer-distance loans. In this section, I will discuss several possible explanations for this absence, as well as offering tentative motivations for certain shared patterns.

The nature of knowledge transmission, in both technical processes and everyday life, may impact upon the amount of linguistic interaction between individuals. Evidence from, *inter alia*, history, ethnoarchaeology and ethnography, indicates that "the transmission of technological knowledge in pre-industrial setting was, and is, fundamentally different from that in modern industrial societies" (Killick, 2004: 573). In industrial societies, technological knowledge and skills are acquired largely through language and illustrations, whereas in non-industrial societies, technical skills were, and are, communicated "through a blend of verbal and non-verbal instruction" (Killick, 2004: 573). Pfaffenberger (1992: 501-502) also notes that another key feature of such systems "is their *silence*, the relatively insignificant role played by human language as against nonverbal communication in ritual […] as a coordinator of technical activities." The few studies of specialized crafts requiring apprenticeships (into which metallurgy falls), such as those concerning Liberian tailors (Lave, 1988) and Ghanaian weavers (Goody, 1978), have noted the small part language seems to play in the knowledge transmission process (Bloch, 1992: 186), as well as the tendency for people not to talk about the activities involved. Given that language is not central in the transmission or production processes, we could view the way in which a task is explained as a "*post hoc* overlinguistic rationalization" (Bloch, 1998: 23-24), i.e. a retrospective explanation using (an inherently inadequate) verbal medium to explain a non-verbal action.

Support for the lesser importance of language in the knowledge transmission process is also found in practical, everyday tasks, which can be viewed as culturally specific, complex and embedded in social life (Bloch, 1992: 186, following the renowned French anthropologists of technology Mauss, Leroi-Gourhan and Haudricourt). This lack of linguistic explicitness is particularly observable in the way everyday tasks are taught to children; we do not generally go through a step-by-step verbal explanation of how to do something, we often show by doing. Similarly, the process of becoming an expert in a particular domain "seems to involve the transformation of the [linguistic] propositions of the teacher into fundamentally non-linguistic knowledge" (Bloch, 1992: 187). Nonetheless, even if the explicit language used to explain a process may not constitute the most accurate record of the process itself, the fact that a process can be explained in the language of the society that uses it indicates that the terms can be communicated to members of other [linguistic] groups.

The transfer of existing terms to new metallurgical objects or processes that may be viewed as largely analogous could also account for the small number of loans. In

---

[15] I thank an anonymous reviewer for the second interpretation of the semantic extension, but cannot clarify which is more appropriate for this term.

her discussion of the transfer from stone working to copper working in the Lake Superior basin, Martin (1999: 117), following Cushing (1894), notes that "no new art [in the sense of working new or unaccustomed material] was ever practiced by aboriginal Americans as strictly new". Indeed, Cushing linked metalworking with established technologies using stone, wood, hide, shell and bark (idem.), indications of which we observed in the use of terms for pre-metal objects in Section 4.2. The methods chosen to design and produce metal (and other types of) artefacts are constrained "not only by the practicalities associated with metalworking from raw metal to finished product but also by cultural influences, some of which will have been borrowed from existing material technologies such as ceramics, carpentry and textile manufacture" (McEwan, 2000: 236). This recalls the social constructionist approach to the study of technology (see Killick, 2004 for a short overview) whereby metallurgy, along with all other technologies, is viewed as a social production determined by, or compatible with, other social phenomena (Lemonnier, 1992: 17), and as such develops as part of a particular societal system. This "fully human experience" (Hosler, 1994: 250) both draws our attention to the agency of the actors involved, as well as helping to account for cultural (and linguistic) variation in terminology and patterns of borrowing.

A further point to consider is that the contact situations for metallurgy transmission were simply of insufficient length for borrowing to occur. Lexical (and other) items will only be transferred if they are heard frequently enough; if the contact scenarios for the transfer of metallurgy were relatively short, or if indeed the linguistic element of such interactions was minimised, then the absence of loanwords is to be expected. In the case of the widely diffused terms in the Andes, the use of Quechua as a *lingua franca* and as the language of a large, powerful empire makes the imposition of terms for new materials is more understandable, with reference to linguistic dominance and exposure to new terms.

Turning from the more conceptual to the methodological, an implicit limitation of this study is the lack of data for, in particular, languages of the Ecuadorian and Peruvian coast, from where much of the maritime trade is claimed to have originated. Furthermore, I cannot claim to have included all the languages spoken in the metalworking regions prehispanically, since many of these languages died out before being described. It is well known, for example, that the population of modern-day Mexico fell by around 90% in the first 100 years of Spanish occupation, meaning a large number of languages were also lost forever. Unfortunately, these are gaps in the data that are impossible to fill and have to be accepted in a study such as this.

Nonetheless, certain patterns in the data can be observed in the three areas under study that merit consideration in the wider archaeological-anthropological context. A key factor to note from the outset is the differences in the socio-political situations in the three areas, which can impact on the type of interaction between speaker groups.

The Andes appears to be the only region where widespread lexical borrowing has occurred, for example Quechua *qori* 'gold' is found in a number of other unrelated Andean languages (see Figure 4). In other lexical domains (including basic vocabulary), Quechua influence is observed in many Andean and western Amazonian languages (Adelaar, 2012). This influence can be attributed mainly to Quechua's status as a *lingua franca* in the late stages of the Inca expansion (1470-1532 CE) and during Spanish occupation (1532-1770 CE), where it was used, *inter alia*, for Christianising purposes. As such, Quechua was imposed upon speakers of other indigenous languages, entailing the imposition of new terms perhaps related to new technologies or the knowledge of such technologies. The existence and use of a *lingua franca* also entails more stable and widespread bilingual situations, which in turn lead to the increased likelihood of borrowing. In contrast, Purépecha, the lingua franca of the Tarascan Empire of West Mexico (a heartland of metallurgy in the region), was also used by Spanish friars in the sixteenth and seventeenth centuries for evangelizing purposes (Hamel, 2008: 313), but no comparable widespread lexical borrowing can be observed. One or more of a multitude of factors could account for these differences in borrowing patterns, but direct comparisons are clearly hard to draw.

Indeed, the major dynasties of Postclassic Mesoamerica – notably the Aztec Triple Alliance and the Tarascan State – co-existed along bellicose lines until contact with the Spanish in 1519. Despite at least four languages being spoken in the Tarascan Empire (Purépecha, Otomí, Nahuatl and Cuitlatec), there is very little evidence of lexical borrowing between them, not even from Purépecha, the language of the rulers who also managed mineral resources (Pollard, 1987), to other languages.[16] The lack of borrowing is perhaps all the more surprising when we consider that Mesoamerica, which includes all of West Mexico, has been held up as a prime example of both a linguistic area (LA; Campbell, Kaufmann & Smith-Stark, 1986) and a cultural area (Kirchhoff, 1943). Of the five core features that define Mesoamerica as a LA, four are grammatical while the fifth constitutes a number of semantic calques such as 'head of leg' for 'knee' and 'stone/bone of bird' for 'egg' (Kaufman, Campbell & Smith-Stark, 1986: 554), indicating a certain amount of conceptual diffusion. We might expect more conceptual diffusion then, even if lexical borrowing *per se* is not as widely attested across the area.

A feature not included in the LA diagnostic traits, but also quite widespread, is the association of particular colours with cardinal points or directions (See De Wolf, 1994).[17] Colour symbolism is shared in the metallurgy

---

[16] But see Cuitlatec (isolate) *navajo* 'knife', from Puebla Nahuatl (Uto-Aztecan), a term that also found its way into Spanish and continues to be used across Mexico; RAE, 2014.

[17] De Wolf (1994: 182) states that "the terms for cardinal points – as rather important representatives of the cultural vocabulary of a people – can give us information about cultural contacts and in some cases about the migration paths of the ancestors of the speakers of a language." (My translation).

domain by, for example, Purépecha and Nahuatl, as in 'copper, lit. red metal/iron', as well as with Huastec, a Mayan outlier that most probably acquired metalworking from central Mexico (probably through Nahuatl speakers; see Hosler & Stresser-Pean, 1992). Yet Highland Mixtec (Oto-Manguean), also said to be part of the LA, makes use of a compound including the term 'yellow' to describe the same metal. That said, colour as a naming strategy is not restricted to Mesoamerica, or the Americas more broadly; indeed, many African languages refer to copper as "red metal" or "red iron" (Herbert, 1984: 10). Yet this variety in conceptual associations is not unusual, even in an area well connected through commercial networks such as Mesoamerica and its neighbouring regions (Weigand, 2001).

Similarly, the small number of borrowings in the languages of the Intermediate Area is intriguing, especially since the region has long been a locus of long-distance exchange and a commercial nexus (O'Connor, 2014: 77). Equally interesting is the high number of cognates per term: take for example the term 'gold' which offers at least eight cognate sets in the Chibchan languages alone. This may seem odd at first sight, given how genetically (Barrantes et al., 1992) and linguistically (Constenla, 1991) stable the region has been since the earliest stages of its continuous inhabitation some 10-12,000 years ago (O'Connor, 2014: 77). Moreover, Bray (1992, in Hoopes & Fonseca, 2003: 64) describes the region as "one metallurgical province", encompassing both Chibchan and Chocoan speakers, on the basis of stylistic similarities termed the 'International Style'. Nonetheless, the similarities in material culture and belief systems, coupled with long-term conflict, have led to the region being described as a "diffuse unity" (Fonseca & Hoopes, 2003). Bray (1984, in O'Connor, 2014: 80) again counters that the cultures in the area remained distinct despite constant contact (and conflict), accepting, for example, new technologies, practices and artefacts, but adapting and reproducing them in line with locally relevant cultural contexts. This scenario echoes the social constructionist view regarding the nature of technology, and indeed such an analysis might favour the use of existing terms or neologisms over terms from neighbouring ethnolinguistic groups.

The variation and multiplicity of terms, coupled with the lack of loanwords in the domain of metallurgy, might lead one to question the validity of an argument for the diffusion of the technology from South America to West Mexico. Certainly, "[...] the idea of multiple sources and multiples centres of secondary dispersion [of metalworking in Black Africa] is altogether plausible, especially in the light of the linguistic complexity [...] in connection with metalworking vocabulary" (Herbert, 1984: 9). We may wish to consider, then, whether the sheer variety of forms found for metallurgical terms in the three regions of extractive metalworking in the prehispanic Americas may also be due to multiple sources and centres or production (see, e.g. de Grinberg, 1990). Such a scenario, coupled with the largely non-verbal nature of knowledge transfer, may help to account for the linguistic data observed in this sample.

6. Conclusion

This paper has shown that the lexicon of metallurgy, in this sample at least, is not able to demonstrate contact at the macro-level between South America and West Mexico to the extent that data in archaeology and genetics have. At the regional level, it has highlighted different patterns of lexical diffusion, with the Andes displaying more widespread borrowing compared with the other two areas. Certain naming strategies for terms, such as the colours for metal terms, follow similar patterns but seem to display no particular regional biases. This finding echoes Lechtman's (2007: 344) statement that "Precolumbian metallurgy was Pan-American", in the sense that it comprised certain shared salient features. These features were (i) an emphasis on the development of specific colours or colour ranges in metals and alloys (as well as for gems and other precious stones), (ii) a stress on shininess, reflectivity, and the iridescence of metallic surfaces, following Saunders' (2003: 20) "aesthetic of brilliance" that also applied to other natural resources and objects, and (iii) the predominant use of copper, silver and gold and their alloys. These production and stylistic similarities are then adapted to individual cultural contexts, encouraging the diversity – or diffuse unity in the Chibchan sense – observable across the metalworking regions.

As indicated in the discussion, the small amount of borrowing may be due to knowledge transfer practices in non-industrialised societies and everyday situations more generally, where the non-verbal takes precedence over the verbal. Given that patterns have emerged at the regional level of analysis in this study, it is worth recalling Geurds and Van Broekhoven (2010: 68), who state that the analysis of social interaction, of which linguistic interaction is clearly a part, should include "an appreciation of localized processes of development at the level of technology, material procurement and semiotic patterns before the regional system can be elucidated." As such, future linguistic investigations could benefit from a more post-processual approach, focussing on more micro-level situations, before trying to address the larger-scale questions of interaction.

References

Aceves, Raúl. 2005. Teiteri Wayeiyari: Glosario de Cultura Huichola, Guadalajara: Secretaría de Cultura de Jalisco.

Adams, Richard E. W. 1977. Prehistoric Mesoamerica. Boston: Little, Brown.

Adelaar, Willem F.H. 2006. "The Quechua impact in Amuesha, an Arawak language of the Peruvian Amazon". In: A.Y. Aikhenvald & R.M.W. Dixon (eds.), Grammars in Contact. A Cross-Linguistic Typology, Oxford and New York: Oxford University Press, pp. 290-312.

Albiez-Wieck, Sarah. 2011. Contactos exteriores del Estado tarasco: Influencias desde dentro y fuera de Mesoamérica. PhD Dissertation, Rheinisch Friedrich-Wilhelms-Universität zu Bonn.

de Alcalá, F. Jeronimó. 1988 [1541]. La relación de Michoacán, México D.F.: Secretaría de Educación Pública.

Anawalt, Patricia Rieff. 1992.Ancient Cultural Contacts between Ecuador, West Mexico, and the American Southwest: Clothing Similarities, Latin American Antiquity 3(2): 114-129.

Anawalt, Patricia Rieff. 1998. "They Came to Trade Exquisite Things", in Richard F. Townsend (ed.), Ancient West Mexico: Art and Archaeology of the Unknown Past, New York: Thames and Hudson & Chicago: Art Institute of Chicago.

Arsandaux, H. and Paul Rivet. Contribution à l'étude de la métallurgie mexicaine, Journal de la Société des Américanistes, 13(2): 261-280.

Barrantes, Ramiro, Peter E. Smouse, Harvey W. Mohrenwesier, Henry Gershowitz, Jorge Azofeifa, Tomas . Arias and James V. Neel. 1990. Microevolution in Lower Central America: Genetic Characterization of the Chibcha-speaking Groups of Costa Rica and Panama, and a Consensus Taxonomy Based on Genetic and Linguistic Affinity, American Journal of Human Genetics 46: 63-84.

Blackiston, A. Hooton. 1910. Recent Discoveries in Honduras, American Anthropologist,12(4): 536-541.

Bloch, Maurice E. F.. 1998. How We Think They Think: Anthropological Approaches to Cognition, Memory, and Literacy, Boulder, Colorado: Westview Press.

Bloch, Maurice. 1992. Language, Anthropology and Cognitive Science, Man 26: 183-198.

de Borhegyi, Stefan F. 1961. Pre-Columbian Cultural Connections between Mesoamerica and Ecuador. In: Middle American Research Records, Vol. II, No. 6, pp. 142-154.

Brucato, Nicolas, Kate Bellamy, Rita Eloranta, Søren Wichmann & Willem Adelaar. 2015. Native American Gene Flow Between Mesoamerica and the Andes, poster presented at the Ninth ISABS Conference on Forensic and Anthropologic Genetics conference, Brač (Croatia), 22-26/06/2015.

Cadogan, Léon. 1992. Diccionario Mbya-Guaraní - Castellano, Asunción: Editora Litocolor S.R.L.

Callaghan, Richard T. 2003. Prehistoric Trade between Ecuador and West Mexico: A Computer Simulation of Coastal Voyages, Antiquity 77 (298): 796-804.

Campbell, Lyle. 1997. American Indian Languages: the Historical Linguistics of Native America, Oxford & New York: Oxford University Press.

Campbell, Lyle. 1998. Historical Linguistics: An Introduction, Edinburgh : Edinburgh University Press.

Campbell, Lyle, Terrence Kaufman and Thomas C. Smith-Stark. 1986. Meso-America as a Linguistic Area, Language 62(3): 530-570.

Chan, Eugene. 2016. Numeral Systems of the World's Languages, Jena: Max Planck Institute for the Science of Human History. https://mpi-lingweb.shh.mpg.de/numeral/.

Coe, Michael D. and Rex Koontz. 2008. Mexico: From the Olmecs to the Aztecs, Sixth Edition, London: Thames and Hudson.

Constenla Umaña, Adolfo. 1991. Las lenguas del área intermedia: Introducción a su estudio areal, San José: Editorial de la Universidad de Costa Rica.

Conzemius, Eduard. 1932. Ethnographical survey of the Miskito and Sumu Indians of Honduras and Nicaragua, Washington : United States Government Printing Office.

Cooke, Richard G. and Warwick M. Bray. 1985. "The Goldwork of Panama: An Iconographic and Chronological Perspective." In: J. Jones (ed.), The Art of Precolumbian Gold: The Jan Mitchell Collection, London: Wiedenfeld and Nicolson, pp. 35–49.

Cushing, Frank Hamilton. 1894. Primitive Copper Working: An Experimental Study, American Anthropologist 7(1): 93-117.

Edwards, Clinton R. 1965. Aboriginal Sail in the New World, Southwestern Journal of Anthropology 21(4):351-358.

Edwards, Clinton R. 1960. Sailing Rafts of Sechura: History and Problems of Origin, Southwestern Journal of Anthropology 16(3): 368-391.

García Icazbalceta, Joaquín. 2010. Carta del contador Rodrigo de Albornoz, al. emperador, Editorial del cardo.

Gerhard, Peter. 1993. A Guide to the Historical Geography of New Spain, Revised Edition, Norman, OK: University of Oklahoma Press.

Geurds, Alexander and Laura N. K. Van Broekhoven. 2010. The Similarity Trap: Engineering the Greater-Caribbean, A Perspective from the Isthmo-Columbian Area, Journal of Caribbean Archaeology Special Publication 3: 52-75.

Gilberti, Maturino. 1962 [1559]. Diccionario de la lengua tarasca o de Michoacán, México, D.F.: Tipografía de la Oficina impresora de estampillas.

Goody, E. 1978. "Towards a Theory of Questions." In: E. Goody (ed.), Questions and Politeness: Strategies in Social Interaction, Cambridge: Cambridge University Press.

Gorenstein, Shirley Slotkin and Helen Perlstein Pollard. 1983. The Tarascan Civilization: A Late Prehispanic Cultural System, Nashville: Vanderbilt University.

Greenberg, Joseph H. 1987. Language in the Americas, Stanford, CA: Stanford University Press.

de Grinberg, Dora M.K. 1990. Los señores del metal: Minería y metalurgia en Mesoamerica, México, D.F.: Pangea Editores.

Hamel, R. E. 2008. "Bilingual Education for Indigenous Communities in Mexico." In: J. Cummins & N.H. Hornberger (eds.), Encyclopaedia of Language and Education, 2nd Edition, Volume 5: Bilingual Education, 311-322.

Haspelmath, Martin and Uri Tadmor (eds.), 2009. Loanwords in the World's Languages: A Comparative Handbook. Berlin and New York: Mouton de Gruyter.

Heine-Geldern, Robert. 1954. Die asiatische herkunft der südamerikanischen metalltechnik, Paideuma 5(7/8): 347-423.

Helms, Mary W. 1979. Ancient Panama: Chiefs in Search of Power, Austin: University of Texas Press.

Hendrichs, Pedro. 1944-1945. Por tierras ignotas : viajes y observaciones en la región del Río de las Balsas, México, D.F.: Editorial Cultura.

Herbert, Eugenia W. 1984. Red Gold of Africa: Copper in Precolonial History and Culture, Madison and London: University of Wisconsin Press.

Highfield, Arnold R. 1997. "Some Observations on the Taíno Language." In: Samuel M. Wilson (ed.), The Indigenous People of the Caribbean, Gainesville: University of Florida Press.

Hoopes, John W. & Oscar M. Fonseca Z. 2003. "Goldwork and Chibchan Identity: Endogenous Change and Diffuse Unity in the Isthmo-Columbian Area". In: Jeffrey Quilter & John W. Hoopes (eds.), Gold and Power in Ancient Costa Roca, Panama, and Colombia, Washington D.C.: Dumbarton Oaks Research Library and Collection, pp. 49-89.

Horcasitas de Barros, María Luisa. 1981. Una artesanía con Raíces Prehispánicas en Santa Clara del Cobre, México: Instituto Nacional de Antropología e Historia.

Hosler, Dorothy. 2009. West Mexican Metallurgy: Revisited and Revised, Journal of World Prehistory 22: 185-212.

Hosler, Dorothy. 1994. The Sounds and Colors of Power: The Sacred Metallurgical Technology of Ancient West Mexico, Cambridge, MA & London: MIT Press.

Hosler, Dorothy and Sean Stresser-Pean. 1992. The Huastec Region: A Second Locus for the Production of Bronze Alloys in Ancient Mesoamerica, Science 257: 1215-1220.

Hosler, Dorothy, Heather Lechtman and Olaf Holm. 1990. Axe-Monies and their Relatives, Studies in Pre-Columbian Art & Archaeology 30, Washington D.C.: Dumbarton Oaks Research Library and Collection.

Kaufman, Terrence. 2007. Meso-America. In: R.E. Asher, Chris Moseley and Giles Darkes (eds.), Atlas of the World's Languages, Second Edition, London: Routledge.

Kelly, Isabel. 1980. Ceramic Sequence in Colima: Capacha, An Early Phase, Tucson: The University of Arizona Press.

Kelly, Isabel. 1974. "Stirrup Pots from Colima: Some Implications". In: Betty Bell (ed.), The Archaeology of West Mexico, Jalisco, México: Sociedad de Estudios Avanzados del Occidente de México.

Key, Mary Ritchie and Bernard Comrie. 2007. The Intercontinental Dictionary Series, http://lingweb.eva.mpg.de/ids/.

Killick, David. 2004. Social Constructionist Approaches to the Study of Technology, World Archaeology, 36(4): 571-578.

Kirchhoff, Paul. 1960 [1943]. Mesoamérica: Sus Límites Geográficos, Composición Étnica y Caracteres Culturales, México: Tlatoani.

Lave, J. 1988. Cognition in Practice. Cambridge: Cambridge University Press.

Lechtman, Heather. 2014. "Andean Metallurgy in Prehistory." In: B.W. Roberts, C. P. Thornton (eds.), Archaeometallurgy in Global Perspective, New York: Springer.

Lechtman, Heather. 2007. "The Inka, and Andean Metallurgical Tradition". In: Richard L. Burger, Craig Morris and Ramiro Matos Mendieta (eds.), Variations in the Expression of Inka Power, Washington D.C.: Dumbarton Oaks Research Library and Collection.

Lemonnier, Pierre. 1992. Elements for an Anthropology of Technology, Ann Arbor: University of Michigan.

Lewis, M. Paul, Gary F. Simons, and Charles D. Fennig (eds.). 2015. Ethnologue: Languages of the World, Eighteenth edition. Dallas, Texas: SIL International. Online version: http://www.ethnologue.com.

Maldonado, Blanca. 2012. "Mesoamerican Metallurgical Technology and Production." In: Deborah L. Nichols (ed.), The Oxford Handbook of Mesoamerican Archaeology, Oxford: Oxford University Press.

Mapunda, Bertram. 2013. "The Appearance and Development of Metallurgy South of the Sahara." Oxford Handbooks Online. Accessed: 26/09/ 2016, http://www.oxfordhandbooks.com/view/10.1093/oxfordhb/9780199569885.001.0001/oxfordhb-9780199569885-e-42.

Marcos, J.G. 1977-78. Cruising to Acapulco and back with the Thorny oyster set, Journal of the Steward Anthropological Society, 91-2): 99-132.

Martin, Susan R. Wonderful Power: The Story of Ancient Copper Working in the Lake Superior Basin, Detroit, Michigan: Wayne State University Press.

McClaran, Marlys. 1976. " Mexico." In: Thomas Sebeok (ed.), Native Languages of the Americas, Volume 2, New York: Plenum Press, pp. 141-155.

McEwan, Colin. 2000. "Introduction." In: Colin McEwan (ed.), Precolumbian Gold: Technology, Style and Iconography, Chicago/London: Fitzroy Dearborn Publishers.

McGuire, Randall. 2011. Mesoamerica, the Northwest of México and the Southwest United States, English version of "Mesoamérica, el noroeste de México y el suroeste de Estados Unidos." In E. Williams, M. García Sánchez, and M. Gándara (eds.), Mesoamérica: Debates y Perspectivas, El Colegio de Michoacán, Zamora, pp.79-94.

Nettle, Daniel. 1998. Is the rate of linguistic change constant? Lingua, 108: 119-136.

Nigra, Ben, Terrah Jones, Jacob Bongers, Charles Stanish, Henry Tantaleán and Kelita Pérez. 2014. The Chincha Kingdom: The Archaeology and Ethnohistory of the Late Intermediate Period South Coast, Peru, Backdirt, pp. 36-47.

O'Connor, Loretta. 2014. "Structural Features and Language Contact in the Isthmo-Colombian Area." In: Loretta O'Connor and Pieter Muysken (eds.), The Native Languages of South America: Origins, Development, Typology, Cambridge: Cambridge University Press, pp. 73-101.

Paris, Elizabeth H. 2008. Metallurgy, Mayapan, and the Postclassic Mesoamerican World System, Ancient Mesoamerica, 19(1): 43-66.

Pérez Pamatz, Felipe and Benjamin Lucas. 2004. "Glosario del cobre martillado." In: Michele Feder-Nadoff (ed.), Ritmo del Fuego: El arte y los artesanos de Santa Clara del Cobre, Michoacán, México, Chicago: Fundación Cuentos.

Pfaffenberger, Bryan. 1992. Social Anthropology of Technology, Annual Review of Anthropology 21:491-516.

Pinart, Alphonse. 1897. Vocabulario castellano-chocoe (baudo citarae), Paris: Ernest Leroux.

Quilter, Jeffrey. 2003. "Introduction: The Golden Bridge of Darien". In: Jeffrey Quilter & John W. Hoopes (eds.), Gold and Power in Ancient Costa Roca, Panama, and Colombia, Washington D.C.: Dumbarton Oaks Research Library and Collection, pp. 1-14.

Radivojević, Miljana, Thilo Rehren, Ernst Pernicka, Dušan Sljivar, Michael Brauns and Dušan Borić. 2010. On the origins of extractive metallurgy: new evidence from Europe, Journal of Archaeological Science 37: 2775-2787.

Real Académica Española. 2014. Diccionario de la lengua española, http://dle.rae.es/?w=diccionario.

Roskamp, Hans. 2013. El Lienzo de Jucutacatola historia sagrada de los nahuas de Jicalán, Michoacán, Arqueología mexicana, 21(123): 47-54.

Roskamp, Hans. 2010. God of Metals: Tlatlauhqui Tezcatlipoca and the Sacred Symbolism of Metallurgy in Michoacán, West Mexico, Ancient Mesoamerica 21(1): 69-78.

Roskamp, Hans. 2005. Pre-Hispanic and Colonial Metallurgy in Jicalán, Michoacán, México: An Archaeological Survey, Mexico: FAMSI.

Roskamp, Hans. 1998. La historiografía indígena de Michoacán : el Lienzo de Jucutácato y los títulos de Carapan, PhD Dissertation, Leiden University.

Salomon, Frank. 1986. Native lords of Quito in the age of the Incas: the political economy of north Andean chiefdoms, Cambridge: Cambridge University Press.

Sánchez-Díaz, Gerardo. (1999). "En torno a una discusión centenaria: el origen sudamericano de los tarascos" en Gerardo Sánchez Díaz y R. León Alanís (coords.), Historiografía michoacana, acercamientos y balances, Universidad Michoacana de San Nicolás de Hidalgo, Morelia, pp. 33-48.

Saunders, Nicholas J. 2003. ""Catching the Light": Technologies of Power and Enchantment in Pre-Columbian Goldworking." In: Jeffrey Quilter and John W. Hoopes (eds.), Gold and Power in Ancient Costa Rica, Panama, and Colombia, Washington, D.C.: Dumbarton Oaks Research Library and Collection.

Schulze, Nicholas. 2008. El proceso de producción metalúrgica en su contexto cultural: los cascabeles de cobre del Templo Mayor de Tenochtitlan, PhD Thesis, Universidad Autónoma de México.

Shimada, Izumi. 1994. "Pre-Hispanic Metallurgy and Mining in the Andes: Recent Advances and Future Tasks." In: Alan K. Craig & Robert C. West (eds.), In Quest of Mineral Wealth: Aboriginal and Colonial Mining and Metallurgy in Spanish America, Baton Rouge: Geoscience Publications, Louisiana State University.

da Silva Maia, António. 1959. Dicionário complementar Português-Kimbundu-Kikongo, Cucujães: Editorial Missões.

Smith, Michael E. 1978. A Model for the Diffusion of the Shaft Tomb Complex from South America to West Mexico, Journal of the Steward Anthropological Society 9(1-2): 179-204.

Stubbs, Brian D. 2011. Uto-Aztecan: A Comparative Vocabulary, Flower Mound, Texas: Shumway Family History Services & Blanding, Utah: Rocky Mountain Books and Productions.

Swadesh, Morris. 1971. The Origin and Diversification of Language (posthumous), Joel Sherzer (ed.), Chicago: Aldine.

Swadesh, Morris. 1967. Lexicostatistic Classification, in Robert Wauchope and Norman A. McQuown (eds.), The Handbook of Middle American Indians, Vol. 5: Linguistics, Austin: University of Texas Press.

Swadesh, Morris. 1964. "Linguistic Overview". In: Jesse David Jennings and Edward Norbeck (eds.), Prehistoric Man in the New World, Papers of a Symposium held at Rice University in Houston on Nov. 9-10, 1962, Chicago: University of Chicago Press.

Swadesh, Morris. 1956. Problems of Long-Range Comparison in Penutian, Language, 32: 17-41.

Thomason, Sarah Grey. 2001. Language contact: An introduction, Edinburgh: Edinburgh University Press.

Warren, Joseph Benedict. 1991. Diccionario grande de la lengua de Michoacán, 2 Vols., Morelia, Mich., Mexico: Fimax.

Weaver, Muriel Porter. 1972. The Aztecs, Maya, and Their Predecessors. Archaeology of Mesoamerica, New York: Seminar. Studies in Archeology.

Weigand, Phil C. 2001. El norte mesoamericano, Arqueología mexicana IX(51):34-39.

West, Robert C. 1994. "Aboriginal Metalworking in Spanish America: A Brief Overview." In: Alan K. Craig & Robert C. West (eds.), In Quest of Mineral Wealth: Aboriginal and Colonial Mining and Metallurgy in Spanish America, Baton Rouge: Geoscience Publications, Louisiana State University.

Wiebe, Neil & Wiebe, Ruth. 2015. Cayapa dictionary. In: Key, Mary Ritchie & Comrie, Bernard (eds.), The Intercontinental Dictionary Series. Leipzig: Max Planck Institute for Evolutionary Anthropology. (Available online at http://ids.clld.org/contributions/245. Accessed on 2016-09-21.)

Williams, Eduardo. 2004. Prehispanic West México: A Mesoamerican Culture Area, FAMSI (http://www.famsi.org/research/williams/).

de Wolf, Paul. 1994. Los términos para los puntos cardinales en phorhé. In: Tercer Encuentro de Lingüística en el Noroeste. Memorias, Vol. 1, Tomo 1, Hermosillo: Universidad de Sonora, pp. 181-202.

Appendix A: Language sample and references consulted

Aymara
Deza Galindo, Juan Francisco. 1989. Diccionario Aymara-Castellano, Castellano-Aymara, Lima: Graphos 100 Editores.

Awa- Pit/Cuaiquer
Lehmann, Walther. 1920. Zentral-Amerika: Die Sprachen Zentral-Amerikas. (I.) Berlin: Dietrich Reimer.

Curnow, Timothy Jowan. 1997. A grammar of Awa Pit (Cuaiquer): An indigenous language of south-western Colombia. University of Canberra. Canberra: Australian National University.

Barí
de Villamañán, Adolfo. 1975. Vocabulario barí comparado: Comparación de los vocabularios del Fr. Francisco de Catarroja (1730) y Fr. Francisco Javier Alfaro (1788) con el barí actual, Caracas: Editorial Arte.

Rivet, Paul & Cesáreo de Armellada. 1950. Les Indiens Motilones, Journal de la Société des Américanistes 39: 15-58.

Bocotá/Buglere
Margery Peña, Enrique & Mariana Arias Rodríguez. 2005. Vocabulario español-bocotá, Lingüística Chibcha XXIV: 87-121.

Boruca
von Thiel, Bernhard August. 1886. Vocabularium der Sprachen der Boruca-, Terraba-. und Guatuso-Indianer in Costa Rica, Archiv für Antropologi, XVI Band.

Quesada Pacheco, Miguel Angel & Carmen Rojas Chaves. 1999. Diccionario boruca-español, español-boruca, San José: Editorial de la Universidad de Costa Rica.

Bribri
Constenla Umaña, Adolfo, Feliciano Elizondo Figueroa & Francisco Pereira Mora. 1998. Curso básico de Bribri, San José: Editorial de la Universidad de Costa Rica.

Gabb, William M. 1875. On the Indian Tribes and Languages of Costa Rica, Proceedings of the American Philosophical Society, 14(95): 483-602.

Arroyo, Víctor Manuel. 1972. Lenguas indígenas costarricenses, San José: Editorial Universitaria Centroamericana (EDUCA).

Cabécar
Arroyo, Víctor Manuel. 1972. Lenguas indígenas costarricenses, San José: Editorial Universitaria Centroamericana (EDUCA).

Margery, Enrique. 1989. Diccionario Cabécar-Español, Español-Cabécar, San José: Editorial de la Universidad de Costa Rica.

Gabb, William M. 1875. On the Indian Tribes and Languages of Costa Rica, Proceedings of the American Philosophical Society, 14(95): 483-602.

Catacaos
Loukotka, Cestmír. 1949. Sur quelques langues inconnues de l'Amérique du Sud. Lingua Posnaniensis I. 53-82.

Changuena
Pinart, Alphonse L. 1890. Diccionario castellano-dorasque, dialectos Chumulu, Gualaca y Changuina, Paris: Ernest Leroux.

Chapalaa/Cayapa
Lindskoog, John N. 1964. Vocabulario cayapa, compilado. Serie de vocabularios indígenas, Mariano Silva y Aceves (ed.)núm. 9., México D.F.: Summer Institute of Linguistics.

Chibcha/Muisca
González de Pérez, María Stella. 1987. Diccionario y Gramática Chibcha: Manuscrito Anónimo de la Biblioteca Nacional de Colombia, Yerbabuena: Instituto Caro y Cuervo.

Acosta Ortegon, Joaquin. 1938. El Idioma Chibcha: Aborigen de Cundinamarca, Bogotá: Imprenta del Departamento.

Quesada Pacheco, Miguel Angel. 1991. El vocabulario mosco de 1612, Lingüïstica Chibcha 10: 29-99.

Uricoechea, Ezekiel. 1871. Gramática, Vocabulario, Catecismo y Confesionario de la lengua Chibcha, Paris: Maisonneuve.

Chichimeca Jonaz
Lastra, Yolanda. 2009.Vocabulario piloto Chichimeco, México, D.F: Universidad Autónoma de México, Instituto de Investigaciones Antropólogicas.

Soustelle, Jacques. 1951. Documents sur les langages Pame et Jonaz du Mexique central (Hidalgo, Querétaro, San Luis Potosí), Journal de la Société des Américanistes 40: 1-20.

Chimila
Trillos Amaya, María. 1996. Categorías gramaticales del Ette Taara, Lengua de los chimilas, Bogotá: Editorial Artes Ltda.

Celedón, Rafael. 1968 [1886]. Gramatica de la lengua Köggaba con Vocabularios y Catecismos, Nendeln/Liechtenstein: Kraus Reprint.

Lehmann, Walther. 1920. Zentral-Amerika: Die Sprachen Zentral-Amerikas. (I.) Berlin: Dietrich Reimer.

Chiriguano
Wolf Dietrich. 2015 [2007]. Chiriguano dictionary. In: Key, Mary Ritchie & Comrie, Bernard (eds.) The Intercontinental Dictionary Series. Leipzig: Max Planck Institute for Evolutionary Anthropology. (Available online at http://ids.clld.org/contributions/289, Accessed on 2016-09-19.)

Cholón
Alexander-Bakkerus, Astrid. 2005. Eighteenth-Century Cholón, Utrecht: LOT

Classical Aymara
Bertonio, Ludovico. 2005, 2006 [1612]. Vocabulario de la Lengua Aymara, Arequipa: Ediciones El Lector.

Classical Huastec
Zenteno, Carlos de Tapia. 1975 [1767]. Noticia de la Lengua Huasteca, Heppenheim: Franz Wolf.

de Quirós, Seberino Bernardo. 2013 [1711]. Arte y vocabulario del idioma huasteco, Edición crítica con anotaciones filológicas de Bernhard Hurch, México D.F.: Bonilla Artigas Editores S.A. de C.V.

Classical Kaqchikel
Coto, Tomás de, Fray. 1983. Thesaurus Verboru: Vocabulario de la lengua cakchiquel v[el] guatemalteca, nuevamente hecho y recopilado con sumo estudio, trabajo y erudición, México: Universidad Nacional Autónoma de México.

Classical Nahuatl
Molina, Fray Alonso de. 1966 [1571]. Vocabulario Nahuatl-Castellano, Castellano-Nahuatl, México D. F.: Ediciones Colofon S. A.

de Arenas, Pedro. 1982 [1661]. Vocabulario Manual de las Lenguas Castellana y Mexicana, México: Universidad Nacional Autónoma de México.

Soriano, Fr. Juan Guadalupe. 2012. Tratado del arte y unión de los idiomas Otomí y Pame; Vocabularios de los idiomas Pame, Otomí, Mexicano y Jonaz, paleografiado y editado por Yolanda Lastra, México, D.F.: Instituto de Investigaciones Antropológicas, Universidad Nacional Autónoma de México.

Classical Quechua
González Holguin, Diego. 1989 [1605]. Vocabvlario de la Lengva General de todo el Perv llamada Lengua Qquichua o del Inca, Edición facsimilar de la versión de 1952, Incluye addenda, Lima: Universidad Nacional Mayor de San Marcos

Cofán
Loukotka, Cestmír. 1949. Sur quelques langues inconnues de l'Amérique du Sud. Lingua Posnaniensis I. 53-82

Colorado/Tsafiki
Buchwald, Otto von. 1908. Vocabular der Colorados von Ecuador, Zeitschrift für Ethnologie, 40:70-82.

Moore, Bruce R. 1979. Método para aprender el idioma colorado, Quito: Instituto Lingüístico de Verano bajo convenio con el Ministerio de Educación y Cultura del Ecuador.

Dickinson, Connie. 2002. Complex Predicates in Tsafiki, PhD Thesis: University of Oregon.

Moore, Brice R. 1966. Diccionario castellano-colorado, colorado-castellano, Quito: Instituto Lingüístico de Verano.

Cora
McMahon, Ambrosio & Aiton de McMahon, María. 1959. Vocabulario Cora (Cora y Español), México D.F.: Instituto Lingüístico de Verano.

Preuss, K. Th. 1935. Wörterbuch Cora-Deutsch, International Journal of American Linguistics, 8(2): 81-102.

Soustelle, Jacques. 1938. Un vocabulaire cora: Manuscrit inédit publié par J. Soustelle. Journal de la Société des Américanistes 30(1): 141-145.

Cuitlatec
Escalante Hernández, Roberto. 1962. El Cuitlateco, México: Instituto Nacinoal de Antropología e Historia.

Hendrichs Perez, Pedro R. 1946. Por Tierras Ignotas: Viajes y Observaciones en la Region del Río de las Balsas, Tomo II. México, D.F.: Editorial Cvltvra.

Léon, Nicholas. 1903. Vocabulario en Lengua Cuitlateca, de Totolapam, Estado de Guerrero. Anales del Museo Nacional, Tomo VII.

Damana (Guamaca)
Trillos Amaya, Maria. 1999. Damana, Munich: Lincom Europa.

Celedon, Rafael. 1878.Palabras de la lengua guamaca que se habla en el pueblo del Rosario i en Marocasa, Collection Linguistique Américaine, Tome V, Paris: Libreros-Editores (reprint 1968 Nendeln/Liechtenstein: Kraus Reprint).

Desano
Tulio Alemán M., Reinaldo López H. & Marion Miller. 2000. Wirá ya, Peamasa ya werekuri, desano-español diccionario bilingüe de 896 palabras, Santafé de Bogotá, Colombia: Editorial Alberto Lleras Camargo.

de Lima Silva, Wilson. 2012. A Descriptive Grammar of Desano, PhD Dissertation: University of Utah

Kate Bellamy

Dorasque
Pinart, Alphonse L. 1890. Diccionario castellano-dorasque, dialectos Chumulu, Gualaca y Changuina, Paris: Ernest Leroux

Duit
Lehmann, Walther. 1920. Zentral-Amerika: Die Sprachen Zentral-Amerikas. (I.) Berlin: Dietrich Reimer.

Emberá/Katío
Sara, Solomon. 2001. A Tri-Lingual Dictionary of Emberá-Spanish-English, Munich: Lincom Europa.

Atienza, Ángel Cayo. 2002 [1936]. El idioma katío, Edición de Ignacio Arellano y Gabriel Arellano, Madrid/Frankfurt am Main: Iberoamericana/Vervuert.

Pinto García, Constancio. 1974. Los indios katíos: su cultura, su lengua, volumen segundo: la lengua katía, Medellín: Editorial Granamerica.

Pinart, Alphonse. 1897. Vocabulario castellano-chocoe (baudo citarae), Paris: Ernest Leroux.

Esmeraldeño
Seler, Eduard. 1902. Gesammelte Abhandlungen der Amerikanischen Sprach- und Alterthumskunde, Erster Band, Berlin: A. Asher & Co.

Guajiro
Jusayú, Miguel Angel & Jesús Olza Zubiri. 1981. Diccionario de la Lengua Guajira, Castellano-Guajiro, Caracas: Universidad Católica Andres Bello, Centro de Lenguas Indígenas.

Captain, David M. and Linda B. Captain. 2005. Diccionario Básico: Ilustrado ; Wayuunaiki-Espanol ; Espanol-Wayuunaiki. Bogota: Edit. Fundación para el Desarrollo de los Pueblos Marginados.

Guambiano
Otero, Jesús María. 1952. Los indions Guambianos. In: Etnología caucana. Estudio sobre los orígenes, vida, costumbres y dialectos de las tribus indígenas del Departamento del Cauca. Popayán: Editorial Universidad del Cauca, pp. 243-322.

Guatuso
Constenla Umaña, Adolfo. 1982. Algunos aspectos de la etnografía del habla de los indios guatusos.

Constenla Umaña, Adolfo. 1998. Gramática de la lengua guatusa, Heredia, Costa Rica: Editorial de la Universidad Nacional.

von Thiel, Bernhard August. 1886. Vocabularium der Sprachen der Boruca-, Terraba-. und Guatuso-Indianer in Costa Rica, Archiv für Antropologi, XVI Band.

Lehmann, Walther. 1920. Zentral-Amerika: Die Sprachen Zentral-Amerikas. (I.) Berlin: Dietrich Reimer.

Conzemius, E. 1930. Une tribu inconnue du Costa-Rica: Les indiens rama du río Zapote, Anthropologie 40: 93-108.

Guaymí/Ngäbe
Quesada Pacheco, Miguel Ángel. 2008. Gramática de la lengua guaymí, Munich: Lincom Europa.

Pinart, Alphonse L. 1897. Vocabulario Guaymie: Dialectos Murıre-Bukueta, Mouı y Sabanero, Paris: Ernest Leroux.

Huastec
Alejandre, Marcelo. 1889. Cartilla Huasteca con su Gramática, Diccionario, y varias Reglas para Aprender el Idioma, México: Oficina Tip. de la Secretaria de Fomento.

Larsen, Ramón. 1997 [1955]. Vocabulario Huasteco del Estado de San Luis Potosí, México, D.F.: Instituto Lingüístico de Verano.

Huichol
McIntosh, Juan B. & José Grimes. 1954. Niuqui 'Ïquisicayari: Vixárica niuquiyári Teivári niuquiyari hepáïsita, Vocabulario Huichol-castellano, Castellano-huichol, México, D.F.: Instituto Lingüístico de Verano.

Aceves, Raúl. 2005. Teiteri Wayeiyari: Glosario de Cultura Huichola, Guadalajara: Secretaría de Cultura de Jalisco.

Ika/Arhuaco
Celedón, Rafael. 1892. Vocabulario de la lengua de Bintukua. In: Actas del 8 Congreso Internacional de Americanistas, 600-611. Paris.

Jacaru
Belleza Castro, Neli. 1995. Vocabulario Jacaru-Castellano, Castellano-Jacaru (Aimara tupino), Cuzco: Centro de Estudios Regionales Andinos "Bartolomé de Las Casas".

Farfán, J.M.B. 1955. Estudio de un vocabulario de las Lenguas Quechua, Aymara y Haqe-aru, Revista del Museo Nacional, Tomo XXIV: 81-110.

Kallawaya
Girault, Louis. 1989. Kallawaya: El Idioma Secreto de los Incas, Bolivia: Talleres Gráficos de "Mundy Color" S.R.L.

Kaqchikel
Blair, Robert W., John S. Robertson, Larry Richman, Greg Sansom, Julio Salazar, Juan Yool & Alejandro Choc. 1981. Diccionario Español-Cakchiquel-Inglés, New York and London: Garland Publishing Inc.

Rodríguez Guaján, Demetrio, Leopoldo Tzian Guantá & José Obispo Rodríguez Guaján. 1990. Ch'uticholtzij Maya-Kaqchikel, Vocabulario Kaqchikel-Español, Vocabulario Español-Kaqchikel, Guatemala: Ediciones Cocadi & PLFM.,

K'iche'
Christenson, Allen J. Unpublished manuscript. K'iche'-English Dictionary and Guide to Pronunciation of the K'iche'-Maya Alphabet, FAMSI.

Kogi
Celedón, Rafael. 1968 [1886]. Gramática de la lengua Köggaba con Vocabularios y Catecismos, Nendeln/Liechtenstein: Kraus Reprint.

Kuna
Pinart, Alphonse Louis. 1890. Vocabulario Castellano-Cuna, Paris: Ernest Leroux.

Puig, P. Manuel María. 1944. Diccionario de la Lengua Caribe-Cuna, Panama, R. de P.: La Estrella de Panama.

Kunza
Vaïsse, Emilio, Félix Hoyos and Aníbal Echeverría y Reyes. 1896. Glosario de la lengua atacameña. Santiago de Chile: Imprenta Cervantes (first published in 1895 in Anales de la Universidad de Chile 91, pp. 527–56, Santiago de Chile).

Schuller, Rodolfo R. 1908. Vocabularios y nuevos materiales para el estudio de la lengua de los indios Lican-Antai (Atacameños) Calchaqui. (Biblioteca de Lingüística Americana, II.) Santiago: F. Becerra M.

Kurripako
Cardona Puig, Felix. 1945. Vocabulario del dialecto karro del río guainia, Acta Venezolana 1(2): 221-230.

Granadillo, Tania. 2006. An Ethnographic Account of Language Documentation Among the Kurripako of Venezuela, PhD Dissertation: University of Arizona.

Mosonyi, Esteban Emilio. 2000. Breve Caracterización conjunta de las lenguas Curripaco y Piapoco. In González de Pérez, María Stella and Rodríguez de Montes, María Luisa (eds.), Lenguas indígenas de Colombia: una visión descriptiva, 641-656. Santafé de Bogotá: Instituto Caro y Cuervo.

Lengua de Michoacán
Warren, Benedict J. 1991. Diccionario Grande de la Lengua de Michoacán, 2 Vols., Morelia, Fimax.

Mapuche
Espósito, María. 2003. Diccionario Mapuche-Castellano, Castellano-Mapuche, Buenos Aires: Editorial Guadal S.A.

Barbará, Federico. 1944. Manual de la lengua pampa, Buenos Aires: Emecé Editores, S.A.

Matlatzinca
Basalenque, Fray Diego. 1975 [1642]. Vocabulario de la Lengua Castellana vuelto a la Matlaltzinga, Revisión Paleográfica, Nota Introductora, y Apéndice por Leonardo Manrique C., México: Biblioteca Enciclopédica del Estado de Mexico.

De Guevara, Fray Miguel. 1863 [1638]. Arte Doctrinal y Modo General para Aprender la Lengua Matlaltzinga, Boletín de la Sociedad Mexicana de Geografía y Estadística, México: Sociedad Mexicana de Geografía y Estadística.

Mazahua
Kiemele Muro, Mildred. 1975. Vocabulario Mazahua-Español y Español-Mazahua, Edición preparada por Mario Colín, México: Biblioteca Enciclopédica del Estado de México.

Colegio de Lenguas y Literatura Indígenas. 1997. Diccionario Mazahua-Español, Toluca: Instituto Mexiquense de Cultura.

Benítez Reyna, Rufino. 2002. Vocabulario práctico bilingüe mazahuua-español, México D.F.: Instituto Nacional Indigenista.

Manso, Francisco. 1637. Doctrina y Enseñança en la Lengua Maçahua, México: Iuan Ruyz.

Cárdenas Martínez, Celestino & Yolanda Lastra. 2011. Mazahua de San Pedro el Alto, Temascalcingo, Estado de México, México D.F.: El Colegio de México.

Miskito
Centro de Investigación y Documentación de la Costa Atlántica. 1986. Diccionario elemental Miskito-Español, Español-Miskito, Managua: División de Comunicaciones – MIDINRA.

Mixteca alta
Beaty de Farris, Kathryn (compiler), Pablo García Sánchez, Rubén García Sánchez, Jesús Ojeda Sánxhez, Augustín San Pablo García and Apolonio Santiago Jiménez (colaboradores mixtecos). 2012. Diccionario básico del Mixteco de Yosondúa, Oaxaca, Coyoacán, D.F.: Instituto Lingüístico de Verano.

Dyk, Anne and Betty Stoudt. 1965. Vocabulario Mixteco de San Miguel El Grande, México, D.F.: Instituto Lingüístico de Verano.

Mixteca costiera
Stark Campbell, Sara, Andrea Johnson Peterson and Filiberto Lorenzo Cruz (Compiladores), Catalina López de García and Daniel Fidencio García Alavez (Colaboradores mixtecos). 1986. Diccionario mixteco de San Juan Colorado, México, D.F.: Instituto Lingüístico de Verano.

Pensinger, Brenda J. (Compiladora). 1974. Diccionario Mixteco-Español, Español-Mixteco, México, D.F.: Insituto Lingüístico de Verano.

Mochica
Brüning, Hans Heinrich. 2004. Mochica Wörterbuch, Diccionario Mochica: Mochica - Castellano, Castellano - Mochica, Lima: Universidad de San Martín de Porres.

Villareal, Federico. 2013 [1921]. La lengua yunga, Pueblo Libre: Editorial Universitaria UNFV.

Salas, José Antonio. 2002. Diccionario Mochica-Castellano, Castellano-Mochica, Lima: Universidad de San Martín de Porres, Escuela Profesional de Turismo y Hotelería.

Nahuatl
Ramírez de Alejandro, Cleofas & Karen Dakin. 1979. Vocabulario náhuatl de Xalitla, Guerrero, Centro de Investigaciones Superiores del INAH.

Brewer Forrest & Jean G. Brewer. 1971. Vocabulario Mexicano de Tetelcingo, Morelos, México D.F.: Instituto Lingüístico de Verano.

Old Guajiro (C19)
Celedon, Rafael. 1878. Catecismo I Vocabulario de la Lengua Goajira, Collection Linguistique Américaine, Tome V, Paris: Libreros-Editores (reprint 1968 Nendeln/Liechtenstein: Kraus Reprint).

Otomí
Hekking, Ewald & Severiano Andrés de Jesús. 1989. Diccionario Español-Otomí de Santiago Mexquititlán, Querétaro: Universidad Autónoma de Querétaro.

Lopez Yepes, Fr. Joaquin. 1826. Catecismo y Declaración de la Doctrina Cristiana en Lengua Otomí con un Vocabulario del Mismo Idioma, Megico: Alejandro Valdés.

Soriano, Fr. Juan Guadalupe. 2012. Tratado del arte y unión de los idiomas Otomí y Pame; Vocabularios de los idiomas Pame, Otomí, Mexicano y Jonaz, paleografiado y editado por Yolanda Lastra, México, D.F.: Instituto de Investigaciones Antropológicas, Universidad Nacional Autónoma de México.

Paez
Pittier de Fabrega, Henry. 1907. Ethnographic and Linguistic Notes on the Paez Indians of Tierra Adentro, Cauca, Colombia.

Slocum, Marianna C. and Gerdel, Florence L. 1983. Diccionario páez-español, español-páez. Lomalinda: Editorial Townsend.

del Castillo i Orosco, Eujenio. 1877. Vocabulario Páez-Castellano, Paris: Librairie-Éditeur J. Maisonneuve.

Pame (general)
Soustelle, Jacques. 1937. La Famille Otomi-Pame du Mexique Central, Paris: Institut d'Ethnologie.

Soriano, Fr. Juan Guadalupe. 2012. Tratado del arte y unión de los idiomas Otomí y Pame; Vocabularios de los idiomas Pame, Otomí, Mexicano y Jonaz, paleografiado y editado por Yolanda Lastra, México, D.F.: Instituto de Investigaciones Antropológicas, Universidad Nacional Autónoma de México.

Soustelle, Jacques. 1951. Documents sur les langages Pame et Jonaz du Mexique central (Hidalgo, Querétaro, San Luis Potosí), Journal de la Société des Américanistes 40: 1-20.

Pame, Central
Gibson, Lorna F. N.d. Pame Pedagogical Grammar, Summer Institute of Linguistics, unpublished manuscript.

Gibson, Lorna F. N.d. Pame Noun Paradigms, Summer Institute of Linguistics.

Pame, Northern
Berthiaume, Scott Charles. 2003. A Phonological Grammar of Northern Pame, PhD Dissertation, University of Texas at Arlington

Pame, Southern
Manrique C., Leonardo. 1967. Jiliapan Pame, in Norman A. McQuown (ed.), Handbook of Middle American Indians, Volume 5: Linguistics, Austin: University of Texas Press, pp. 331-348.

Puquina
Aguiló, P. Federico. 2000. El Idioma del Pueblo Puquina: Un enigma que va aclarándose, Quito: Imprefepp.

Adelaar, Willem F.H. with Pieter C. Musyken. 2004. The Languages of the Andes, Cambridge: Cambridge University Press.

Purépecha
Velásquez Gallardo, Pablo. 1978. Diccionario de la Lengua Phorepecha, Español-Phorepecha, Phorepecha-Español, México D.F.: Fondo de Cultura Económica.

Pérez Pamatz, Felipe and Benjamin Lucas. 2004. Glossary of Coppersmithing. In: Michele Feder-Nadoff (ed.), Ritmo del Fuego, México: Morevallado Editores.

Horcasitas de Barros, María Luisa. 1981. Una artesanía con Raíces Prehispánicas en Santa Clara del Cobre, Addenda 1980, México D.F.: Instituto Nacional de Antropología e Historia.

Horcasitas de Barros, María Luisa. 1974. Cobre Martillado: Vocabulario Tradicional, Utillaje y Técnicas de Manufactura, México D.F.: Instituto Nacional de Antropología e Historia.

Quechua, Ancash
Parker, Gary J. & Amancio Chávez. 1976. Diccionario Quechua: Ancash-Huailas, Lima: Ministerio de Educación/Instituto de Estudios Peruanos.

Julca Guerrero, Félix. 2009. Quechua Ancashino: Una Mirada Actual, Lima: CARE Perú.

Quechua (all modern)
Ladrón de Guevara, Laura. 1998. Diccionario Quechua de las Regiones: Ayacucho - Cuzco - Junin - Ancash - Cajamarca, Lima: Editorial Brasa S.A.

Quechua, Cajamarca
Quesada Castillo, Felix. 1976. Diccionario Quechua: Cajamarca-Cañaris, Lima: Ministerio de Educación/Instituto de Estudios Peruanos

Quechua, Cusco
Hornberger, Esteban S. & Nancy H. Hornberger. 1978. Diccionario tri-lingue: Quechua of Cusco/English/Spanish, Volume III Español Quechua, Qosqo: Imprenta Prelatura de Sicuani.

Rama
Rigby, Nora & Robin Schneider. 1989. Dictionary of the Rama Language, Berlin: Dietrich Reimer Verlag.

Conzemius, E. 1930. Une tribu inconnue du Costa-Rica: Les indiens rama du río Zapote, Anthropologie 40: 93-108.

Sechura
Loukotka, Cestmír. 1949. Sur quelques langues inconnues de l'Amérique du Sud. Lingua Posnaniensis I. 53-82

Sirionó
Schermair, E. Anselmo. 1962. Vocabulario Castellano-Sirionó, Vienna: Mechitaristen-Druckerei.

Cadogan, Léon. 1992. Diccionario Mbya-Guaraní - Castellano, Asunción: Editora Litocolor S.R.L.

Holmberg, Allan R. 1950. Nomads of the Long Bow: The Siriono of Eastern Bolivia, Washington:L United States Government Printing Office.

Taíno
Granberry, Julian & Gary S. Vescelius. 2004. Languages of the Pre-Columbian Antilles, Tuscaloosa: University of Alabama Press.

Gaztambide Arrillaga, Carlos. 1992. Diccionario Gaztambide Taíno-Español/Español Taíno (Tomo XXIII), Puerto Rico: Ramallo Bros. Printing Inc.

Highfield, Arnold R. 1997. Some Observations on the Taíno Language. In: Samuel M. Wilson (ed.), The Indigenous People of the Caribbean, Gainesville: University of Florida Press.

Teribe
Diego Quesada, J. 2000. A Grammar of Teribe, Munich: Lincom Europa.

Heinze, Carol. 1979. Cursillo de Asimilación - Teribe, Panamá: Editorial de la Nación.

von Thiel, Bernhard August. 1886. Vocabularium der Sprachen der Boruca-, Terraba-. und Guatuso-Indianer in Costa Rica, Archiv für Antropologi, XVI Band.

Arroyo, Víctor Manuel. 1972. Lenguas indígenas costarricenses, San José: Editorial Universitaria Centroamericana (EDUCA).

Gabb, William M. 1875. On the Indian Tribes and Languages of Costa Rica, Proceedings of the American Philosophical Society, 14(95): 483-602.

Tlapanec
Suárez, Jorge A. 1983. La Lengua Tlapaneca de Malinaltepec, México: Universidad Nacional Autónoma de México.

Suárez, Jorge A. 1988. Tlapaneco de Malinaltepec, México, D.F.: El Colegio de México.

Radin, Paul. 1935. Notes on the Tlappanecan Language of Guerrero, International Journal of American Linguistics 8(1): 45-72.

Romero Castillo, Moisés. 1966. Vocabulario Chichimeco-Jonaz. In: Summa Anthropological, Un homenaje a Roberto J. Weitlaner. (Editor Unknown), pp. 501-532, Mexico: Instituto Nacional de Antropologia e Historia.

Tukano
Beuchat & Rivet. 1911-1912. La Famille Betoya ou Tucano, Mémoires de la Société de Linguistique de Paris XVII, pp. 117-136, 162-190.

Gíacone, A. 1949. Os Tucanos e Outras Tribus do Rio Vaupés Afluente do Rio Negro-amazones, Sâo Paolo: Imprensa Ofical do Estado.

Ramirez, Herni. 1997. A Fala Tukano dos Ye'pâ-Masa, Tomo II Dicionário, Manaus: Inspetoria Salesiana Missionária da Amazônia CEDEM.

Koch-Grunberg, Theodor. 1912. Betoya-Sprachen Nordwestbrasiliens und der angrenzenden Gebiete, Anthropos 7: 429-462.

Tunebo
Headland, Edna Romayne. 1997. Diccionario Bilingüe Uw Cuwa (Tunebo) - Español, Español - Uw Cuwa (Tunebo) con una Grámatica Uw Cuwa (Tunebo), Santafé de Bogotá: Editorial Buena Semilla.

Rivet, Paul & Victor Oppenheim. 1943. La lengua tunebo. Revista del Instituto Etnológico Nacional 1: 47-53.

Ulwa
Green, Thomas Michael. 1999. A Lexicographic Study of Ulwa, PhD Thesis: Massachusetts Institute of Technology.

Uru
Aguiló, P. Federico.1986. El Idioma de los Urus. Editora Centro Portales.

Métraux, Alfred. 1935. Contribution à l'ethnographie et à la linguistique des Indiens Uro d'Ancoaqui (Bolivie), Journal de la Société des Américanistes, 27(1): 75-110.

Polo, José Toribio. 1901. Indios Uros del Perú y Bolivia, Boletín de la Sociedad Geográfica de Lima 10: 445-482.

Posnansky, Arthur. 1915. La lengua "chipaya" (Carangas, Bolivia). In: XIX Congreso Internacional de Americanistas, La Paz, (Bolivia) 15-20 de Diciembre 1914: I Entrega, 1-27. La Paz.

Warao
de Barral, Basilio. 1957. Diccionario Guarao - Español, Español - Guarao, Caracas: Editorial Sucre.

Williams, James. 1928. The Warau Indians of Guiana and Vocabulary of their Language, Journal de la Société des Américanistes 20: 193-252.

Williams, James. 1929. The Warau Indians of Guiana and Vocabulary of their Language, Journal de la Société des Américanistes 21: 201-261.

Waunana
Binder, Reinaldo. 1977. Una gramática pedagógica del waunana (primera parte), Panamá: Editora de la Nación.

Holmer, Nils M. 1963. Gramática comparada de un dialecto del chocó (con textos, índice y vocabulario), Etnologiska Studier 26, Göteborg: Elanderus Boktryckeri Aktiebolag.

Lotero Villa, Luz. 19XXX. Monografía de los indígenas noanama: tribu de una región colombiana.

Binder, Ronald, Phillip Lee Harms & Chindío Peña Ismare. 1995. Vocabulario ilustrado wounmeu-español-epena pedee, tomo 2, Santafé de Bogotá: Editorial Alberto Lleras Camargo.

Zapotec
Munro, Pamela and Felipe H. López with Olivia V. Méndez, Rodrigo García and Michael R. Grant. 1999. Di'csyonaary X:tèe'n Dìi'zh Sah Sann Lu'uc, San Lucas Quiaviní Zapotec Dictionary, Volume II, English and Spanish Indices, Los Angeles (CA): Chicano Studies Research Center Publications.

Pickett, Vilma and collaborators. 1971. Vocabulario Zapoteco del Istmo Castellano-Zapoteco, Zapoteco-Castellano, México, D.F.: Instituto Lingüístico de Verano.

Appendix B: Wordlist

Alloy, anvil, arrow [point], arsenic, awl, axe, axe money / naipe, axehead, balance / scale(s), bead, bell (different types), bellows, blade, curved (for cleaning plancha), blowtube, bowl, bracelet, brazier / clay furnace, breastplate, bronze, brooch, burin, button, cast / mould, chisel, cinnabar, clamps, c-clamps, compass, copper, crown, crucible, deposit (of ore/mineral), digging stick tip, disc / coin, disc, flat used in electric grinders, disc, flat and thick of hammered copper, ear spool, earring, enamel, fan (electric), file (iron or steel for smoothing), finger ring, fire, firewood, fishhook, form / stake used to give a piece form, fuel, furnace, gilding, gold, hammer, head ornament, helmet, hoe, hot, ingot, iron, knife, lip plug, labret, lost wax casting, metalworker, mine, moneychanger, barterer, moveable metal stake, necklace, needle, nose ring, open ring, ore, outline/trace, pin, pit, pliers, pole, wooden for removing impurities, rattle, rocks around mouth of cendrada, scraping pole, scribed guidelines, shears, shield, silver, silversmith, slag, sledgehammer, smelter, smithy, smoke, soldering, spear head / point, stick for cleaning molten copper, stones for containing old metal, sword, temperature, tin, to add height to walls of vessel whilst deepening, to alloy, to cast, to crush [slag], to even up, to fold object's edge, to gild, to give the object (cazo) the desired height, to hammer, to locate ore, to melt, to mine, to polish / shine / burnish, to shape, to silver-plate, to smelt, to solder, weld, to stretch, extend, to work metal, tongs, tool blade, tumbaga, tweezers, vessel, wide-mouthed, wax, white hot, woodblock, dapping bench, wooden piece for tracing circles, workshop.

(Re)considering the Archaeo-linguistics of Mesoamerica

Kathryn M. Hudson, University at Buffalo and John S. Henderson, Cornell University

The history of archaeo-linguistic research in Mesoamerica has been fraught with forced correspondences between archaeological and linguistic data as well as inherited assumptions about cultural primacy. These difficulties are particularly problematic in the region's southeastern periphery, where such tendencies are exacerbated by a dearth of linguistic data as well as an ongoing adherence to core-periphery models in which influence – including, arguably, linguistic influence – is assumed to have flowed from seemingly more 'advanced' population centers to their supposedly less-developed neighbors. The indicators of this advancement unsurprisingly reflect the kinds of features that appeal to archaeologists and the institutions that support them, and the resulting assumptions concerning their significance create a skewed historical perspective in which cultural and political identities are easily conflated.

The comparative methodology dominant in considerations of Mesoamerican linguistic history exacerbates these homogenizing tendencies. Such work is frequently based primarily on historical documentary sources whose contents are, by nature, skewed to emphasize or illustrate particular kinds of features. The incorporation of data from contemporary linguistic fieldwork is also potentially problematic, since many surviving indigenous populations in the region are facing language endangerment, death, or collective consolidation in an attempt to retain some measure of social or political influence. This is not to say that comparative studies have nothing to offer; in fact, when done well, such research can shed considerable light on ancient associations. However, the successful use of such methodologies requires a critical perspective and robust understanding of the nature of the available data, what they can and cannot reveal, and the scope of their applicability.

This paper will focus on the southeastern periphery of Mesoamerica, presenting a preliminary review of ongoing research focused on the intersections of the region's archaeological and linguistic heritages. This work, which juxtaposes information on non-elite material remains – particularly ceramics – with data concerning linguistic distributions and patterns of relatedness, is part of an ongoing field project, directed by the authors, in the lower Ulúa Valley of Honduras. Its focus on non-elite materials reflects a conscious attempt to correct for the socio-political conflation inherent in many orthodox analyses and a firm belief that non-elite materials offer a more reliable indication of the linguistic and cultural practices most common in a region than their elite counterparts. While it remains a work in progress, these analyses can nonetheless illustrate the problems inherent in traditional methodologies and indicate potentially fruitful avenues for future research.

On the Intersections of Language and the Archaeological Record

Using the perspectives of historical linguistics in conjunction with material remains has been an enduring dimension of archaeology, but its popularity has varied wildly across subdisciplines and geographic regions, and through time. In areas with ancient writing systems, especially the Mediterranean and Near East, analysis of texts and philological approaches to reconstructing the past have been central to the archaeological enterprise since its inception as a recognizable academic discipline. "Linguistic palaeontology" (Heggarty 2007), like the "Wörter und Sachen" approach – employing reconstructed lexicons of early languages in combination with material remains to reconstruct past cultures – has never gone entirely out of fashion. The popularity of other kinds of analyses based on the assessment of congruences between historical linguistic reconstructions and the archaeological record has fluctuated wildly. By the mid-20th century, most archeologists, especially those working on prehistoric periods in the Americas, had come to be deeply suspicious of the plausibility of relating material remains to language in any significant way. At the same time, Swadesh (1950, 1955) was developing his glottochronological methodology for adding an absolute time dimension to reconstructed histories of language families. The later 20th century saw general rejection of glottochronology in linguistics just as language history re-emerged as a major theme in archaeology.

With Renfrew's popular *Archaeology and Language: The Puzzle of Indo-European Origins* (1987), the potential of combining historical linguistics and archaeological analysis, always apparent to those interested in the early history of speakers of Indo-European languages, began to attract broader attention in archaeology. The renewed interest in the Indo-European world has continued (Mallory 1989; Mallory and Adams 2006; Anthony 2007) and broader hypotheses about relationships between the spread of farming, population movements, and the distribution of particular language families (Bellwood 2001; Bellwood and Renfrew 2002; Bellwood and Diamond 2003) stimulated more general debates in archaeology.

These farming–language dispersal hypotheses involve two key themes in the history of combining historical linguistic and archaeological data to explain the past. One is the use of reconstructed ancient lexicons as a reflection of ancient cultural practices; the other is linking archaeological and linguistic distributional data. These hypotheses maintain that population expansions related to the adoption of agriculture favored the differential expansion – geographically and in terms of the total number of speakers – of particular language families, including the most significant families today. They have stimulated much the same kinds of critiques that have always been leveled at the attempt to associate language history with major cultural transformations seen in the archaeological record. Linguists are inclined to be particularly sharp in their critiques of this kind of deployment of linguistic data, especially by archaeologists, as evidenced by the following observation made by Kaufman and Justeson (2009:224):

> They [Bellwood and Diamond (2003)] use no linguistic data in their arguments, only distillations of the opinions of linguists whose statements seem to be compatible with their model; or in the absence of a definable opinion by linguists, they assume that their temporal and geographical model for the spread of agriculture and languages in a particular area will be borne out by subsequent linguistic investigation.

Other proposed connections between language history and major developments reflected in the archaeological record have often drawn similar critiques to those leveled at attempts to use distributional data – especially non-contiguous distributions of related languages – as an indicator of ancient population movements. These critiques are often rooted in skepticism about lexicostatistical and glottochronological methods which, in turn, raise important issues about analytical methods – such as the recognition of cognates – which are widely used in linguistic analyses.

Many of the criticisms leveled at both lexicostatistics and glottochronology focus on the implications of using wordlists as a means of comparison. Teeter (1963:639, 644) observed that "mere similarity in vocabulary, whether … called 'basic', 'universal', or 'acultural', allows none but the grossest sort of inference" and creates a risk of "mistak[ing] the dictionary for the language." The nature of language development and divergence makes it difficult to date linguistic splits on the basis of lexical interpretation; even non-glottochronological endeavors are marred by the fact that "as distance from the common language increases, cognates come to be dissimilar and externally caused similarities may also increase" (Teeter 1963:639-641). Many have noted the problems in assuming a constant rate of lexical replacement for core vocabulary (e.g. Crowley and Bowern 2010; Dixon 1997); equally troublesome is the observation that "two pairs of languages, while separated by the same period of time, might have dramatically different retention figures," since "it is logically possible for two languages to change the same 19.5% of their core vocabulary every 1,000 years and retain the remaining 80.5% intact over succeeding periods … [and] for the 19.5% to be different in each successive period" (Crowley and Bowern 2010:151). Dimmendaal (2011:73) cited Bergsland and Vogt's (1962) comparison of Old Norse and Modern Icelandic – which showed a glottochronological time depth of only 258 years – to illustrate the dangers of assuming that the rates of language change can be averaged. Teeter (1963:642) noted that "[t]o be usable, the [word]list must be universally valid, and ... must consist of enough items to handle statistically ... [t]hese aims are opposed in practice." To this we would add the observation that wordlists must be culturally situated if they are to be of practical use, particularly in the study of ancient contexts.

This critique was anticipated by Hoijer (1956:49-50), who noted that the wordlist proposed by Swadesh presupposes "meanings universal to all human societies such as must be expressed in every language," even as it conflated "'universal and non-cultural' items" with "categories of forms which are relatively stable in the Indo-European languages." Matisoff (2000:335) similarly described the standard Swadesh lists as "culturally and grammatically inappropriate for many linguistic areas of the world, full of over- and under- differentiations." Both claim that the items in Swadesh's list are not culturally neutral or universal since "each language has not only its own peculiar structure but its own unique set of semantic patterns" (Hoijer 1956:59). Translation of a wordlist does not rectify this problem, since "[e]very attempt to translate the test list into a particular language … is bound to leave a residue of items for which no single, simple term … can be found" (Hoijer 1956:60). In short, it is impossible to create a list appropriate for cross-cultural use; "[i]t is doubtful that any test list … will achieve this objective, for there is no way in which we can rule out … the particularities of individual cultures … [and this] accounts for a good deal of the error in lexicostatistic dating" (Hoijer 1956:60).

Despite these issues, lexicostatistical methods have been productively applied in some cases. Many of these use altered or innovative wordlists, and a variety of modifications to the constituency of the wordlist(s) – many tailored to particular regions – have been proposed. Matisoff (1978, 2000) developed the CALMSEA (Culturally and Linguistically Meaningful for Southeast Asia) list, a 200-item wordlist modeled on the 200-item list proposed by Swadesh but altered to exclude regionally inappropriate terms and include lexical items reflective of concepts salient for speakers of the region's languages. O'Grady (1960) developed a regionally-tailored wordlist for Australia after encountering difficulties with Swadesh's 200-item list, concluding that "no less than 69 of the items are either unsuitable or else need more precise definition in terms of the Australian environment." O'Grady and Klokeid (1969), in their defense of the classification of Australian languages, used a 100-item wordlist to classify Wirangu. Alpher and Nash (1999) compiled a 151-item wordlist for their study of languages from the Cape York Peninsula that combined new additions and lexical items found in O'Grady and Klokeid (1969) with the unpublished wordlists created by Hale (1961) and Black (nd).

Heggarty adopted a slightly different approach in his 150-item CALMA (Culturally and Linguistically Meaningful for the Andes) list for the Andean region (see McMahon, Heggarty, McMahon, and Slaska 2005; McMahon and McMahon 2005:156). The CALMA list can be divided as required, which allows the wordlist to accommodate cases where languages differentiate between meanings in a similar way (McMahon and McMahon 2005:156, 167). This permits different forms for two or more sub-senses in the target language to be assigned to a single slot within the wordlist (McMahon and McMahon 2005:167). This "departs from the earlier assumption of 'one meaning, one lexeme' ... [and] represents, in as detailed, sensitive and balanced a way as possible, the exact nature of the overlaps and differences between languages in their lexical semantics" (McMahon, Heggarty, McMahon, and Slaska 2005:156). It represents an attempt to capture semantic categorizations that may affect lexically rooted analyses more accurately. By recognizing a scale of overlap in meaning between correlated items, this model also incorporates weighting and intermediate values in a way that accommodates multiple true synonyms and lexeme pairs composed of multiple morphemes (McMahon, Heggarty, McMahon, and Slaska 158-160).

McMahon and McMahon (2005:48) follow Kroeber and Chrétien (1937:85) and others in advocating an increased use of statistical analyses to "validate and correct insight, or, where insight judgments are in conflict, help decide between them." Such techniques are further said to "increase[ ] objectivity, sharpen[ ] findings, and sometimes force[ ] new problems" (Kroeber and Chrétien 1937:85, in McMahon and McMahon 2005:48); they also have the effect of making lexicostatistical insights more easily compatible with archaeological analyses because they are less subjective, more systematic and so readily analyzed in comparison with archaeological analyses. Embleton (1986:3) has proposed a particular set of refinements in quantitative methods that McMahon and McMahon (2005:49-50) adopt in their review of classificatory approaches to language. Heggarty (2010:310, 317, 318-321) asserts the need to "refine the quantitative sensitivity of ... methods, to sharpen their resolution for measuring *degree* of difference more finely;" he also advocates the use of statistical methodologies in studies of "deep end" objectives or other difficult questions and makes use of linear regression analyses – plotted in terms of stability of meanings – in his consideration of Andean languages.

Heggarty (forthcoming) further recommends referring to correlates between languages – defined as "striking form-to-meaning correspondences which are highly unlikely to be due to chance, but might well reflect either common ancestry or contact" (McMahon and McMahon 2005:168) – rather than cognates in situations where many matches occur between languages but their significance is beyond the reach of comparative methodologies. He suggests that their plausibility should be rated to reflect "how far the degree of phonetic similarity ... appears to constitute a correlation significantly greater than chance" (McMahon and McMahon 2005:168). This evokes Dixon's (1997:37, emphasis added) suggestion that:

> [c]omparison of core vocabularies is not, of course, a useless exercise. It is a very helpful first step when dealing with new languages and may suggest hypotheses about possible *relationships* which can be an aid in planning detailed descriptive and comparative work. But it should never be taken as proof of genetic relationships.

Heggarty (2010:307) also proposes that "[i]t would be perfectly logical for approaches to be devised which use lexicostatistical-type cognate counts ... as measures only of degree of divergence between given languages, by whatever real-world forces that came about from one case to the next." He differentiates lexicostatistical analyses aimed at illustrating degrees of relationship from those focused on showing the existence (i.e. fact) of relationship; the first of these is said to be suitable in cases where the subject languages are known to be related, while the second applies when the goal is to establish preliminary evidence of relatedness (Heggarty 2010:307).

Though the theoretical underpinnings of glottochronology are deeply (perhaps fatally) flawed, systematic measures of relatedness still hold considerable potential to contribute to reconstructing the past. As Kaufman and Justeson (2009:230) point out, despite the clear failure of reality to conform to the assumptions on which glottochronology rests, the method nonetheless seems to provide useful approximations of the timing of language diversification. They also hold out the prospect of substantial improvement in the method itself, notably by calculating individual rates of change for each lexical item. Heggarty (2007:327-337) is not so sanguine about the utility of glottochronology, but insists that systematic measures of relatedness can provide very useful general perspectives on the past. His analysis of Quecha varieties, for example, demonstrates that they embrace far more variability than would be plausible for 500 years of diversification, making it wildly unlikely that Quechua spread throughout the Andes with the expansion of Inka political control. In the same way, a determination that languages with non-contiguous distributions are related is sufficient to indicate population movement.

Arguments for a general congruence between historical-linguistic reconstructions and the archaeological record tend not to stimulate intense critiques; simplistic identifications of artifact types, art styles, and archaeological cultures with languages, especially in combination with over-reliance on postulated migrations, evoke sharp reminders that potsherds are not direct stand-ins for people, and most particularly, that they do not speak.

In fact, shared styles, common image elements and iconographic inventories, similar craft practices and technological habits, inclinations, and tendencies all imply some kind of interaction. The existence of speech communities and language varieties also implies interaction, and congruence between the interaction spheres and their material and linguistic results must be a plausible expectation in some circumstances. The critical analytical step is specifying the conditions under which coincidence may be expected and how it may be reflected in the patterning of material remains. This patterning will be far more complex and nuanced than the equation of pottery types with social groups:

> The most troubling aspect of this type of analysis is not the notion that pottery, *a priori*, may be a direct reflection of social groups, but rather that these types of inferences are based upon a very superficial analysis of the pottery itself. It is simplistic to regard one specific ceramic type as diagnostic of anything larger than its singular behavioural correlate. Any definition of an ethnic group by a ceramic style, or any singular

attribute or behaviour, is reductive and uninformative. In order to meaningfully and accurately correlate pottery to social groups, all aspects of ceramic production and distribution must be considered ... in addition to inter and intra-regional cultural and economic interaction spheres. The articulation of social boundaries based on pottery needs to be subordinated to questions concerning who is producing specific ceramic types, for whom and at what scale. (Dessel and Joffe 2000:44)

Despite these obstacles and the frequent oversimplified equation of pottery types with people, careful attention to the mechanisms of production and more nuanced contextualization at varying scales can allow ceramics to offer productive insights into social groups.

Language and Archaeology in Mesoamerica
Attempts to integrate linguistic and archaeological evidence in reconstructions of the pre-Columbian history of Mesoamerica have a long history and remain an important theme in contemporary syntheses. Epigraphic approaches to early Mesoamerican history have focused heavily on the Maya world, though ancient texts are known in several other regions, notably Oaxaca (Zapotec) and the trans-isthmian zone (Zoque). Traces of past interaction have often been sought in lexical items. Hill (2001, 2010) uses a reconstructed maize vocabulary for proto-Uto-Aztecan to argue for the unconventional thesis that Uto-Aztecan languages spread north from Mesoamerica along with agriculture (see Brown 2010 and Kaufman and Justeson 2009:225-226 for a contrary view). Campbell and Kaufman's (1976) argument that extensive borrowing of Mixe-Zoquean words for key cultural items reflects the impact of Gulf coast Olmecs on the rest of Mesoamerica has been widely influential.

In eastern Mesoamerica, a major factor contributing to the inclination to combine archaeological and linguistic evidence is the widely shared belief that, as Coe (2011:11) put it, "[t]here are few parts of the world where there is such a good 'fit' between language and culture: a line drawn around the Mayan-speaking peoples would contain all those remains, and hieroglyphic texts, assigned to the ancient Maya civilization." Although intended to highlight a linkage between a generic Maya cultural pattern and Mayan languages, this notion is not founded on the identification of a specific set of material traits that were demonstrably in use throughout the area where Mayan languages were spoken. To the degree that this claim has a tangible archaeological referent, it is the architectural, sculptural, and textual apparatus of lowland Maya city-states and their rulers (Henderson and Hudson 2012, 2015; Hudson and Henderson 2014). These are markers of eliteness that are beloved by archaeologists, but there is no reason to suppose that they reflect the identities – linguistic or otherwise – of non-elite population segments. This lowland-city-state-centric perspective is a core element of the perception that adjacent areas to the southeast were peripheral to a Maya core. It carries with it the assumption that, if such correspondences hold for the core, they should also be expected in the southeastern periphery, so that the absence of supposed Maya markers signals the presence of non-Mayan speech communities, which may or may not be identified with particular languages.

The textual dimension of this elite complex is particularly problematic. Epigraphic research has a long history in Mesoamerica that originated with colonial-era observations of Diego de Landa (Tozzer 1941) and his (erroneous) recognition of a Maya "alphabet." More scholarly perspectives began to emerge during the 20th century (see e.g. Whorf (1942); Thompson (1960); Knorozov (1958); and Proskouriakoff (1960, 1961, 1963, 1964)), and recent investigations by Lounsbury, Stuart, Houston, Justeson, and others (see bibliography in Wichmann 2004) have revealed a considerable amount of detail about both the script's orthographic and grammatical conventions and the language(s) that it represents. While these contributions provide a crucial line of evidence that can supplement archaeological inquiries, they are based on a biased data set and are not indicative of broader social and linguistic patterns. Literacy among the ancient Maya appears to have been limited to a small and arguably elite subset of the population (Houston and Stuart 1992; Houston 1994), whose cultural and linguistic practices were shaped by their sociopolitical status rather than their geographic location or the identity of the populations under their rule. Most hieroglyphic texts encode the languages – usually one of the Yucatecan or Cholan languages (Johnson 2013:71) – of the aristocrats whose political ends they serve; the vernacular language was often different. Considered together, these factors clearly indicate that writing is a poor reflection of local linguistic practices.

Compared with the Maya lowlands and with western Mesoamerica, the documentation of languages and their distributions and of the material record (Henderson and Hudson 2012) are distinctly spotty in the southeastern peripheral regions. It is clear, however, that some of the languages spoken in the region are related to languages more widely distributed in western Mesoamerica. Members of the Uto-Aztecan group, especially Pipil, and Otomanguean languages such as Mangue provide the most obvious examples. In addition, Subtiaba is very closely related to Tlapanec, another Otomanguean language spoken in Guerrero. A series of languages whose affiliations are markedly less clear – notably Lenca, Tol, and Xinca – are more problematic. These are sometimes treated as isolates, sometimes grouped together, and sometimes linked tenuously to even more distant families; the recurrent suggestions that Lenca might be related to Xinca or alternatively part of a macro-Penutian grouping is a good example. Whatever the model, the lack of data allows these languages to be more easily slotted into positions that are convenient for the interpretive perspective of the classifier.

A clear illustration of this tendency is the Xile Hypothesis, which grew out of an archaeological project directed by Robert Sharer (1978) at the "site-zone" of Chalchuapa in the highlands of El Salvador. Chalchuapa is one of the largest sites in southeastern Mesoamerica, with 58 large civic structures and nearly 100 smaller buildings, probably domestic, located within a civic core of approximately three square kilometers (Sharer 1978:Vol 1). It was occupied nearly continuously from the terminal Early Preclassic (c. 1200 – 900 BC) until the Spanish invasion in the 16th century AD. The eponymously named central site has been combined with five others – Tazumal, Casa Blanca, El Trapiche, Pampe, and Almulunga – to form the heart of the "site zone," which also includes the cultural activity areas of Laguna Cuzcachapa, Laguna Seca, and Las Victorias.

The Xile Hypothesis reflects an ongoing interest in how Chalchuapa's material remains relate to local and regional relationships, as well as to patterns of interaction and influence. It posits the existence of a single ancestral Xinca-Lenca linguistic unit in and around the site during the Late Preclassic period (i.e. the centuries just before and after 1 AD). This hypothetical language was dubbed Xile, since it was taken as the ancestral variety for both Xinca and Lenca. Sharer (1974) and Lawrence Feldman, from whom he first became aware of this interpretation (personal communication cited in Sharer 1974:175), considered Xile to be a Macro-Mayan language spoken by a population that was fully involved in highland Maya society. This group is said to have split – conveniently – into Xinca and Lenca following the eruption of the Ilopango volcano and the attendant social dislocation in the early centuries AD (Sheets 1983, 2002). The Lenca are said to have moved north, towards the Ulúa Valley, and eastward, where they may have formed the majority population at the site of Quelepa. The remaining Xinca speakers were responsible for eventually rebuilding Chalchuapa, but the disruptions caused by the volcano weakened their economic and political foundations and made it possible for Nahua groups such as the Pipil to establish themselves in the region.

The problems with this interpretation are many and begin with the focus on asserting a linguistic association with Mayan-speaking populations. Neither Xinca nor Lenca is well-documented, but there is nothing obvious in the data that are available to suggest either is a Mayan language or that they are related and descended from a common ancestor belonging to a Macro-Mayan stock. The supposed genetic affiliations of Lenca and Xinca with one another and with the Maya were based on the near-anecdotal perspectives of some – but by no means all – historical linguists. The Xile hypothesis was certainly motivated by an interest in attaching linguistic identities to the archaeological record; it may also have involved a desire to mobilize linguistic arguments to bolster the case for connecting the region with the Maya world and its academic cachet. The proposal did not, however, involve consideration of actual linguistic evidence. Although the proposed Xile territory corresponded roughly to the distributional patterns of some artifact forms and styles, the argument was not grounded in a distributional analysis of a well-defined set of material remains. Both the hypothetically shared elements of material culture and their distributions were under-specified. Essentially, inadequately defined sets of material remains were imagined to correspond to a fictitious linguistic entity, which was in effect created to match the distributions of material traits.

Communities and Social Segments in the Archaeological Record

Some attempts to relate language to archaeological evidence have been received quite positively. This may be in part because – as in Campbell and Kaufman's (1976) hypothesis that speakers of Mixe-Zoquean represented a key component of societies that made up the Olmec world – the hypothesis was proferred by linguists, included specific linguistic data, and remained vague about specific material correlates. The response of one of the commenters on Sharer's (1974) Xile hypothesis reflects what is still a more typical perspective in Mesoamerican archaeology: attempts to draw correlations between material remains and languages reflect an all-too-typical Mayanist fascination with correlating archaeologically defined cultures with linguistic groupings. The most naive expression of this is the flat assertion that "[a] degree of commonality in … material culture … is sufficient to indicate that … two populations were speakers of the same language." Such statements must certainly tax the patience of all readers who learned long ago that there exists no necessary relationship between culture (especially material culture) and language. How could such a proposition ever be verified, or even rationalized? (Rucker in Sharer 1974:181-182)

An alternative approach is possible if specific sets of shared elements of material remains (*not* archaeological cultures) and their distributions are defined without reference to hypothetical patterns of language distribution. This analytical separation is crucial, since it allows the degree of fit between independent material distributions and linguistic distributional analyses to be assessed without construing either data set as the mold into which the other must be fitted. It also helps minimize the likelihood of producing distributions that are skewed by tacitly assumed similarities. This in turn enhances the possibility of recognizing patterns that may be indicative of ancient overlap between material cultural production and linguistic usage.

Approaches to distributional patterning in the archaeological record must be comprehensive and systematic if they are to discriminate sets of material remains that correspond in some way to social groupings such as speech communities from those that reflect exchange relationships, aristocratic social networks, political spheres, and the like. A key consideration is the identification of data sets that incorporate material remains produced by the non-elite social segments that comprise the majority of any community. Most attempts to correlate language distributions and material remains have focused on luxury goods – usually items of personal adornment that were made for and consumed by elites – and on materials that are part of the apparatus of states: stelae with royal portraits and hieroglyphic texts, jewelry made from jade and other scarce exotic raw materials, special ceramic vessels, usually elaborately decorated.

The elite functions of these items make their association with language distributions particularly problematic. For example, in the Maya lowlands – Yucatan, the Petén region of northern Guatemala, and adjacent regions of Belize, eastern Chiapas, and northwestern Honduras – it is abundantly clear that such items were part of an international elite culture that was shared by the aristocratic segments of many societies spread across an area in which several languages of the Yucatecan and Cholan sub-groups of the Mayan family were spoken. There is clear evidence in material remains and hieroglyphic texts that members of such elites were very mobile and quite often came to reside among populations with different identities and different vernacular languages. Since individuals are often accompanied by their material possessions when they move, it is necessary to realize that the material items found in a particular location did not necessarily originate from that place and so do not necessarily reflect the population(s) native to it. Additionally, very portable items such as jewelry were sometimes simply items of exchange or gifts, so that their distributions may reflect economic or social networks with no implications at all about cultural identity or language.

With particular reference to pottery – by far the most abundant class of archaeological data in Mesoamerica – the Mixteca-Puebla style provides a very clear case. Defined mainly in terms of shared stylistic and iconographic features of highly decorated elite serving vessels, Mixteca-Puebla pottery – along with mural paintings, books, and portable objects of adornment in the same style – is distributed across Mesoamerica from western Mexico to Costa Rica (Boone and Smith 2003; Day 1984; Escalante 2012; Masson 2003; Nicholson 1960, 1982; Nicholson and Quiñones 1994; Pohl and Masson 2003; Stone 1982; von Winning 1977). It originated late in the first millennium AD in the Cholula region of Puebla and was quickly adopted in the Mixteca region of western Oaxaca; it remained the preferred elite serving ware in these regions until the time of the Spanish invasion. In this core region, Mixteca-Puebla pottery was produced and consumed by speakers of Mixtec and Nahuatl. In West Mexico, it was used by speakers of several Uto-Aztecan languages, and in southeastern Mesoamerica, it occurs among speakers of several languages of varied affiliation. Mixteca-Puebla pottery did not correspond to a particular cultural or linguistic identity but rather indicated a socio-economic status that was shared only by elites with varied cultural, ethnic, and linguistic affiliations. It can thus be conceptualized as a group marker superimposed onto an array of identity categories.

Very different parameters control the manufacture, distribution, and consumption of ordinary ceramic vessels for routine use as part of household practice. We propose that shared features of manufacturing practice – especially form, surface treatment, and decoration – in non-elite household pottery represent the most useful material evidence to consider in relation to language distributions. Jars, bottles, bowls, and plates designed and used for everyday storage, cooking, and household food serving were made for local consumption; they were rarely, if ever, exchanged beyond the local community. Nor were they manufactured in centralized production facilities under the control of and reflecting the preferences of a ruling group or an economic aristocracy.

It is important to note that the status of any given ceramic complex as elite or non-elite is an empirical question that must be addressed with distributional data in each region. Luxury wares made for and consumed by aristocrats cannot be recognized simply on the basis of how they are decorated (e.g., Henderson 1992). Very elaborate polychrome painted pottery in the lower Ulúa valley, for example, looks like the kind of pottery that was limited to high-ranking households in the Maya world; imported examples at Copán were, in fact, luxury wares with extremely restricted distributions. In the lower Ulúa valley itself, where they were made, Ulúa Polychrome vessels were in use in households of all socio-economic ranks despite the fact that, in terms of labor required for their manufacture, they were quite expensive.

Even within a local region, non-elite household pottery was shaped, decorated, and fired in many production sites and was independent of the taste preferences of any particular economic, social, or political group. When household pottery assemblages within a region incorporate similar features of form, surface treatment, and decoration, it is clear that the common features reflect concepts of how such vessels should look that were shared by the bulk of the population within a particular region. They must reflect some dimension of shared identity. When these kinds of features are shared across a very large area, incorporating many local regions, ideas about how such vessels should appear were shared by hundreds of ceramic production facilities in many dozens of communities and by the populations that consumed them. Widely shared preferences of this kind – particularly when they are stable over long time spans (on the scale of centuries) – must correspond to an important shared dimension of identity. Language is the most obvious aspect of identity that is shared by non-elite populations on that scale. This kind of similarity implies not only shared preferences, but also intense long-term communication among potters, and a common language would have facilitated interaction. This does not mean that every widely distributed long-lasting style of utilitarian pottery necessarily corresponds to a particular language group, but it does provide a warrant for entertaining the possibility of such a connection. The critical issue is what other kinds of data may be taken to be compatible with such a relationship.

Quotidian Pottery and Vernacular Language in Southeastern Mesoamerica

The ceramic history of the southeastern periphery of Mesoamerica provides a particularly clear example of a widely distributed and long-lasting household ceramic tradition. From the initial appearance of pottery before 1500 BC, communities in the southeastern periphery shared a series of preferences for particular shapes and surface treatments for their household pottery (Henderson and Beaudry-Corbett 1993). By the last centuries of the first millennium BC, these general preferences crystallized into a distinctive set of features that would be shared throughout the southeastern periphery for more than a millennium. Ceramic vessels for quotidian use featured particular forms of small and medium-sized bowls, plates, jars, and cylinders, as well as ollas large and small. Surface treatments involved specific modes of plastic decoration and painted designs.

These kinds of similarities form the basis for defining ceramic systems (Henderson and Agurcia1987; Beaudry-Corbett, Henderson, and Joyce 1993), a useful but rarely operationalized aspect of Mesoamerican formal ceramic classification. Two sets of ceramic systems (Henderson 1993; Andrews 1976; Baudez and Becquelin 1973; Beaudry-Corbett et al 1993; Hirth, Kennedy, and Cliff 1989, 1993; Nakamura, Aoyama, and Uratsuji 1991; Sato 1993; Sharer 1978: Vol 3; Urban 1993a, 1993b, 1993; Viel 1993a, 1993b) in use during the Classic period (ca AD 250 – 1000) show very heavily overlapping distributions (Fig. 1):

1) unslipped ollas with either similar patterns of brushing, gouging, and incising or with designs involving very similar elements and structures painted in red on smoothed surfaces (the Jicatuyo supersystem; Fig. 2)
2) smaller jars, bowls, and plates with orange slips, decorated with a variety of shared techniques and modes of decoration, including specific red-painted designs and Usulután resist decoration (the Choloma supersystem; Fig. 3)

The distribution pattern of these materials is a general match for the historically attested distribution of Lenca (Fig. 4). Lenca, an isolate that became extinct early in the second half of the 20th century, is attested in a small array of historical documents and ethnographic accounts. All of the documented varieties are demonstrably related, though their status as dialects or distinct languages remains unclear. The lingering uncertainty concerning the particularities of these distinctions will be set aside here and the term Lenca will be used to refer to a collective whole encompassing all attested Lencan varieties.

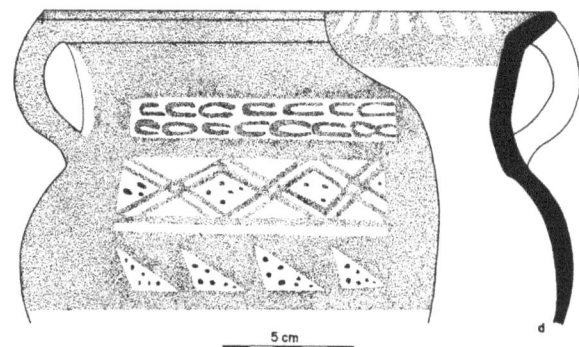

Fig. 2: Magdalena Red-painted olla (Jicatuyo supersystem).

Fig. 3: Conejo Bichrome bowl (Choloma supersystem).

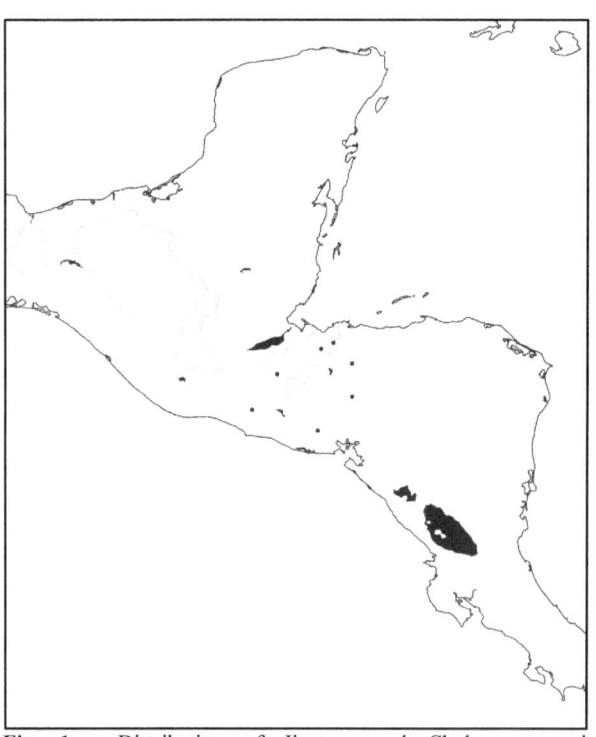

Fig. 1: Distribution of Jicatuyo and Choloma ceramic supersystems.

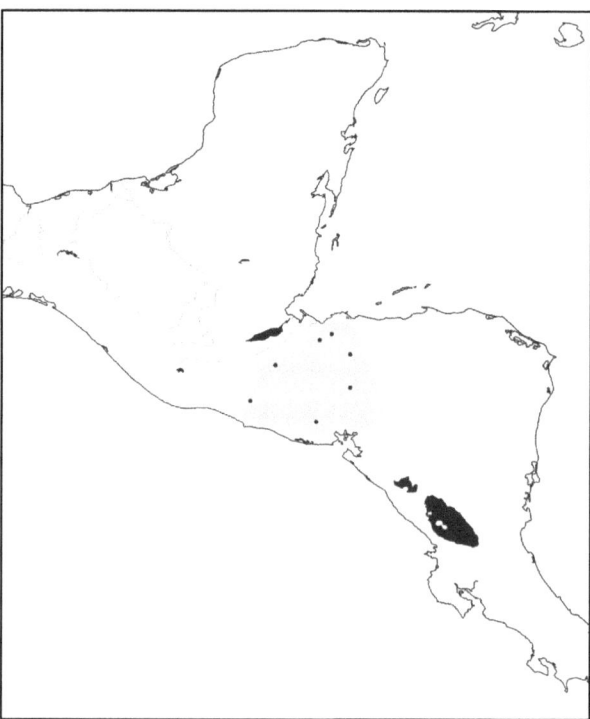

Fig. 4: Distribution of Lenca varieties.

Since a series of local speech communities with related languages/dialects implies descent from a common ancestral language and usually some degree of continuing interaction among their speakers, the distribution of Lenca can be seen as indicative of a network of related communities. The fact that the geographic distribution of the locations in which these varieties were spoken is strikingly similar to that of the household ceramics described above indicates that the corresponding populations of speakers were likely culturally and linguistically related. This is not to suggest, of course, that everyone in the region or in any of its communities spoke only Lenca. Ethnographic and ethnohistorical sources indicate that Mesoamerican communities, families, and individuals were very often multi-lingual, though a single language can usually be identified as dominant within a community. Communities in the southeastern periphery were not homogeneous culturally or linguistically, and near the limits of the distribution of Lenca, intra-community linguistic diversity would have been considerable. Nonetheless, they certainly interacted intensively over a very long period. Similarities in material production among non-elites – unlikely unless the producers participate in the same interaction sphere – would have been facilitated by a common dominant language.

The incorporation of Cacaopera produces an even closer correspondence. Cacaopera is generally classified as a Misumalpan language of the Sumu-Cacaopera-Matagalpa type, but historical and ethnographic records indicate that speakers occasionally self-identified themselves and their language as Lenca, at least in the early part of the twentieth century. Although such auto-classification is not necessarily reflective of actual relatedness, the available lexical data suggest that Cacaopera and Lenca shared a considerable amount of vocabulary indicative of relatively intense interaction. This language – though not necessarily genetically related to Lenca itself – must be taken into account if a full linguistic picture of the southeastern periphery is to be developed. Its geographic positions in the sphere indicated by material commonality, in combination with their attested relationships with known Lenca varieties, indicate a clear association with the archaeologically attested cultural sphere.

The history of ceramic preferences at the Maya city of Copán, in combination with other facets of its material remains, provides a suggestive case study in the correlation between language and non-elite material culture. From the 5th through the 8th centuries AD, Copán was the capital of a substantial regional state near the eastern edge of the Maya world in what is today northwestern Honduras (Andrews and Fash 2005; Fash 2001). Beginning by the mid-to-late first millennium BC, the population of the Copán valley shared the widespread preferences for the particular kinds of utilitarian pottery vessels that define the southeastern sphere. During the 5th century AD, the "Maya royal complex" – a distinctive set of styles of monumental architecture and political art that functioned to bolster the authority of rulers – appeared at Copán without discernible local antecedents. It was arguably imported from the Tikal region of the central Petén (Sharer 2003, 2009), and its appearance was likely accompanied by the arrival of speakers of the Mayan language of that region.

Ceramic innovations accompanying this episode are limited in scale; they clearly involve the appearance of new kinds of pottery, some imported from city-states in the Petén region and some locally manufactured cognates. New kinds of ceramics are far less frequent than local utilitarian containers, particularly in households outside the site core; they certainly did not displace long-standing vessel types. Household vessels at Copán continued to reflect the shared preferences of the southeastern periphery tradition for at least another 500 years; as elsewhere in the southeast, this tradition persisted through the 9th and 10th century transition that brought an end to the centralized political order reflected in Maya city-states. Although archaeological documentation of the last centuries of the pre-Columbian period is sparse, at least some aspects of the southeastern utilitarian tradition survived until the time of the Spanish invasion.

A narrow emphasis on the elite and state-related novelties would lead to the inference that Mayan speech had displaced Lenca – in a manner analogous to the ways in which foreign Maya elites displaced local counterparts – at least in Copán valley, but the continuous production and utilization of utilitarian wares suggests otherwise. There is evidence that speakers of a Mayan language – most probably a language of the Cholan group, and likely an ancestral version of Chort'i – were newly present in the valley. The hieroglyphic texts that demonstrate this are closely associated with the emergence of the new Copán state and the elite group that controlled it. The most plausible inference is that the newly attested language was that of a new ruling group but not the language of the populace.

Concluding Remarks
There appears to be a close parallel between the distribution of a set of widely shared features of household pottery, stable over a period of more than a millennium, on the one hand, and the distribution of Lenca and likely related varieties on the other. This parallel patterning does not establish a definitive one-to-one relationship between preferences for certain features of household ceramic vessels and a particular language, but it is sufficient to warrant serious consideration of the hypothesis that pottery of this tradition was produced in and for a network of communities in which shared Lenca speech facilitated long-term intense interaction.

Support for the hypothesis can be sought in more detailed documentation of variability in both data sets. In the case of the southeastern household ceramic tradition, the most obvious step is to undertake a more detailed analysis of the technology of the pottery comprising the constituent ceramic systems, a dimension of ceramic analysis that rarely receives adequate analytical attention even within local regions. Patterns of variability in the characteristics of production have considerable potential to signal the existence of more localized interaction networks and social groupings within the southeastern sphere. Although continuities from the Classic period to the Spanish invasion in household ceramic production and consumption – especially in red-painted and incised ollas – can be detected in a few regions where the material record is particularly full, better documentation of shared preferences for particular kinds of household pottery during the last centuries of the pre-Columbian era will provide a better bridge to the first direct documentation of languages in the early Colonial period.

The distributional patterning of variation in these decorated serving vessels must be contextualized in terms of the variability in two other classes of pottery in use in the same communities. Distributional patterning in technological dimensions of undecorated utilitarian vessels may be expected to parallel that seen in analogous features of decorated serving vessels, and to reflect more localized networks as well. Shared patterns in elaborately decorated serving vessels, especially Ulúa polychrome varieties, are likely to reflect commerce as well as common preferences resulting from long-term social interaction among prosperous social segments.

Parallels between the distribution of these kinds of features and the distribution of specific varieties of Lenca speech would constitute strong support for the hypothesis that the southeastern tradition of utilitarian pottery reflects, at least in a general way, social groupings characterized not only by interaction but by shared aspects of identity that likely included speech. Unfortunately, it is no longer possible to create language and dialect maps on the basis of contemporary linguistic documentation. Recognition of distinct varieties of Lenca and determination of their distributions must come from painstaking analysis of notoriously incomplete and inconsistent observations about language culled from ethnographic accounts and ethnohistorical sources. These analyses are the focus of our on-going work in southeastern Mesoamerica.

References
Alpher, Barry and David Nash. 1999. Lexical replacement and cognate equilibrium in Australia. *Australian Journal of Linguistics* 19:5-56.

Andrews, E. Wyllys. 1976. *The Archaeology of Quelepa, El Salvador*. Middle American Research Institute, Publication 42. New Orleans: Tulane University.

Andrews, E. Wyllys and William L. Fash (eds.), 2005 *Copán: The History of an Ancient Maya Kingdom*. Santa Fe: School of American Research.

Anthony, David. 2007 *The Horse, the Wheel, and Language: How Bronze-Age Riders from the Eurasian Steppes Shaped the Modern World*. Princeton: Princeton University Press.

Beaudry-Corbett, Marilyn P., Pauline Caputi, John S. Henderson, Rosemary A. Joyce, Eugenia J. Robinson, and Anthony Wonderley. 1993. Lower Ulúa region. In *Pottery of Prehistoric Honduras: Regional Classification and Analysis*. John S. Henderson and Marilyn P. Beaudry-Corbett (eds.), pp.64-135. Institute of Archaeology, Monograph 35. Los Angeles: UCLA.

Beaudry-Corbett, Marilyn P., John S. Henderson, and Rosemary A. Joyce. 1993. Approaches to the analysis of pre-columbian Honduran ceramics. In *Pottery of Prehistoric Honduras: Regional Classification and Analysis*. John S. Henderson and Marilyn P. Beaudry-Corbett (eds.), pp. 3-6. Institute of Archaeology, Monograph 35. Los Angeles: UCLA.

Bellwood, Peter S. 2001. Early agriculturalist population diasporas? Farming, languages, and genes. *Annual Review of Anthropology* 30:

Bellwood, Peter S. and Colin Renfrew (eds.). 2002 *Examining the Farming/Language Dispersal Hypothesis*. Cambridge: McDonald Institute for Archaeological Research, University of Cambridge.

Bellwood, Peter S. and Jared Diamond. 2003. Farmers and their languages: the first expansions. *Science* 300:597-603.

Bergsland, Knut and Hans Vogt. 1962. On the validity of glottochronology. *Current Anthropology* 3: 115–129.

Black, Paul. n.d. *Lexicostatistical lists: Kokaper (with Kokbabonk)*. Unpublished manuscript.

Brown, Cecil H. 2010. Lack of linguistic support for Proto-Uto-Aztecan at 8900 BP. *Proceedings of the National Academy of Sciences* 107(15):E34.

Campbell, Lyle R. and Terrence Kaufman. 1976. A linguistic look at the Olmecs. *American Antiquity* 41:80-89.

Campbell, Lyle R., Terrence Kaufman, and Thomas C. Smith-Stark. 1986. Meso-America as a linguistic area. *Language* 62(3):530-570.

Coe, Michael D. 2011. *The Maya*. 8th ed. New York: Thames & Hudson.

Crowley, Terry and Claire Bowern. 2010. *An Introduction to Historical Linguistics*. 4th Edition. New York: Oxford University Press.

Day, Jane Stevenson. 1984. *New Approaches in Stylistic Analysis: The Late Polychrome Period Ceramics from Hacienda Tempisque, Guanacaste Province, Costa Rica*. PhD dissertation, Department of Anthropology. Boulder: University of Colorado.

Dessel, J. P. and Alexander H. Joffe. 2000. Alternative approaches to Early Bronze Age pottery. In *Ceramics and Change in the Early Bronze Age of the Southern Levant*. Graham Philip and Douglas Baird (eds.), pp. 31-58. Sheffield: Sheffield Academic Press.

Dimmendaal, Gerrit Jan. 2011. *Historical Linguistics and the Comparative Study of African Languages*. Philadelphia: John Benjamin's Publishing Company.

Dixon, Robert M. W. 1997. *The rise and fall of languages*. Cambridge: Cambridge University Press.

Embleton, Sheila M. 1986. *Statistics in Historical Linguistics*. Bochum: Brockmeyer.

Escalante Gonzalbo, Pablo. 2012. The Mixteca-Puebla tradition and H. B. Nicholson. In *Fanning the Sacred Flame: Mesoamerican Studies in Honor of H. B. Nicholson*. Matthew A. Boxt and Brian D. Dillon (eds.), pp. 293-307. Boulder: University Press of Colorado.

Fash, William L. 2001. *Scribes, Warriors, and Kings: The City of Copán and the Ancient Maya*. revised ed. New York: Thames and Hudson.

Hale, K. L. 1961. *Attestations of 100-word list in 33 Cape York languages* [also exists under *Vocabularies and Cognation Judgments for 30 Cape York Peninsula Languages*]. Unpublished manuscript.

Heggarty, Paul. 2007. Linguistics for archaeologists: principles, methods and the case of the Incas. *Cambridge Archaeological Journal* 17(3):311-340.

2010. Beyond Lexicostatistics: How to get more out of 'word list' comparisons. *Diachronica* 27(2): 301-324.

Henderson, John S. 1993. Classification schema. In *Pottery of Prehistoric Honduras: Regional Classification and Analysis*. John S. Henderson and Marilyn P. Beaudry-Corbett (eds.), pp. 281-296. Institute of Archaeology, Monograph 35. Los Angeles: UCLA.

1992. Elites and ethnicity along the southeastern fringe of Mesoamerica. In *Mesoamerican Elites: An Archaeological Assessment*, Diane Z. Chase and Arlen F. Chase (eds.), pp. 157-168. Norman: University of Oklahoma Press.

Henderson, John S. and Ricardo Agurcia F. 1987. Ceramic systems: facilitating comparison in type-variety analysis. In *Maya Ceramics: Papers from the 1985 Maya Ceramic Conference*, Prudence M. Rice and Robert J. Sharer (eds.), pp. 431-438. BAR International Series, 345.

Henderson, John S. and Marilyn P. Beaudry-Corbett (eds.). 1993. *Pottery of Prehistoric Honduras: Regional Classification and Analysis*. Institute of Archaeology, Monograph 35. Los Angeles: UCLA.

Henderson, John S. and Kathryn M. Hudson. 2012. The southeastern fringe of Mesoamerica. In *The Oxford Handbook of Mesoamerican Archaeology*. Deborah L. Nichols and Christopher A. Pool (eds.), pp. 482-494. New York: Oxford University Press.

2015. The myth of Maya: archaeology and the construction of Mesoamerican histories. In Harri Kettunen and Christophe Helmke (eds.), *On Methods: How We Know What We Think We Know About the Maya*, pp. 7-24. Acta Mesoamericana Vol. 28. Markt Schwaben: Verlag Anton Saurwein.

Hill, Jane H. 2001. Proto-Uto-Aztecan. *American Anthropologist* 103(4):913–934.

2010. New evidence for a Mesoamerican homeland for Proto-Uto-Aztecan. *Proceedings of the National Academy of Sciences* 107 (11):E33.

Hirth, Kenneth, Nedenia Kennedy, and Maynard Cliff. 1989. Chronology and ceramic variability within the El Cajon region. In *Archaeological Research in the El Cajon Region*, Vol. 1. Kenneth Hirth, Gloria Lara Pinto, and George Hasemann (eds.), pp. 207-232. Memoirs in Latin American Archaeology, No. 1. Pittsburgh: University of Pittsburgh.

1993. El Cajón region. In *Pottery of Prehistoric Honduras: Regional Classification and Analysis*. John S. Henderson and Marilyn P. Beaudry-Corbett (eds.), pp. 214-232. Institute of Archaeology, Monograph 35. Los Angeles: UCLA.

Hoijer, Harry. 1956. Lexicostatistics: A critique. *Language* 32: 49-60.

Houston, Stephen D. 1994. Literacy among the pre-columbian Maya: a comparative perspective. In *Writing Without Words: Alternative Literacies in Mesoamerica and the Andes*. Elizabeth H. Boone and Walter D. Mignolo (eds.), pp. 27-49. Durham: Duke University Press.

Houston, Stephen D, and David Stuart. 1992. On Maya hieroglyphic literacy. *Current Anthropology* 33(5):589-593.

Hudson, Kathryn M. and John S. Henderson. 2014. Life on the edge: identity and interaction in the Land of Ulúa and the Maya world. In *Sounds Like Theory*. Janne Ikäheimo, Anna-Kaisa Salmi, and Tiina Äikäs (eds.), pp. 151-171.

Johnson, Scott A. J. 2013. *Translating Maya Hieroglyphs*. Norman: University of Oklahoma Press.

Kaufman, Terrence and John Justeson. 2009. Historical linguistics and pre-columbian Mesoamerica. *Ancient Mesoamerica* 20(2):221-231.

Knorozov, Yuri V. 1958. The problem of the study of the Maya hieroglyphic writing. translated by Sophie D. Coe. *American Antiquity* 23(3):284-291.

Kroeber, Alfred L. and C. D. Chrétien. 1937. Quantitative Classification of Indo-European Languages. *Language* 13(2):83-103.

Mallory, James Patrick. 1989. *In Search of the Indo-Europeans: Language, Archaeology and Myth*. London: Thames & Hudson.

Mallory, James Patrick and Douglas Q. Adams. 2006. *The Oxford Introduction to Proto-Indo-European and the Proto-Indo-European World*. Oxford: Oxford University Press.

Masson, Marilyn. 2003. The Late Postclassic symbol sets in the Maya area. In *The Postclassic Mesoamerican World*. Michael E. Smith and Frances F. Berdan (eds.), pp. 194-200. Salt Lake City: University of Utah Press.

Matisoff, James A. 2000. On the uselessness of glottochronology for the subgrouping of Tibeto-Burman. In *Time Depth in Historical Linguistics*, eds. Colin Renfrew, April McMahon, and Larry Trask, pp. 333–372. Cambridge: McDonald Institute for Archaeological Research.

McMahon, April, Paul Heggarty, Robert McMahon, and Natalia Slaska. 2005. Swadesh sublists and the benefits of borrowing: an Andean case study. *Transactions of the Philological Society* 103(2): p.147–170.

McMahon, April and Robert McMahon. 2005 *Language Classification by Numbers*. Oxford: Oxford University Press.

Nakamura, Seiichi, Kazuo Aoyama, and Eiji Uratsuji (eds.). 1991. *Investigaciones Arqueológicas en la Región de La Entrada*. San Pedro Sula: Instituto Hondureño de Antropología e Historia.

Nicholson, Henry B. 1960. The Mixteca-Puebla concept in Mesoamerican archaeology: a re-examination. In *Men and Cultures: Selected Papers from the 5th International Congress of Anthropological and Ethnological Sciences, Philadelphia, September 1-9, 1956*. Anthony F. C. Wallace (ed.), pp. 612-617. Philadelphia: University of Pennsylvania.

1982. The Mixteca-Puebla concept revisited. In *The Art and Iconography of Late Postclassic Central Mexico*. Elizabeth H. Boone (ed.), pp. 227-254. Washington: Dumbarton Oaks.

Nicholson, Henry B. and Eloise Quiñones Keber (eds.). 1994. *Mixteca-Puebla: Discoveries and Researches in Mesoamerican Art and Archaeology*. Culver City: Labyrinthos.

O'Grady, Geoffrey, and Terry Klokeid. 1969. Australian Linguistic Classification: A Plea for Coordination of Effort. *Oceania* 39(4): 298-311.

Pohl, John M. D. 2003. Ritual and iconographic variability in Mixteca-Puebla Polychrome pottery. In *The Postclassic Mesoamerican World*. Michael E. Smith and Frances F. Berdan (eds.), pp. 201-206. Salt Lake City: University of Utah Press.

Proskouriakoff, Tatiana. 1960. Historical implications of a pattern of dates at Piedras Negras, Guatemala. *American Antiquity* 25(4):454-75.

1961. Portraits of women in Maya art. In *Essays in Pre-Columbian Art and Archaeology*. Samuel K. Lothrop, et al. (eds.), pp. 81-99. Cambridge: Harvard University Press.

1963. Historical data in the inscriptions of Yaxchilán, Pt. 1. *Estudios de Cultura Maya* 3:149-67.

1964. Historical data in the inscriptions of Yaxchilán, Pt. 2. *Estudios de Cultura Maya* 4:177-201.

Renfrew, Colin. 1987. *Archaeology and Language: The Puzzle of Indo-European Origins*. Cambridge: Cambridge University Press.

Sato, Etsuo. 1993. La Entrada region. In *Pottery of Prehistoric Honduras: Regional Classification and Analysis*. John S. Henderson and Marilyn P. Beaudry-Corbett (eds.), pp. 20-29. Institute of Archaeology, Monograph 35. Los Angeles: UCLA.

Sharer, Robert J. 1974. The prehistory of the southeastern Maya periphery. *Current Anthropology* 15:165-187.

1978. *The Prehistory of Chalchuapa, El Salvador*. 3 vols. Philadelphia: University of Pennsylvania Press.

2003. Tikal and the Copán dynastic founding. In *Tikal: Dynasties, Foreigners, and Affairs of State.* Jeremy A. Sabloff, ed. Pp. 319-354. Santa Fe: School of American Research.

2009. The Ch'orti' past : an archaeological perspective. In *The Ch'orti Maya Area: Past and Present.* Brent E. Metz, Cameron L. McNeil, and Kerry M. Hull (eds.), pp. 124-133. Gainesville: University Press of Florida.

Sheets, Payson D. (ed.). 1983. *Archaeology and Volcanism in Central America: The Zapotitlan Valley of El Salvador.* Austin: University of Texas Press.

2002. *Before the Volcano Erupted: The Ancient Cerén Village in Central America.* Austin: University of Texas Press.

Smith-Stark, Thomas C. 1994. Mesoamerican calques. In *Investigaciones lingüísticas en Mesoamérica.* Carolyn J. MacKay and Verónica Vásquez (eds.), pp. 15-50. Mexico: Universidad Nacional Autónoma de México.

Stone, Doris Z. 1982. Cultural radiations from the central and southern highlands of Mexico into Costa Rica. In *Aspects of the Mixteca-Puebla Style and Mixtec and Central Mexican Culture in Southern Mesoamerica.* Middle American Research Institute, Occasional Paper 4:61-70. New Orleans: Tulane University.

Swadesh, Morris. 1950. Salish Internal Relationships. *International Journal of American Linguistics* 16(4): 157-167.

1955. Towards Greater Accuracy in Lexicostatistic Dating. *International Journal of American Linguistics* 21 (2): 121-137.

Teeter, Karl. 1963. Lexicostatistics and genetic relationship. *Language* 39:638-648.

Thompson, J. Eric S. 1960. *Maya Hieroglyphic Writing: An Introduction.* Rev. ed. Norman: University of Oklahoma Press.

Tozzer, Alfred M. (ed.). 1941. *Landa's Relacion de las Cosas de Yucatan.* Cambridge: Harvard University, Peabody Museum Papers 18

Urban, Patricia A. 1993a. Naco Valley. In *Pottery of Prehistoric Honduras: Regional Classification and Analysis.* John S. Henderson and Marilyn P. Beaudry-Corbett (eds.), pp. 30-63. Institute of Archaeology, Monograph 35. Los Angeles: UCLA.

1993b. Central Santa Bárbara region. In *Pottery of Prehistoric Honduras: Regional Classification and Analysis.* John S. Henderson and Marilyn P. Beaudry-Corbett (eds.), pp. 136-171. Institute of Archaeology, Monograph 35. Los Angeles: UCLA.

1993c. Southwestern Honduras. In *Pottery of Prehistoric Honduras: Regional Classification and Analysis.* John S. Henderson and Marilyn P. Beaudry-Corbett (eds.), pp. 172-179. Institute of Archaeology, Monograph 35. Los Angeles: UCLA.

Viel, René. 1993a. Copán Valley. In *Pottery of Prehistoric Honduras: Regional Classification and Analysis.* John S. Henderson and Marilyn P. Beaudry-Corbett (eds.), pp. 12-18. Institute of Archaeology, Monograph 35. Los Angeles: UCLA.

1993b. *Evolución de la Cerámica de Copán, Honduras.* Tegucigalpa: Instituto Hondureño de Antropología e Historia.

von Winning, Hasso. 1977. Rituals depicted on polychrome ceramics from Nayarit. In *Pre-Columbian Art History.* Alana Cordy-Collins and Jean Stern (eds.), pp. 121-134. Palo Alto: Peek Publications.

Whorf, Benjamin Lee. 1942. Decipherment of the linguistic portions of the Maya hieroglyphs. *Annual Report for 1941*, pp. 479-502. Washington: Smithsonian Institution.

Wichmann, Soren (ed.). 2004. *The Linguistics of Maya Writing.* Salt Lake City: University of Utah Press.

Studies on the genetic make-up of the Aleut are equally inconclusive at this point (compare Achilli et al. 2013, suggesting haplogroup A2a, typical of EA, arose in Alaska, with Crawford, Rubicz, and Zlojutro 2010:712 suggesting that the Alaskan Eskimo may have come from Siberia in a separate migration). They do suggest that the eastern Aleut and Southwestern Alaskan mainland area had more genetic diversity than previously thought, with the diversity increasing over time and involving possible admixture from neighboring Eskimo and Na-Dene groups (Raff, et al. 2010:687); that the Aleut have been a distinctive population for about 3000 years; and that the Eastern Aleut show affinities with the Siberian Yupit and Chukchi, and the Western Aleut with Alaskan Yupit (Crawford, Rubicz, and Zlojutro 2010, Reich et al. 2012). One study suggests some connection between the Bering Island Aleut, the Sireniki, and the Paleo-Eskimo Saqqaq of almost 4000 B.P., but the connection is not direct (Gilbert et al., 2008). Various models have been proposed to explain the peopling of the Aleutians (Crawford et al. 2010, citing Zlojutro et al. 2006), ranging from early Paleo-Aleut presence with Aleut genetic markers, to early pan-Beringian presence, to early Na-Dene presence, but all involving subsequent population incursions westward along the Aleutian Chain, particularly around 6000 B.P.; this date coincides with the earliest period of cultural change in the archaeological record.

There is also genetic evidence for the third period of cultural change. For example, Smith et al. (2009) find evidence for a replacement of the maternal line about 1000 B.P., coinciding with the presence of Neo-Aleut cranial types. There are also suggestions that in 500 B.P., the Aleut type was found far to the east of present-day acknowledged Aleut territory, and that an influx of newcomers, possibly Thule Eskimos, arrived in the Eastern Aleut territory about 1000 B.P. and began moving westward (Crawford, Rubicz, and Zlojutro 2010, Hatfield 2010).

3.3 Ethnohistory
Evidence for both cultural and physical contact, at least for the latest period of contact from ca. 1000 B.P., is bolstered by the earliest historical records, which show that the Aleut, the people of Southeast Alaska, and those of the Northwest Coast shared mythologies, cultural practices, and socio-economic organization. The Aleut, like the Eyak, Tlingit, Haida, and Tsimshian, but unlike the Yupit, had a stratified society with up to five social classes, including slaves (Liapunova, 1996:138). The institution of slavery was well established, old, and most developed in the more densely populated eastern Aleutians. Both material goods and slaves, most often women and children, were acquired by frequent trade or war from the Kodiak Islanders, the Chugach, Tlingit, and Dena'ina communities to the east, and from neighboring Aleut communities on the chain (Veniaminov 1984). Some families may have had a slave for each member of the family, and as many as 20 slaves have been recorded in a family (Liuapunova 1996:138ff). The norm may have resembled the northern Northwest Coast, where despite considerable variability within and between communities, the number of slaves was enough to have a considerable socio-economic and political impact on a community (Donald, 1997:197). Thus, at least in the Eastern Aleutians, Aleut speakers were in close contact with non-Aleut speakers for extended periods of time. Aleut men would have had exposure to other languages during their travels, and women and children would have had exposure to other languages through slaves in their homes.

4. Eskimo-Aleut Linguistics and Language Contact
All the non-linguistic evidence makes it difficult to maintain certain assumptions about the linguistic history of EA. Thus, separate dispersals may mean that the genesis of EA was not necessarily on the Seward Peninsula; a shorter time period of EA divergence may not account for the sharp differences between Eskimo and Aleut; and extensive cultural contact between the Aleut and their neighbors make it difficult to rely on language-internal developments alone to account for language change in Aleut.

In addition, since the 1980's, there have been a number of advances in our understanding of how languages change as well as in the methodologies available to examine relationships between languages. A number of studies (i.a. Thomason and Kaufman 1988, Hickey 2003, Heine & Kuteva 2005) have highlighted the role of language contact in language change, the different types of contact and their expected outcomes, and the types of evidence of contact that we might expect to find. In particular, certain patterns are strongly suggestive of certain types of contact. For example, long-term stable bilingualism can be expected to have a different effect than rapid language shift or language mixing. The former tends to show more evidence of lexical borrowing and what Ross (2003) terms 'metatypy', or grammatical convergence, while the latter may show significant structural changes, multiple sources of inheritance, etc. A conspicuous reason to look for evidence of language contact is especially the inability to account for significant amounts of data with the comparative method, including apparent cognates with irregular sound correspondences, radical differences between related languages, unexplained typological similarities with neighboring languages, etc. (cf. Ross 2003:174). In addition, there has been a shift from a preference for the most parsimonious explanation of a linguistic change, often equivalent to a language internal explanation, to a preference for the best explanation, which may include language external motivations (cf. Filppula 2003:161).

It therefore makes sense to re-examine the relationship between Aleut and Eskimo for evidence of language contact. As the reconstruction of EA is based largely on similarities in the phonological and morphological systems and on the cognate status of some 15-25% of the lexicon, I focus here on lexical and phonological evidence, although as noted above, several studies have proposed grammatical evidence. Possible evidence for contact can be found in loanwords between neighboring languages, distribution patterns of Eskimo and Aleut

#	Loan from		Loan into	
1	Athabaskan	Dena'ina *nini* (cf. Koyukon *noone*) 'porcupine'	Aleut	*nuunax̂* 'porcupine'
2	Athabaskan	Dena'ina *k'qushiya* 'marmot'	Aleut	*qusx̂ix̂* marmot
3	Aleut	*chaqalkan* 'kind of seaweed	Dena'ina Athabaskan (via Eskimo); also in Eyak, Tlingit, Tsimshian, Kwakiutl	*jaqal'qa* 'dulse'
4	Aleut	*saquchikdax̂* 'fly'	Dena'ina Athabaskan	*tsaqunka* 'common flea'
5	Aleut	*agaayuux̂* 'cormorant'	Eyak	*àwáiyàq* 'cormorant'

Table 1. Prehistoric loanwords between Aleut and non-Eskimo languages.

cognates, the existence of large numbers of synonyms, irregular sound correspondences, phonological variability, and lexical constructions more typical of Athabaskan languages.

4.1 Loanwords

To date, there is little evidence of language contact in the form of loanwords. This is one of the main reasons given for assuming a high degree of relative isolation of the Eskimo, Aleut, and neighboring groups. Bergsland (1994) lists both loans from other languages into Aleut and loans from Aleut into neighboring languages. The vast majority of loans so far identified are shared between Central Alaskan Yupik or Alutiiq Eskimo and Aleut, in particular Eastern Aleut. Of the 110 shared terms, 80% come from Aleut and relate to flora, fauna, and material culture. As Aleut was a greater source than recipient of borrowing, this could indicate that the Aleut homeland was further east at one point (see 3.2).

Only a handful of lexical items common to Aleut and Athabaskan or Pacific Northwest Coast languages from the pre-Russian contact period have been identified (Table 1; from Bergsland 1986, 1994); loans between Aleut and non-Eskimo languages may have been introduced via Eskimo:

The lack of obvious loanwords may not be as important in determining prehistoric language contact as has been assumed, as "lexical borrowing is not a necessary condition or concomitant of contact-induced change' (Ross 2003:193). However, preliminary studies suggest the probability of finding additional loans, and further that other types of borrowing, e.g. calques, may have been more important (see 4.6).

4.2 Distribution of EA cognates to non-cognates

Bergsland (1986) claims that between 15-25% of the Eskimo and Aleut vocabularies are cognate. The fact that many terms are non-cognate does not by itself suggest an external source. Some may be the result of old taboo systems, slang, or metaphorical extensions, as in Eastern Aleut *agna-x̂* 'tongue', possibly related to *agi-* 'to open', but Eastern Aleut *umsu-x̂* 'fluke, whale's tail'; cf. Atkan and later Eastern *umsu-x̂*, Attuan *uvsu-x̂* 'tongue.' However, close studies of the lexicon (Bergsland 1986, Berge 2012, 2014) reveal an apparent split between the grammatical and more lexical domains of the lexicon: the former (inflection, deixis, basic postpositions) are mostly cognate; lexical domains so far examined are mostly non-cognate, with some notable exceptions. Of those reviewed so far, only some male domains (relating to boats and hunting tools) show more cognate than non-cognate terminology, although only by slight margins. Otherwise, over half of the basic 200-word Swadesh list is non-cognate, and terms for kinship, flora and fauna, clothing, house, war, basketry, sewing, and social status are mostly non-cognate. Many cognates are not the most basic; thus the roots of Aleut *chaĝalix* 'seal pup' and Eskimo *carliaq* 'baby, young of animal' are cognate, and Aleut *agdaaĝux̂* 'young of hair seal' is a term derived from a possible cognate root *hax-six* 'to grow, grow up' (cf. perhaps Yupik *makete-* Inuit *makit-* 'to get up'), but none of the basic Aleut terms for seal are cognate, e.g. Aleut *iglagayax̂* 'ribbon seal' vs. Central Alaskan Yupik *qasrulik* or northern Inupiaq *qaiqulik* 'ribbon seal.' And while the most basic positional nouns (e.g. Aleut *il-* 'inside,' Proto-Eskimo *ilu* 'inside'), which function as postpositions in Aleut, are shared between Aleut and Eskimo, Aleut has generalized the category so that there are now more than 50 postpositions. While some of these are cognate or possibly cognate with roots in Eskimo (e.g. Aleut *chuq(i)-* 'root, bottom, area beneath', Proto-Eskimo (PE) *cuqlay-* 'root (edible)', over half are non-cognate (see 4.6).

These patterns are not unlike what is found in cases of language shift or in mixed languages where the vocabulary is predominantly from one source (the target language) and the grammar predominantly from another (the source language; cf. Winford 2003). This seems to suggest that speakers of an EA language shifted to a non-EA language, rather than vice versa (contra Fortescue 1998:187, who hypothesizes that an original non-EA population adopted an incoming EA language; Fortescue's proposed shift, however, is about 4000 B.P.).

4.3 Existence of large numbers of synonyms

For 199 terms on the Swadesh 200-word basic vocabulary list (one term, 'woods', is not represented), there are 530 close equivalents, including dialectal variants and synonyms. All but 68 of the 199 terms have one or more synonyms; for many synonym pairs, no obvious distributional or semantic differences are noted in Bergsland (1994), although one is often a default term. Some examples are given below:

'one'	taĝatax̂	ataqan (PE cognate)
'belly'	sanĝux̂	kilmax̂
'to breathe'	axsmilix	anĝilix (PE cognate)
'cold'	achunax̂	ichingunal (possible PE cognate)
'to dig'	kamgulix	hangulix

Not infrequently, there are multiple synonyms; the term 'cold', for example, is represented by four terms, with no obvious difference in usage: Atkan and Attuan *achuna-*, not cognate with Eskimo, *ichinguna-* and *ikuna-*, both in Atkan only and both possible cognates with Eskimo, and Eastern and Atkan *qingana-*, not cognate. Synonymy may arise for a number of reasons, including dialect diversity, specialized vocabulary as a reflection of social and cultural complexity, and importantly, language contact. A more detailed investigation of synonyms and their sources is needed, however.

4.4 Irregular Sound Correspondences

Despite a number of important works on the phonological and morphological reconstruction of Eskimo and Aleut, particularly in the 20th century (and most recently by Bergsland 1986, Fortescue 1998, Fortescue et al. 2012, and Alonso de la Fuenta 2010), there is still no comprehensive reconstruction of proto-Aleut (as opposed to proto-Eskimo), and many reconstructions of Aleut words are extremely tentative. Bergsland (1986:66ff) writes that some 10% of his reconstructed EA cognates assume irregular development. For example, there is no regular Aleut *$*d$* ~ Yupik *$*t$* correspondence, although Aleut *ada-* 'father' is labeled a possible irregular cognate of Yupik and Seward Peninsula Inupiaq *ata* 'father' (Bergsland 1994:11). In an otherwise straightforward phonological system with voiceless stops corresponding to voiced fricatives, the reconstructions of *$*t$, c, č, s (Bergsland 1994; Fortescue et al. 2010 reconstruct *$*t_1$, *$*t_2$, *$*c_1$, and *$*c_2$) are unclear – they do not all straightforwardly correspond to voiced fricatives – and the many noted correspondences are problematic, with only partial conditioning environments. Thus, 'the difference between [the following] remains obscure' (Bergsland 1986:11):

Aleut *asax̂* 'name', *asaa* 'his name'	Yupik *ateq*	PE *$*atər$
Aleut *itix̂* 'anus', *ichaa* 'his anus'	Yupik *teq*, *texxa*	PE *$*ətər$

There are many other irregular correspondences. It is as yet unclear whether they suggest as yet unexplored internal sound changes or whether they are evidence of ancient loans between Eskimo and Aleut.

4.5 Phonological variability

The Eskimo and Aleut phonological systems are obviously similar to each other both in their inventories of sounds and in their phonotactics, and they are relatively simple in comparison with the neighboring Athabaskan languages. However, Aleut allows a degree of phonological variability in the production of various morphemes and lexical items that is unknown in the Eskimo languages. Thus, either or both vowel quality and length may vary, and velar and uvular phonemes may be interchanged in some words or morphemes. The variability in vowel quality and length may be related to sometimes competing rules of accentuation, syncopation, epenthesis, and vowel harmony, although the details remain to be worked out. For example, the main accent tends to be penultimate and may perceptually lengthen a vowel; the number of syllables and vowel length may affect syncopation, as in *ukux̂takux̂* 'he/she sees' vs. *ukux̂t'kuqing* 'I see'; epenthetic vowels may be realized as /i/ or as /a/; in Eastern Aleut, /a/ vowels tend to be influenced by neighboring high vowels, as in *tayaĝux̂* → *tayuĝux̂* 'man', or *itxaygix̂* → *itxiygix̂* 'reindeer.' As a result, a single word may have a number of different pronunciations, as in the following extreme case, which illustrates both vowel and velar/uvular variability:

Eastern Aleut *uuĝ(u)mik(i)dax, uuĝ(u)mika(a)dax, uuĝamikadax, uumx̂ikaadax, uumĝika(a)dax̂, uunĝimkaadax̂, uuĝnimkaadax̂, aaĝumkidax* 'blowfly' (Bergsland 1994:426)

This variability is noted for some Athabaskan-Eyak-Tlingit (AET) languages (e.g. Eyak, cf. Krauss 2012, although the nature of variability in Eyak may arise for unrelated reasons and needs further investigation).

4.6 Lexical constructions

There are a number of lexical constructions that, while found in both Eskimo and Aleut, have become far more common and generalized in Aleut, including noun and postpositional phrases. Both Eskimo and Aleut have derivational morphology for nominal modification; likewise, both have periphrastic noun phrases based on possessive constructions. Eskimo languages tend to prefer derivation, however, while Aleut generalizes the possessive construction. Derived nouns in Aleut tend to have some lexicalized meaning, as illustrated below:

Greenlandic derived N	**Aleut derived N**
illu-ssuaq	*ula-lgu-x̂*
house-BIG.ABS	house-big-ABS
'the big house'	lit. 'the big house', used to denote 'hotel', or other big building

As in Eskimo (cf. Fortescue 1984:330), periphrastic noun phrases may sometimes result in quasi-compounds, such as *kamgam ulaa* 'feast house', now lexicalized as 'church' and the basis of verbalizations, as in [*kamgam ula*]*ĝilix* 'to have a church', but with no unusual morphophonology (cf. *ulaĝilix* 'to have a house, to live…'). Unlike Eskimo, however, Aleut also makes extensive use of quasi-compounds rather than derived nouns for a wide variety of concepts, ranging from native flora, place and personal names to body parts (Bergsland 1994, 1998), as in *aanisnaadam saaxarangin* 'Indian paintbrush flower' (lit. 'bumblebee's sugar');' these types of compounds are widely found in the neighboring Athabaskan languages, cf. Dena'ina *nantl'iłi t'una* 'arctic lupine' (lit. 'bee's plant'). Other Aleut examples are given below:

a. *tanam chngatuu* 'kind of beetle' (lit. 'land's hair, fur')
b. *agalum kitangis* 'roots (lit. feet) of the teeth'
c. *Qugam itxa* (place name on Umnak Island, lit. 'demon's tail')
d. *Alitxum aalicha* (person name, lit. 'Army's landing place')

There are strong reasons for reconstructing case marking in both Eskimo and Aleut, although it is extremely reduced in the latter. Instead, Aleut makes use of postpositional phrases, the postpositions having developed from positional nouns. Noun phrases involving positional nouns are found in both Eskimo and Aleut languages, although in Eskimo, case-marked nouns such as *illu-mi* 'house- LOCATIVE'= 'in the house' are more typical:

Greenlandic derived N	**Greenlandic NP**	**Aleut NP → PP**
illu-mi	*illu-up ilu-ani*	*ula-m il-an*
house-LOC	house-REL inside-3SG.POS.LOC	house-REL inside-LOC
'in the house'	'inside the house'	'in the house, inside the house'

While there are seven cognate positional nouns between Eskimo and Aleut, there are over 50 postpositions in Aleut. Interestingly, the same types of positional noun phrases are found in AET; they are structured similarly, consisting of a noun or pronoun and a postpositional element that may have been a positional noun in origin; and there are around 35 of them, e.g. *-layɛ* 'on top of', from a nominal stem meaning 'end, top' compounded with the preceding element (Sapir 1915:547). In both Aleut and AET, positional nouns are frequently used with unexpressed nouns; postpositions may head a nominalization or a relative clause, e.g. Aleut *ukux̂tagan ilan* 'look.at.NOMZ.3SG.REL in' = 'while he was looking at her' (Bergsland 1997a:317; cf. Chipewyan *hi-l-tc! ɛ-t!a* 'because he was angry', from *hi-l-tc!ɛ* 'he was angry' and postpositive *–t!a* 'with, on account of', Sapir 1915:549); postpositions may be combined, even merging into compounds in Aleut, e.g. Eastern Aleut *qusamadaa* 'upward direction' from *qusam hadaa* 'above toward' (Bergsland 1997a:69; cf. Tlingit *t'a·ɹi* 'under' from *ɹi* 'down in' and presumably something related to Ath *-t'a* 'among,' Sapir 1915:548); and postpositions can take locational case marking (Bergsland 1997a:67; Sapir 1915:547).

Thus, Aleut has (over-)generalized an EA pattern of noun phrase construction (Heine and Kuteva 2005); this pattern is also prevalent in AET. It is quite possible that this generalization was driven by both language internal and external motivations.

5. Conclusions
The linguistic features described above are only circumstantial evidence of language contact, and certainly require more targeted studies. However, taken together, and in conjunction with non-linguistic evidence, they are suggestive of contact effects. Of the three prehistoric periods of cultural contact, the last two, approximately 3000 B.P. and 1000 B.P., are most relevant for EA. Two layers of Eskimo contact effects might explain similarities between discontinuous groups, e.g. between Atkan Aleut and Central Alaskan Yupik, and between Eastern and Central Siberian Yupik. The latest contact may have had the greatest effect: everything points to a major upheaval between 1000-600 B.P., including the Thule advance, the development of new technology, and cultural upheavals possibly as a result of climatic factors such as population expansion, crash, and subsequent repopulation. Cultural changes affected the whole Pacific coast area and included the arrival not only of Thule influence from the northwest but also of the Dena'ina Athabaskans the Eyak from the east, and the Tlingit from the south, and increased social complexity, warfare, and trade. Although there is no obvious evidence of large-scale population replacement (cf. Heggarty 2015), this may have involved the absorption, to varying degrees, of incoming groups.

Given the advances in multiple fields, it seems clear that we need to reassess long-held ideas regarding the history and development of EA. Some important components of such work should include 1) a systematic historical reconstruction of Proto-Aleut, 2) a clarification of the cognate status of lexical items with irregular sound correspondences, 3) a detailed and comprehensive examination of the non-sourced vocabulary, and 4) collaboration with ongoing investigations in all relevant fields. With respect to the latter, the linguistic understanding of EA would be better informed by more archaeology in the Aleut area, more clarity in the molecular and physical anthropological findings, and the incorporation of new methodologies in historical linguistics including language contact and prehistory, lexicostratigraphy, and linguistic phylogeny. With respect to the latter, an important and relatively new contribution to our understanding of language change is the increasingly refined use of large data sets to model language relationships. Phylogenetic studies are already proving useful in evaluating different Beringian migration theories (Sicoli and Holton, 2014), and they confirm the oddity of Aleut (Wichmann et al. 2014).

Abbreviations
ABS = absolutive, LOC = locative, N = noun, NOMZ = nominalizer, NP = noun phrase, POS = possessive, PP = postpositional phrase, REL = relative, SG = singular

References
Achilli, Alessandro, et al. 2013. Reconciling migration models to the Americas with the variation of north American native mitogenomes. *Proceedings of the National Academy of Sciences of the United States of America* 110:35:14308-14313. doi:10.1073/pnas.1306290110.

Alonso de la Fuente, José Andrés. 2010. Proto-Eskimo-Aleut */ə/ and the origin of Aleut pre-aspirated consonants. *Revista Española de Antropología Americana* 40:1:139-159.

Berge, Anna. Forthcoming. Polysynthesis in Aleut (Unangam Tunuu). *Asian and African Languages and Linguistics*.

Berge, Anna. 2010. Origins of linguistic diversity in the Aleutian Islands, in Crawford, M.H. et. al., 557-582.

Bergsland, Knut. 1986. Comparative Eskimo-Aleut phonology and lexicon. *Journal de la Société Finno-ougrienne* 80:63-137.

Bergsland, Knut. 1989. Comparative aspects of Aleut syntax. *Journal de la Société Finno-ougrienne* 82:7-80.

Bergsland, Knut, compiler. 1994. *Aleut Dictionary : Unangam Tunudgusii*. Fairbanks: ANLC.

Bergsland, Knut. 1997b. How Did the Aleut Language Become Different from the Eskimo Languages? In *Languages of the North Pacific Rim 2,* Osahito Miyaoka and Minoru Oshima, eds. Sakyo-ku: Kyoto University, Graduate School of Letters, 1-17.

Bergsland, Knut, and Vogt, Hans. 1962. On the validity of Glottochronology. *Current Anthropology*, April 1962, vol 3(2):115-153.

Corbett, Debra, West, Dixie, and Lefèvre, Christine, eds. 2010. The People at the End of the World: The Western Aleutians Project and the Archaeology of Shemya Island. *Alaska Anthropological Association Monograph Series VIII*. Anchorage: Aurora.

Crawford, M. H., West, Dixie L., O'Rourke, Dennis H. 2010. Special Issue on the Origins of the Populations of the Aleutian Islands. *Human Biology* 82:5-6.

Crawford, Michael H., Rubicz, Rohina C., and Zlojutro, Mark. 2010. Origins of Aleuts and the genetic structure of populations of the archipelago: Molecular and archaeological perspectives, in Crawford, M.H. et. al., 2010. 695-717.

Davis, Richard S. and Knecht, Richard A. 2010. Continuity and change in the Eastern Aleutian archaeological sequence, in Crawford, M.H. et. al., 507-524.

Donald, Leland. 1997. *Aboriginal Slavery on the Northwest Coast of North America*. Berkeley: University of California.

Dumond, Don. 1965. On Eskaleutian linguistics, Archaeology, and Prehistory. *American Anthropologist* 67(5):1231–1257.

Dumond, Don. 1987. A reexamination of Aleut prehistory. *American Anthropologist* 89:1:32-56.

Dumond, Don. 2001. Toward a (yet) newer view of the (pre)history of the Aleutians. In *Archaeology in the Aleut Zone of Alaska, Some Recent Research*, D. E. Dumond, ed. University of Oregon Anthropological Papers 58. Eugene: University of Oregon Press, 298-309.

Fortescue, Michael. 1998. *Language Relations Across Bering Strait: Reappraising the Archaeological and Linguistic Evidence.* London: Cassell.

Fortescue, Michael. 2002. The Rise and fall of Eskimo-Aleut polysynthesis. In *Problems of Polysynthesis*, Nicholas Evans and Hans-Jürgen Sasse, eds. Berlin: Akademie Verlag, GmbH, 257-276.

Fortescue, Michael, Steven Jacobson, Lawrence Kaplan. 1994. *Comparative Eskimo Dictionary with Aleut Cognates*. Fairbanks: ANLC.

Foster, Michael K. 1996. Languages and the Culture History of North America. In *Handbook of North America Indians* vol. 17, Ives Goddard, vol. ed. Washington, D.C.: Smithsonian Institution, 64-110.

Gilbert MTP, Kivisild T, Grønnow B, Andersen PK, Metspalu E, Reidla M, Tamm E, Axelsson E, Götherström A, Campos PF, Rasmussen M, Metspalu M, Higham TFG, Schwenninger J-L, Nathan R, De Hoog C-J, Koch A, Møller LN, Andreasen C, Meldgaard M, Villems R, Bendixen C, and Willerslev E (2008) Paleo-Eskimo mtDNA Genome Reveals Matrilineal Discontinuity in Greenland. *Science* 320: 1787-1789.

Golovko, Evgenij Vasil'evic. 1996. Aleut and the Aleuts in Contact with Other Languages and Peoples. In *Atlas of Language of Intercultural Communication in the Pacific, Asia, and the Americas.* S.A. Wurm, P. Muhlhausler, D.T. Tryon (eds.). Berlin; New York: Mouton de Gruyter, 1095–1101

Hatfield, Virginia L. 2010. Material culture across the Aleutian Archipelago, in Crawford, M.H. et al., 525-556.

Heggarty, Paul. 2015. Prehistory through Language and Archaeology, in *The Routledge Handbook of Historical Linguistics,* Claire Bowern and Bethwyn Evans, eds. London: Routledge. 595-626.

Heine, Bernd, and Kuteva, Tania. 2005. *Language Contact and Grammatical Change*. Cambridge Approaches to Language Contact. Cambridge: Cambridge University.

Hrdlička, A. 1945. *The Aleutian and Commander Islands and Their Inhabitants.* Philadelphia: Wistar Institute of Anatomy and Biology.

Krauss, Michael E. 1979. Na-Dene and Eskimo. In *The languages of Native America: Historical and Comparative Assessment,* L. Campbell & M. Mithun, eds. Austin: University of Texas Press, 803-901.

Krauss, Michael. 1990. Typology and change in Alaskan languages. In Language Typology 1987: Systematic Balance in Language, Papers from the Linguistic Typology Symposium, Berkeley, 1-3 December 1987. Current Issues in Linguistic Theory 67, Winfred P. Lehmann, ed. Amsterdam: John Benjamins, 147-159.

Krauss, Michael. 2012. Eyak Dictionary draft. http://www.uafanlc.arsc.edu/data/Online/EY961K2011/Eyak_Dictionary_2012-05-01.pdf

Laughlin, W.S. 1951. The Alaska Gateway viewed from the Aleutian Islands. In *Papers on the Physical Anthropology of the American Indian,* W.S. Laughlin, ed. New York: Viking Fund, 98-126.

Laughlin, W.S. 1952. The Aleut-Eskimo Community. *Anthropological Papers of the University of Alaska* 1(1):25-46.

Laughlin, William S. 1980. *Aleuts: Survivors of the Bering Land Bridge*. Forth Worth: Hartcourt Brace.

Leer, Jeff. 1991. Evidence for a Northwest Coast language area: promiscuous number marking and periphrastic possessive constructions in Haida, Eyak, and Aleut. *IJAL* 57.2:158-193.

Liapunova, Roza G. 1996. *Essays on the ethnography of the Aleuts : at the end of the eighteenth and the first half of the nineteenth century*. Translated by Jerry Shelest, edited by William B. Workman and Lydia T. Black. Fairbanks : University of Alaska, c1996.

Marsh, Gordon, and Swadesh, Morris. 1951. Kleinschmidt Centennial V: Eskimo Aleut Correspondences. *IJAL* 17:4:209-216.

Maschner, Herbert D. G. and Reedy-Maschner, Katherine L. 1999. Raid, Retreat, Defend (Repeat): The Archaeology and Ethnohistory of Warfare on the North Pacific Rim. *Journal of Anthropological Archaeology* 17:19–51.

Mason, Owen K. 2009. Flight from the Bering Strait: Did Siberian Punuk/Thule Military Cadres Conquer Northwest Alaska? In *The Northern World, AD 900-1400*, Herbert Maschner Owen Mason, and Robert McGhee, eds. Salt Lake: University of Utah, 76-127.

Miyaoka, Osahito. 2012. *A Grammar of Central Alaskan Yupik (CAY).* Mouton Grammar Library 58. Berlin: Mouton De Gruyter.

Ross, Malcom. 2003. Diagnosing prehistoric language contact. In *Motives for Language Change,* Raymond Hickey, ed. Cambridge: Cambridge University Press, 174-198.

Sapir, E. 1916. Time Perspective in Aboriginal American Culture, A Study in Method. *Anthropological Studies 13*. Ottowa: Government Printing Bureau.

Sicoli MA, Holton G (2014) Linguistic Phylogenies Support Back-Migration from Beringia to Asia. PLoS ONE 9(3): e91722. doi:10.1371/journal.pone.0091722.

Smith, Silvia E., Hayes, M. Geoffrey, Cabana, Graciela S., Huff, Chad, Coltrain, Joan Brenner, O'Rourke, Dennis H. 2009. Inferring Population Continuity Versus Replacement with aDNA: A Cautionary Tale from the Aleutian Islands. *Human Biology* 31:4:407-426.

Thomason, Sarah Grey and Kaufman, Terrence. 1988. *Language Contact, Creolization, and Genetic Linguistics.* Berkeley: University of California.

Veltre, Douglas W. 2001. Korovinsky: Archaeological and Ethnographical Investigations of a Pre- and Post-Contact Aleut and Russian Settlement on Atka Island, in *Archaeology in the Aleut Zone of Alaska*, Don Dumond, ed. Eugene: University of Oregon Anthropological Papers 58:187-213.

Wichmann, Søren, André Müller, Annkathrin Wett, Viveka Velupillai, Julia Bischoffberger, Cecil H. Brown, Eric W. Holman, Sebastian Sauppe, Zarina Molochieva, Pamela Brown, Harald Hammarström, Oleg Belyaev, Johann-Mattis List, Dik Bakker, Dmitry Egorov, Matthias Urban, Robert Mailhammer, Agustina Carrizo, Matthew S. Dryer, Evgenia Korovina, David Beck, Helen Geyer, Pattie Epps, Anthony Grant, and Pilar Valenzuela. 2013. The ASJP Database (version 16). Listss16_nw.pdf. Accessed at https://archive.org/details/asjp-database-16, 05/10/2015.

Winford, Ronald. 2003. *An Introduction to Contact Linguistics.* Oxford: Blackwell.

Woodbury, Anthony. 1984. Eskimo and Aleut Languages. In *Handbook of North American 42 Indians, Vol. 5: Arctic*, David Damas, ed. Washington, D.C.: Smithsonian, 49-63.

An Archaeology of Air

Jeff Benjamin, Columbia University

Anaximenes held that the world is perishable.
-Aëtius (Wheelwright 1966, 63)

Doesn't a breath of the air that pervaded earlier days caress us as well?
In the voices we hear, isn't there an echo of now silent ones?
- Walter Benjamin 1940, 390

A cherished feature of the "World Air Guitar Championships" held annually in Oulu, Finland – as stated by one of its participants – is the fact that the event defiantly eludes academic intervention – it simply can't be taken seriously. While outside of the purview of this paper, I would gladly approach this challenge in ever so many ways, but to mention simply one, it seems that 'air guitar' accomplishes a great deal by momentarily making the *invisible visible* through an heroic effort of human amusement, the creation of an active performative space where this epiphany of consciousness quite justifiably belongs. Competitors in this event come from all over the world and then take to the stage, cradling and playing imaginary guitars with great enthusiasm and skill. Their performances are judged based on the standards of technical virtuosity and 'air-ness', an undefinable category which allows for considerable latitude among the judges. Another endearing quality of this competition (and the basis for its origin as articulated by its founders) is the stated ideal of creating world peace, with the thought that if everyone simply played air guitar there would be no more war, because nobody could hold guns (Varley 2016).

For the purposes of this paper, I will describe *air* as a variegated, complexly layered, multiply textured substance covering the earth's surface. It is of diverse densities and temperatures, exhibiting qualities of form and formlessness, motion and stasis, and carrying within it all forms of various gases, spores and pollen from plants, dust, sediment and soil, birds, insects, microbes of all kinds. It is, in fact, a repository of archaeological knowledge as rich and informative as the subsurface matrix. As a portion of the earth's stratigraphy, the atmosphere (where most air resides) "is more of a visceral, thickened, and ponderous presence, weighing more than five thousand trillion tons and rife with life, activity, and movement" (Macauley 2010, 29). Although existing as a fluid, the airscape is highly structured and has the capacity for maintaining strictly delineated form. One particular event serves to illustrate this property. On April 25, 1953, a nuclear bomb test in Nevada sent a mushroom cloud 44,000 feet into the sky. The high winds of the jetstream, reaching 115 miles per hour, caught this cloud of airborne radioactive material and transported it as an intact mass, where a storm then deposited it "out of the air and into the ground" (Wald 2003) upon the city of Troy, New York, more than two thousand miles from its source.

The contemplation of air as an object, or "hyper-object" (Morton 2013, see below) of archaeological inquiry immediately evokes the challenge of invisibility: objects of archaeological concern are generally visible. This suggests a possible expansion of allowable qualities associated with archaeological objects, or artifacts. Air eludes the grasp of archaeologists in many respects, although there has been notable progress regarding the fluid, dynamic qualities of large-scale objects (Edgeworth 2011). Because of its invisible nature, in colloquial expressions air is treated as an homogenous entity, a consistent and uniform field, an empty space, a void, where matter and things abide and move *through*. However it is clearly true that air moves within us (through the process of respiration), just as we move within it. As Macauley has noted, it is upon realizing that the entire planet is quite literally "conspiring" together that we might reach a greater understanding: "to contemplate this fact can dramatically change our lives to reveal new ways that human others and nonhuman otherness are woven into the very elemental conditions of our existence" (Macauley 26).

Interpreted strictly, an 'archaeology of air' could refer directly to the critically important climatological practice of analyzing air bubbles in ice core samples to determine the constitution past atmospheres, but it is perhaps through an investigation of the aeolian artifacts that exist within the dynamic, flowing substance of above-ground air where we can best start to understand how to approach language archaeologically. It is within air, this finite aeolian midden, that speech and language seem to play a particularly important role in the geological era now generally accepted as the anthropocene (arising from a rapidly accelerating human influence on planetary systems). Speech is simply one of several human material interventions into this precarious matrix of air; it is just one of a multitude of anthropogenic aeolian forms, particularly within the troposphere, the lowest layer of the earth's atmosphere where most human activity occurs. Increasingly covered by an ever deepening skin of anthropogenic matter, it has now been proposed that the upper levels of the earth's surface constitute what could be termed the "archaeosphere" (Edgeworth 2014), a rather modest proposal suggesting that the entire planet is now a region of archaeological concern. Instead of differentiating, I would include the aeolian realm within this concept, since, as previously mentioned, the atmosphere is rife with anthropogenic influence. We are, as Goethe has observed, "'people of the air-ocean' (Völker des Luftmeers)... Our bodies are, in other words, fully immersed in air and shaped by this seemingly invisible form of matter all around us, through which we move." (Sullivan 2014, 85).

Air, as an extensively distributed substance, could easily qualify for the term "hyperobject," since is it "viscous, non-local, interobjective" (Morton 2013, 1). Morton's neologism can be seen as an attempt to both apprehend and explain the vastness of phenomena that seem to confound human understanding. For this reason, it is a useful conceptual model that could be employed towards an effort to come to terms with something as unfathomable as climate change itself. However, it should be noted that there has also been a fair amount of antecedent work on the topic of expansive natural entities, including air. In Western philosophy this extends back to early Greek philosophers and their invested engagement with the four basic *elements* of air, water, earth and fire. This partition finds its first written expression in Western literature in the work of Empedocles (Kingsley 1995, 1), though it should be stated that he did not invent them; the four separate elements were already in common use within Greek thought (Macauley 2010, 108). Kingsley elucidates the significant amount of debate and confusion regarding Empedocles' use of the terms "aither" and "aer," and which one was intended to indicate what is commonly considered to be the realm of air, that which we breathe. Interestingly, it is the former term, "aither," which was intended for this (Kingsley 24), though centuries of misinterpretations have led to the use of the latter, which was originally intended to indicate moisture, mist, vapor (35).

Anaximenes' prophetic warning at the beginning of this article makes one question whether we should study the words of those who failed or those who warned – those who could see the danger coming. Anaximenes of Miletus (585-528 BC), a student of Anaximander, held that air is "the principle...out of which come to be things that are coming to be, things that have come to be, and things that will be" (Anaximenes, as quoted by Hippolytus in *Refutation* 1.7.1-3 = DK 13A7; McKirahan 1994, 49). According to Theophrastus, Anaximenes agreed with Anaximander "that the underlying nature is one and APEIRON, but not indeterminate as Anaximander held, but definite, saying that it is air." (Theophrastus, quoted by Simplicius, Commentary on Aristotle's Physics 2.26-25.1 = DK 13A5; McKirahan 48). Subsequent Greek observations of sound and the human voice are subsumed within the earliest scientific investigations into air. In a fascinating series of queries into various natural and social phenomena, Aristotle expresses puzzlement regarding the echoing human voice:

Why, if indeed voice is air that has been given shape and while traveling its shape is often dissolved, does echo occur when such (air) strikes against something hard and it is not dissolved, but we hear it clearly? Is it because (echo) is refraction, but not dispersion? In this way the whole persists, and the two parts that are similar shapes arise from it; for refraction occurs at a similar angle. And this is why the voice of the echo is similar to the original (Aristotle 369).

With an acknowledgement of this early Greek engagement with air as an element – an entity widely distributed through space and time (an early expression of "hyperobject") – permission may be granted to take air seriously as a zone of archaeological inquiry, along with its corresponding anthropogenic configurations, not the least of which is human speech and language.

The Aeolian Artifacts of Industry: Sound and Speech
The symbol for the American Society for Industrial Archaeology is the gasholder in Troy, New York. Constructed by the Troy Gas Light Company in 1912, this structure held coal gas used for industrial and street lighting in the early twentieth century. The Troy structure is typical for the time: a thick round brick shell with decorative window wells which housed a large iron tank with an open bottom that raised up and down on a pool of water, keeping the trapped gas at a steady pressure (Pyne 1989, 55). The symbol of the gasholder is an appropriate segue, because the very term "gasholder" is a term that Benjamin Lee Whorf would have highly approved of, since its function (and subsequent dangerous implications) is properly captured in language. Working as an employee of a fire insurance company, Whorf's linguistic discoveries had their genesis in an investigation of pragmatic and imprudent word choices in industrial applications, "analyzing many hundreds of reports of circumstances surrounding the start of fires, and in some cases, of explosions" (Whorf 1956, 135). In particular, Whorf draws attention to the erroneous use of the word "empty" when speaking of – or worse yet – labeling gasoline tanks that have been emptied of their fluid contents:

Thus, around a storage of what are called "gasoline drums" behavior will tend to a certain type, that is, great care will be exercised; while around a storage of what are called "empty gasoline drums," it will tend to be different – careless, with little repression of smoking or of tossing cigarette stubs about. Yet the "empty" drums are perhaps the more dangerous, since they contain explosive vapor (Whorf 135).

Whorf's observations demonstrate that words and language are materially contiguous with visible, tangible forms, meriting similar treatment and creating commensurate effects. As noted by Poincaré, words are incendiary artifacts in themselves. Reflecting upon a particular human susceptibility to language, Poincaré writes of human beings: "they can be moved by a single word and remain indifferent to everything else. I have no way of knowing if this decisive word is not the one which you are about to say, and I would forbid you to say it!" (Poincaré 1963, 116). In an interesting study tracing the historical and political trajectory of particular words, Gluck and Tsing note that "words are like swords, sometimes becoming so rigid that the words and practices of power can hardly be separated" (Gluck and Tsing, 13). The material propinquity and contiguity of words with tangible force suggests that the opposite is also true: words could have a profoundly ameliorative effect. Moreover, I would submit that it is the manner in which the invisible, gaseous realm of air is addressed by language (and archaeological text) that might offer instructive options for the present ecological crisis. In the meantime, failure to adequately contend with climate change is also a failure of language (as well as everything else). Just as we can hardly expect existing repeated and tangible anthropogenic forms such as streets, windows, cars, buildings, empty lots, light poles, cell phones to offer any functional counteractive to the present situation, it is similarly unlikely that the existing repeated linguistic forms could produce any substantial effect. Language can now be treated just like all other aspects of repetitive material culture. In a discussion of the 'statement' as an elementary unit of discourse, Foucault writes:

> This repeatable materiality that characterizes the enunciative function reveals the statement as a specific and paradoxical object, but also as one of those objects that men produce, manipulate, use, transform, exchange, combine, decompose and recompose, and possibly destroy (Foucault 1972, 105).

The application of linguistic structuralism upon social and material form has provided a very useful way to differentiate between forms and discern patterns as well as deviations from patterns, but this has traditionally unidirectional. In an analysis of the vernacular architecture of a very specific area in the state of Virginia in the United States, Henry Glassie makes explicit use of the structural linguistic model by looking for a grammar of "architectural competence," an irreducible formal unit that carried through several hundred houses. In this case it was a square, roughly 16 feet by 16 feet. All other aspects of Glassie's grammar were derived from this single unit. Since there were no written records of how the carpenters of this region made their decisions building and partitioning space, Glassie employed a Saussurian linguistic structural model and was able to discern intricate structural patterns to infer the corresponding "patterns in logic" (Glassie 160) of the makers. James Deetz, a student of Glassie, reversed this relationship, stating that words have many properties in common with tangible artifacts, foregrounding the tangible form as a base to draw comparisons (Deetz).

This raises a question: can a model of formal properties of tangible artifacts be used to analyze spoken language? For instance, could the maximum weight of a cubic foot of water laden soil, as an irreducible unit of green roofing practice, provide meaning, direction and structure for language? Can archaeologists study spoken words as artifacts without relying upon written records as an interpretive key? The relationship "between artifacts and text" (Andren 1998) has been well explored, and as noted by Andren "a concern with text emerged simultaneously with archaeology as a discipline" in the form of "philological archaeology" (Andren 16). By physically discovering and recovering written texts, archaeology informs and augments spoken language, one might even say that it produces language. However, spoken words - as units of sound - are materially constituted, and I would submit that they can also be studied archaeologically, separate from their correspondence in text. This archaeological engagement with the sonic forms of words seems to find a place within the disciplinary parameters of contemporary archaeology; an archaeology of the "just now."

Daily sonic experience would suggest that the 'repeated sound' is an elemental component of industrial material and social formation. It is a creative force capable of delineating and erasing social boundaries as well as forming social identities. The history of industrialization itself is often discussed agonistically; as class struggle. This history of contention – sonic and otherwise – cannot be denied, but to this dialogue I would like to draw attention to the considerable amount of evidence that suggests that an understanding of industrializing - and more importantly, *deindustrializing*- processes can be enhanced through an interpretive filter of sonic affect: how industrial sound has, over time, influenced speech patterns and behavior, and vice versa (Eco 1983). In 1854, Thoreau described in a rather celebratory manner the emergent sound of the railroad, and perhaps most salient to the discussion at hand is the social change that Thoreau observed. It is specifically this kind of testimony that helps us, now fully immersed in industrial social forms, to understand just how unique this process was, especially as it pertains to the changes in speech. Thoreau writes: "Do they not talk and think faster in the depot than they did in the stage office? There is something electrifying in the atmosphere of the former place....To do things 'railroad fashion' is now the by-word...." (Thoreau 2004, 202). The literary treatment of this sonic transition by other authors, such as Nathaniel Hawthorne, are laced with foreboding. I would submit that such historical observations can help us listen to our own changing soundscape. What are the emerging sonifacts of de-industrialization, and how can this be verified?

Within the sonic space of the act of building or even dismantling, within the repeated pounding, tapping, positioning of like materials, the fastening of the built environment to the earth, there are words. These words tend to be declaratory, abrupt, short, certainly not expository. In settings of industrial production a word can speak volumes. The words tend to exist within niches created by the absence of sounds of production – extending Krause's "niche hypothesis" into the human realm of "anthrophony" (Krause 2012). In such busy sonic environments we sometimes say that we need to 'get a word in edgewise', and it would seem that this phrase has actual physical merit. In 1912 at Indiana University, Arthur Foley and Wilmer Souder used the principle of light diffraction to photograph sound waves emitting from a clicking device situated between a light source and an emulsion plate. The resulting images captured the airborne sound waves (Foley and Souder 1912). While these sonic forms are simple and elegant, the sound environment of a construction site or urban environment is very intricate and complex, and of great intensity. In the eighteenth century within the cotton mills of Lancashire, England, an interesting practice developed because of this sonic intensity. Known as "mee-mawing," workers would make eye contact and mouth their words without vocalization, since there was no possibility of speaking over the machinery (Sale 1995, 46).

Speech forms of early industrialization happened within, between, around, over and under these percussive, repetitive, cyclical sound forms of industry, and contributed to the advent of acquired hearing loss as well as a particular kind of internalization of speech. Although by no means making any causal connection to industrialization, Jakobson addresses this tendency towards sonic interiority explicitly, saying:

> We speak to ourselves without emitting and without hearing any sounds. Instead of pronouncing or hearing we imagine ourselves to be pronouncing or hearing. The words of our interior speech are not composed of emitted sounds but of their acoustic and motor images (Jakobson 1978, 37).

In the extreme sonic environment of an assembly line, a kind of self induced anaesthesia ensues. Interviewed by Studs Terkel in his book "Working," a spot welder at a Ford assembly line stated:

> You don't compete against the noise....You pretty much stay with yourself. You get involved with yourself. You dream, you think of things you've done. I drift back continuously to when I was a kid and what me and my brothers did. (Terkel 1974, 222).

In historical accounts, sound is usually a peripheral concern at best, and yet language pertaining to environmental sound inserts itself in a very interesting way. It is probably no coincidence that a town with a sudden increase in industrial activity or urban expansion is frequently referred to as a 'boom-town.' From all of the historical evidence, this term is probably sonically accurate. In a somewhat typical example of economic boosterism, a pamphlet describing the acceleration of manufacturing in mid-nineteenth century Montreal states:

> The whirr of machinery and the booming noise of a thousand hammers echo on every side, we are within a very hive of human industry. (Lewis 2000, 101).

Sharing significantly similar properties of compression and pneumatic release, human speech and the various sonifacts of the machines of the extractive industries existed simultaneously in the aeolian realm of the early industrial era. In the formation of the built environment, a particular group of devices and their sonic counterparts deserve closer scrutiny. Steam hammers, drills, pile drivers and other equipment using pressurized air were a ubiquitous presence in early industrial and urban America. The pile driver, initially employing a heavy weight dropped from a height, was so ubiquitous that very little is actually known about its origins (Boyer 1985: 57). However, in early American accounts, engineers kept meticulous records of the amount of strikes and the weight used to drive piles of varying lengths into varying substrates. Detailed cyclical and periodic information is available for many of these devices in early patents. Considered sonically, musicians could interpret them as musical scores (Benjamin 2013, 55) and simply to imagine their operation one can deduce the implications for sustained human speech; they can even be viewed as an extension or replacement of human speech. The operative features of many hammering tools were obscured from view and proper functioning frequently relied upon a partner providing visual commands. These patent descriptions give us an idea of how speech and listening endured and were transformed within early industrial settings. One engineer's account relates the 9,923 hammer strikes at 65 per minute required to drive a piling into position with a 2800 pound weight (Wellington 1893, 118). The friction of the repeated impact would often cause the top of the pilings to catch fire, especially with the Nasmyth steam pile driver, which did not lift a weight, but rather drove a piston straight down with the force of compressed air onto the head of the piling at a rate of one strike per second (U.S.A.C.E. 1881, 9). We can still see the remains of many of these artifacts, bobbing just above the surface of the water, inverted tree stems, utilizing the tree's natural tapered biological form as a wedge, capped with a ring of iron. In hindsound, it would be tempting to conjure a percussive sonifactual assemblage accompanying the positioning of each piling, but this was not always the way it was done. In fact, most of the successful pilings in the Hudson River along New York City were *pressed* into the silt with the weight of the scow, not driven through impact.

In the mid 1800's when the pilings supporting the brick and stone buildings of early Chicago proved insufficient and the future of the city was threatened by rising water, a 27 year old engineer, George Pullman, took on the task of raising entire buildings out of the swamp, sometimes as much as five meters, city blocks at a time, by supporting the buildings from beneath with timbers and installing thousands of turn jacks. Vocal commands would have been indispensible in this process, since one can stay visually focused on the task at hand while listening for the command that might be very well out of sight. It is almost certain that vocal messages synchronized the incremental turnings of the jacks, and the buildings were slowly raised, with people still working and living in them, windows, furniture all intact (Buder 1967: 5). The importance of speech within the extractive industries as well as early industry can be discerned within the woodblock prints of the treatise of early mining techniques in Agricola's "De Re Metallica" (1556, 1950) and Diderot's "Encyclopedia of Trades and Industry" (1751, 1959). Notable for their inclusion of the human form within illustrations of technical processes, both works carry frequent depictions of workers engaged in the act of the "disciplined perception" (Rose 2004, 73) of listening as well as speaking. The manipulation of atmospheric pressure in devices such as Bessemer furnaces, foundries, pile drivers, steam hammers, pressurized caissons for bridge and building foundations and drills of all kinds for the extractive industries composed a fundamental aeolian force resulting in the fusion of the human built environment to the surface of the earth.

Language as Art

As both the composition and medium of spoken language, air is also an important element for consideration in linguistic theory, for the characteristics of air impart upon speech its necessary elements of form and motion. The lowest level of the atmosphere, the troposphere, extending to about 12 kilometers, is a region where words are formed, exchanged, transformed, hidden, forgotten, remembered; where, as the greek root tropos, or "turn" suggests, they mix and blend with great simultaneity. Due to changes in temperature and humidity, the speed and motion of spoken forms in this region varies considerably. In normal atmospheric conditions, when the air is cooler at higher elevation, sound bends upward as it moves, creating a shadow zone on the ground where it does not reach. In an inversion of this, where there is a warm layer of air above a cool surface layer, sound refracts downward and can travel long distances along the surface. Wind also changes the motion of sound. Spoken into a headwind, words will be directed upwards while spoken downwind they fall to the earth (Simon Fraser University 2015). It is in this realm of constant motion and change, this chaotic medium, that words present themselves, offering a challenge for archaeologists accustomed to a study of static form. Thinking about such dynamic systems as objects – as Edgeworth has done in his archaeological study of rivers – may seem to impart upon them a quality of stasis. But perhaps a consideration of fluid form as artifact could also serve to impart upon static or inert objects a greater dynamism. I would concede that studying words archaeologically does seem to reduce their quality of exigency or urgency, in keeping with Mark Leone's observation regarding the "relative muteness of archaeological data" (Leone 1978, 194). In thinking this way, I have found support in Pierre Schaeffer's concept of the 'sound object' – unit of sound independent of source or receiver. It was Schaeffer's now famous cut-bell experiment that led him to this realization. But the phrase "cut-bell" is in itself misleading, for it was not the bell which was cut, but rather the tape recording of a bell strike, where the attack portion of the sound was removed physically from the tape, and the remaining portion of the tape, when played, sounded like an oboe (Schaeffer 2012, 14). It was this discovery which convinced Schaeffer that sound could be conceived as an object independent of its source or listener.

The proposition that words and speech forms exist in the world as sonic artifacts, or sonifacts (Benjamin 2015) – on par with tangible artifacts – immediately calls to question their place within a heirarchy of concerns. What is the place of linguistic forms within the vast realm of human material culture? The philosopher John Searle is careful to separate language from thought itself. He laments: "Language is typically not seen as an extension of prelinguistic forms of intentionality. On the contrary, language is often seen as the primary form of intentionality, and some philosophers claim that without language, there can be no thought at all. I believe that this view is more than a philosophical error; it is bad biology...." (Searle 2009, 61). Having miraculously maintained their sensitivity, artists and poets tend to confirm the existence and endurance of pre-(or post?) linguistic modes of thought that cannot be expressed in words. Artaud is particularly articulate in this regard:

> There's no correlation for me between words and the exact states of my being....I study myself microscopically....I'm the man who's best felt the astounding disorder of his language in relation to his thought....I am the man who knows the innermost recesses of loss (Artaud 1965, 37).

Zerzan echoes this sense of loss in his essay "Too Marvelous for Words:"

> Language initiates and reproduces a distinction or separation that leads to ever-increasing placelessness...Foucault noted that speech is not merely 'a verbalization of conflicts and systems of domination, but...the very object of man's conflicts.' He didn't develop this point, which is valid and deserves our attention and study" (Zerzan 2008, 6).

Archaeology takes issues of space and place quite seriously, therefore any archaeological treatment of sound and speech can be seen as an attempt to reclaim a place for language, but in order to do this language must be willing to share space with other artifacts – to exist on par with them. Conceived archaeologically, language can be approached as human detritus: reconstituted, recycled and modified as all artifacts and assemblages sustain change of form and context over time. On a more positive note, Ricouer states that the very life force of language is within its forward motion toward change and metamorphosis. The goal of language, as Ricouer sees it, is in "producing new utterances" (Ricouer 1974, 84). "This advance of (ideal) meaning toward the (real) reference is the very soul of language" (87). It would seem that, due to their intrinsic properties of motion and invisibility, sound, language and air will always find ways to evade capture.

The cut-up method of reorganization of words by poets, sounds by musicians, and images by visual artists is simply the manifestation of an unconscious interior process of choice. It is reminiscent of Saussure's observation regarding the associative properties of words: how a word, when uttered, automatically conjures a host of possible relationships with all other words simultaneously. William S. Burroughs, conjecturing that spoken language is actually a virus in a symbiotic relationship with its host, celebrated the cut-up technique as a way for writers to better understand words, by encouraging a "tactile communication" with them, as a way to possibly achieve a form of resistance. The poet Gary Snyder celebrates the "wildness" of language, language as a kind of "uninvited guest," suggesting a foreignness from the human organism, speculating that it came from "someplace else" (Snyder 1977, 177). Burroughs also proposes that the cut-up form of linguistic reorganization even has a prophetic capacity, stating: "Perhaps events are pre-written and pre-recorded and when you cut word lines the future leaks out" (Burroughs 1974, 28).

In a recent talk addressing the multiple temporalities manifest in the archaeological record, Yannis Hamilakis was asked: "How do we engage the future?" To this he responded: "It's a matter of reshaping the discipline to think about what kinds of material we accept in our own domain." (Hamilakis 2015). I would add that if we are to think about the future at all, then why not think about the best possible case scenarios? I mention this because discussions of climate change are already drawing troubling metaphors, even models with distinct military features. For instance, a labor historian has stated that "The scale and scope of change necessary to reach 350 parts per million is surely comparable with that of mobilization for World War II" (Brecher 2014, 3). The human tendency toward repetition is certainly one trait that keeps archaeologists in business, but as Thomas McGovern has observed, we are also in a unique position to discern the material perpetuation of "repeated mistakes" (McGovern 2015), and I would assert that this includes linguistic ones. McGovern specifically addresses this repetition of error concerning resource depletion and waste, showing how error occurs when there is a restriction and narrowing of the stream of knowledge. This quite naturally segues into language. Burroughs has stated "There are certain formulas, word-locks, which will lock up a whole civilization for a thousand years" (Burroughs 1974, 49). But as mentioned earlier, there are also well known techniques for freeing up and loosening language from an artistic standpoint.

It is no mistake that we employ meteorological terms to denote freedom of speech, thought and expression, this is the material culture of air, after all: we try to create a "climate" conducive to free speech, learning and thought: in a gathering, in a classroom, a sonic micro-climate; an attentiveness to competing speech forms, how words coexist or collide. A sensitive archaeological attentiveness to spoken language is well situated to discern these shifting forms.

Starting with the rather modest proposition that language is art, and without being formulaic, it would only seem appropriate for archaeologists to include descriptions of sounds and words in their field notes, abstracted from any preconceived meaning or judgement, so that patterns of maintenance and moments of departure can be discerned. It is possible that, by borrowing systems of classification and analysis from linguistics, acoustics and musicology, an archaeometry of sound and speech forms could perhaps emerge.

> All experiments...represent problems in archaeological material, through incomplete survival, through loss of understanding of purpose, through doubts about presumed function. All begin with reconstruction, and all go on to tests for function or for suitability (Coles 1973, 14).

Spoken dialogue - conversation - is itself an example of experimental archaeology. As thinkers and speakers, we take what we know from the past and then try things out, using words to excavate other words, to prompt the re-emergence of muted speech forms, the latent sounds beneath the visible and tangible, to, at the very least, bear witness to the precarity of this art form known as language (Wuethrich 2000).

References

Agricola, Georgius. *De Re Metallica*. Translated by Herbert Clark Hoover and Lou Henry Hoover. New York: Dover, 1950 (1556).

Andren, Anders. *Between Artifacts and Texts*. New York: Springer, 1998.

Aristotle. *Problems: Books 1-19*. Edited and translated by Robert Mayhew. Cambridge, MA: Harvard University Press, 2011.

Artaud, Antonin. *Anthology*. Edited by Jack Hirschman. San Francisco: City Light Books, 1965.

Beaudry, Mary C. "Words for things: linguistic analysis of probate inventories," in *Documentary Archaeology in the New World*. Edited by Mary C. Beaudry. Cambridge: Cambridge University Press, 1988.

Brecher, Jeremy, Ron Blackwell and Joe Uelein. "If Not Now, When? A Labor Movement Plan to Address Climate Change," in *New Labor Forum* 1, no.7 (2014): 1-8.

Benjamin, Jeff. "Listening to Industrial Silence: Sound as Artifact," in *Reanimating Industrial Spaces*. Edited by Hilary Orange (Walnut Creek, California: Left Coast Press, 2015), 108-124.

Benjamin, Walter. 1940. *Selected Writings, Volume 4, 1938-1940*. Edmund Jephcott et al., trans. Edited by Howard Eiland and Michael W. Jennings. Cambridge, Mass.: The Belknap Press of Harvard University Press.

Benjamin, Jeff. *Sound as Artifact*. Master's Thesis. Houghton: Michigan Technological University, 2013.

Boyer, M.J. "Resistance to Technological Innovation: The History of the Pile Driver through the 18th Century," in *Technology and Culture* 26, no. 1 (Jan., 1985): 55-68.

Buder, Stanley. *Pullman: An experiment in industrial order and community planning 1880 - 1930*. New York: Oxford University Press, 1967.

Burroughs, William S. *The Job*. New York: Penguin, 1974.

Coles, John. *Archaeology by Experiment*. New York: Charles Scribner's and Sons, 1973.

Dickinson, Emily. *The Complete Poems of Emily Dickinson*. Edited by Thomas H. Johnson. New York: Little, Brown and Company, 1890.

Diderot, Denis. *Pictorial Encyclopedia of Trades and Industry*. New York: Dover, 1959.

Eco, Umberto. 'Lumbar Thought', in *Travels in Hyperreality: Essays*. New York: Harcourt, Brace & Company, 1983.

Edgeworth, Matt. *Fluid Pasts: Archaeology of Flow*. London: Bristol Classical Press, 2011.

Edgeworth, Matt. "Extraordinary ground: the emergence of the archaeosphere as hyperobject." Unpublished paper, 2014.

Foley, Arthur L. and Wilmer H. Souder. "A New Method of Photographing Sound Waves," in *Physical Review* 35, no. 5, (1912).

Foucault, Michel. *The Archaeology of Knowledge*. Translated by A.M. Sheridan Smith. New York: Harper Colophon, 1972.

Glassie, Henry. Glassie, Henry. *Folk Housing in Middle Virginia: A Structural Analysis of Historic Artifacts*. Knoxville: University of Tennessee Press, 1975.

Gluck, Carol and Anna Lowenhaupt Tsing. *Words in Motion: Toward a Global Lexicon*. Durham: Duke University Press, 2009.

Hamilakis, Yannis. "Multi-temporal Archaeology: Sensoriality and the ontology of duration." Lecture. Department of Anthropology. Columbia University, April 6, 2015.

Jakobson, Roman. *Six Lectures on Sound and Meaning*. Cambridge: MIT Press, 1978.

Kingsley, Peter. *Ancient Philosophy, Mystery, and Magic: Empedocles and Pythagorean Tradition*. Oxford: Clarendon Press, 1995.

Krause, Bernie L. "The Niche Hypothesis: How Animals Taught Us to Dance and Sing," accessed May 5, 2012 at http://users.auth.gr/paki/files/soundscape/referances/niche.pdf

Leone, Mark. "Archaeology as the Science of Technology: Mormon Town Plans and Fences," in *Historical Archaeology: A guide to Substantive and Theoretical Contributions,* edited by Robert L. Schuyler, 191-200. Farmingdale: Baywood Publishing Co., 1978.

Lewis, Robert. *Manufacturing Montreal: The Making of an Industrial Landscape, 1850 to 1930.* Baltimore: Johns Hopkins Press, 2000.

Lucretius. *The Nature of the Universe.* Translated by R.E. Latham. Baltimore: Penguin Classics, 1960.

Macauley, David. *Elemental Philosophy: Earth, Air, Fire and Water as Environmental Ideas.* Albany: State University of New York Press, 2010.

McGovern, Tom. "Resilience and Sustainability in Interesting Times: Some North Atlantic Lessons." CUNY Anthropology Department Lecture. March 13, 2015.

McKirahan, Richard D., Jr. *Philosophy Before Socrates: An Introduction with Texts and Commentary.* Indianapolis: Hackett Publishing Company, Inc., 1994.

Morton, Timothy. *Hyperobjects: Philosophy and Ecology after the End of the World.* Minneapolis: University of Minnesota Press, 2013.

Poincaré, H. Mathematics and Science: Last Essays. New York: Dover Publications, 1963.

Pyne, Mary E. "New England's Gasholder Houses," in *IA: The Journal of the Society for Industrial Archaeology* 15, no. 1 (1989): 54-62.

Ricouer, Paul. *The Conflict of Interpretations.* Evanston: Northwestern University Press, 1974.

Rose, Mike. *The Mind at Work: Valuing the Intelligence of the American Worker.* New York: Penguin, 2004.

Sale, Kirkpatrick. *Rebels Against the Future: The Luddites and Their War on the Industrial Revolution. Lessons for the Computer Age.* Reading, Mass: Addison-Wesley, 1995.

Schaeffer, Pierre. *In Search of a Concrete Music,* trans. Christine North and John Dack. Berkeley: University of California Press, 2012.

Searle, John R. *Making the Social World: The Structure of Human Civilization.* Oxford: Oxford University Press, 2009.

Simon Fraser University. *Sound Propagation.* http://www.sfu.ca/sonic-studio/handbook/Sound_Propagation.html. Accessed on October 15, 2015.

Snyder, Gary. *The Gary Snyder Reader: Prose, Poetry and Translations 1952-1998.* Washington D.C.: Counterpoint, 1999.

Sullivan, Heather. "The Ecology of Colors: Goethe's Materialist Optics and Ecological Posthumanism," in *Material Ecocriticism,* edited by Serenella Iovino and Serpil Opperman, 80-94. Bloomington: Indiana University Press, 2014.

Terkel, Studs. *Working.* New York: Avon Books, 1974.

Thoreau, Henry David. *Walden and Other Writings.* Edited by Joseph Wood Krutch. New York: Bantam, 2004[1854].

nited States Army Corps of Engineers. Circular of the Office of the Chief of Engineers, November 28, 1881, Pile Foundations and Pile Driving Formulae. 1881.

Varley, Ciaran. 2016. "Meet the man who thinks Air Guitar can bring world peace." BBC. Accessed on October 21, 2016. http://www.bbc.co.uk/bbcthree/item/daa79eb5-4613-46cd-bf62-dbccdf8aa01c

Wald, Matthew L. "Book Examines Nevada Test That Left Fallout in Troy, N.Y.," in The New York Times, April 18, 2003. http://www.nytimes.com/2003/04/18/nyregion/book-examines-nevada-test-that-left-fallout-in-troy-ny.html. Accessed on October 21, 2015.

Wellington, A.M. ed., *Piles and Pile Driving: being a reprint of some of the articles which have appeared in Engineering News on pile driving and the safe load of piles and of the pamphlet on "Bearing piles" by Rudolph Hering.* New York: Engineering News Publishing Co., 1893.

Wheelwright, Philip. *The Presocratics.* New York: Macmillan, 1966.

Whorf, Benjamin Lee. *Language, Thought, and Reality: Selected Writings,* edited by John B. Carroll. Cambridge, MA: MIT Press, 1956.

Wuethrich, Bernice. "Learning the World's Languages - Before They Vanish," in Science 288 (200): 1156-1159.

Zerzan, J. *Twilight of the Machines.* Port Townsend, WA: Feral House Press, 2008.

Maritime Helsinki – Two Case Studies Combining Archaeology and Linguistics in the Helsinki Archipelago

Annukka Debenjak, Marika Luhtala and Paula Kouki
University of Helsinki

Introduction

The prehistoric populations of archaeological cultures are usually assumed to have had some degree of cultural unity. However, linking archaeological cultures with the language spoken by the people that created them is not a straightforward task. Languages are by nature not static; rather, their use fluctuates historically throughout the geographic zones in which they are spoken, and language does not necessarily correlate with ethnicity or group identity as perceived by the people themselves.

One way of approaching the language of past populations is the study of place names, or *toponomastics*, which has a long tradition in Nordic archaeology. Coastal Finland, with its successive settlement by speakers of Sámi, Finnish, and Swedish, lends itself particularly well to this type of study.

The Maritime Helsinki project started in 2014 as a collaboration between the institutes of Finnish Language and Archaeology at the University of Helsinki under the directorship of Docent Terhi Ainiala and Professor Mika Lavento. The main goal of the project was to conduct an in-depth study into the little-known history of the settlement patterns and identities of past populations in the Helsinki archipelago through the use of toponomastics, historical documents (i.e. maps), and archaeological fieldwork. The research concentrated on identifying the temporal stratigraphy of Finnish and Swedish toponyms as reflecting consecutive phases of settlement in the archipelago and being datable by linguistic features and historical documents, as well as on locating the archaeological remains of settlements which had previously received little attention. To ensure information was conveyed effectively, and to avoid pitfalls such as misunderstanding and over-interpretation, the linguists and archaeologists worked side by side both in the archives and in the field.

The archipelago of Helsinki is currently under heavy land-use pressure from the ever-growing capital city. Some islands, such as Kulosaari (Brändö), Laajasalo (Degerö), Lauttasaari (Drumsö), and Tammisalo (Tammelund), have already become urban residential and industrial areas. In 2016, two other islands, Vallisaari and Kuninkaansaari, which had earlier belonged to the Finnish Defence Forces, were opened to tourism and visitors, with a consequent increase in land use and construction (Finnish Ministry of Finance 2014). An even more radical change awaits islands such as Vartiosaari, which the City of Helsinki plans to transform into a residential area to house thousands of people. These changes in the use of the archipelago pose a threat to potentially undiscovered archaeological sites. The Maritime Helsinki project thus also addressed a current and pressing need for rescue archaeology.

In this article, we present two case studies focusing on the archipelago of Helsinki: namely, the results of our research on Vallisaari and Villinki (Fig. 1), two neighbouring islands which nevertheless have very different histories of settlement and land use. In the autumn of 2014, the remains of the marine pilot village on Vallisaari were located by an archaeological survey. An archaeological and toponomastic survey was carried out on Villinki in the spring of 2015. The aim of the archaeological survey

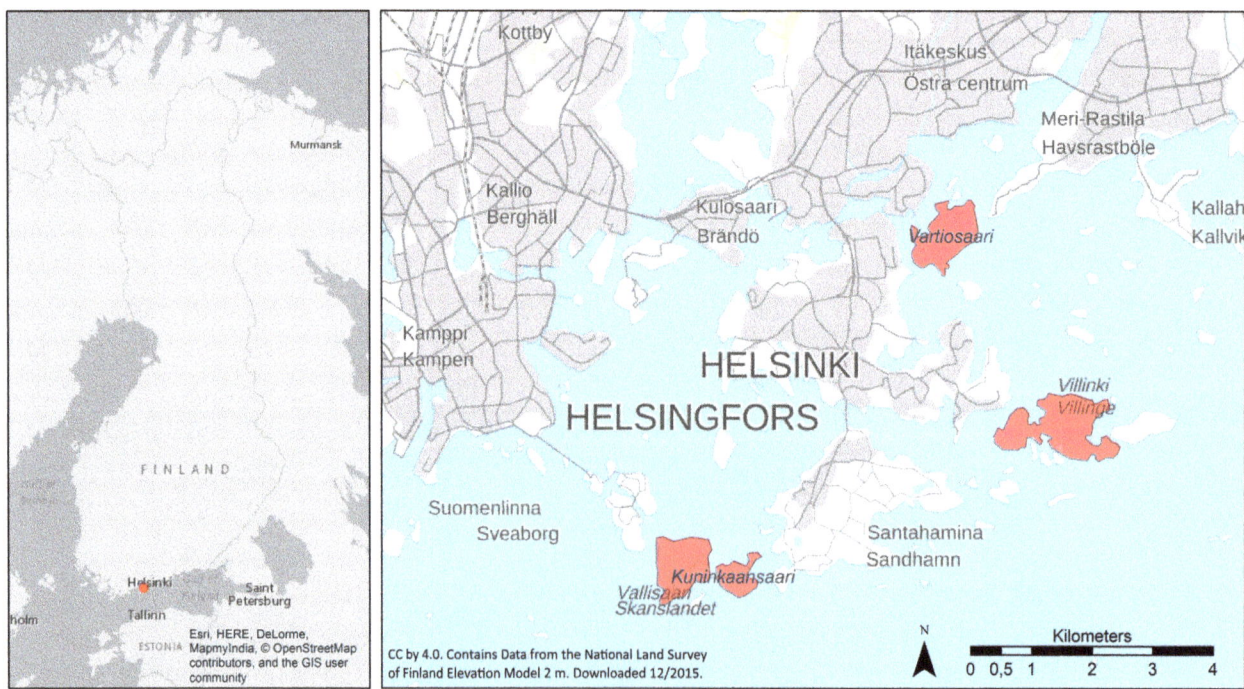

Fig. 1. The Helsinki archipelago. The islands discussed in this article are marked in red. (Map by A. Debenjak.)

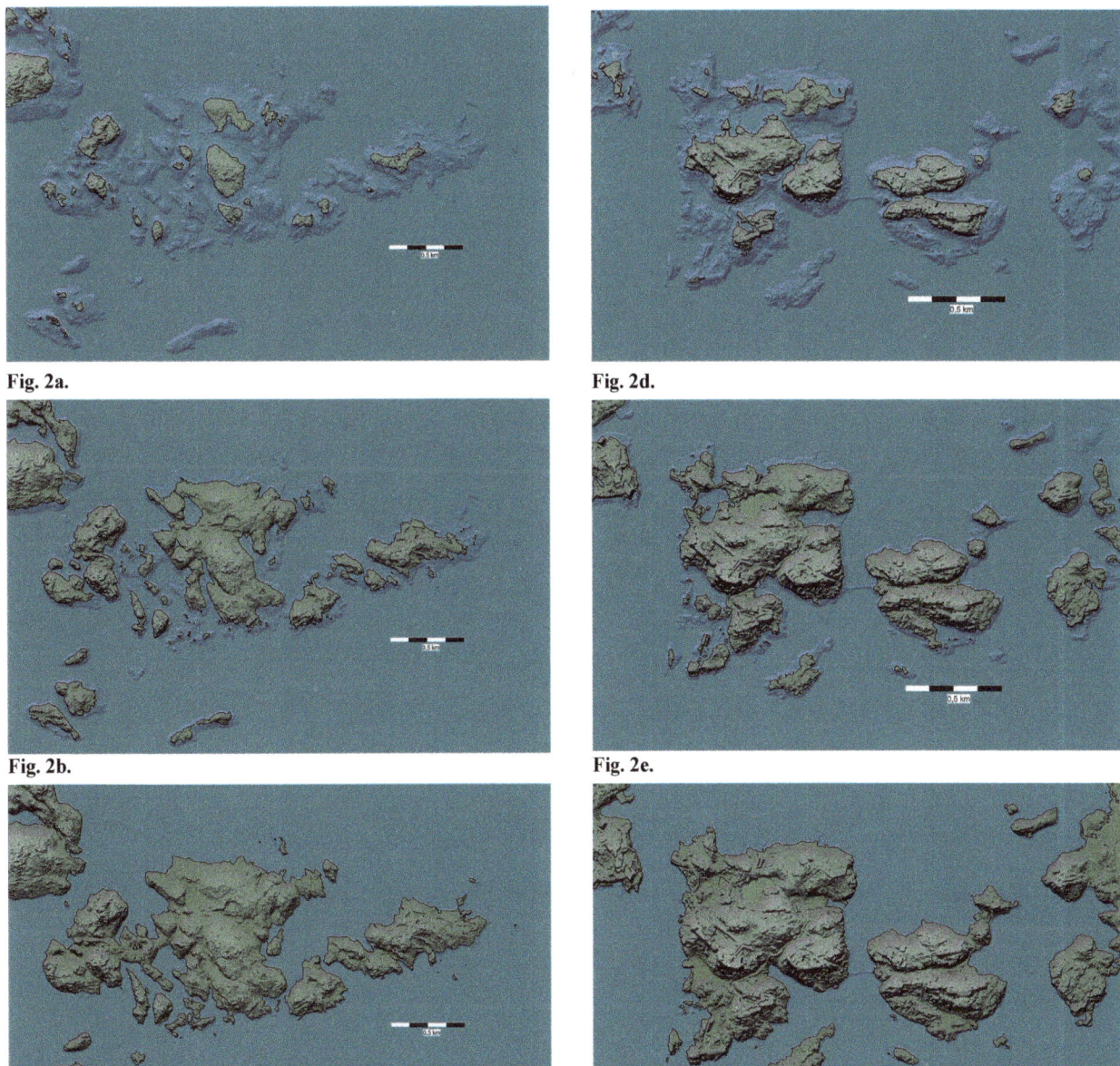

Fig. 2. GIS models of sea level change for Villinki and Vallisaari. 2a) Villinki ca 2000 BCE 2b) Villinki ca 1 CE 2c) Villinki ca 1500 CE 2d) Vallisaari ca 2000 BCE 2e) Vallisaari ca 1 CE 2f) Vallisaari ca 1500 CE (Maps by A. Debenjak.)

on Villinki was to detect previously undiscovered prehistoric sites, as well as to clarify, if possible, the location and extent of historical settlement on the island before the establishment of late nineteenth and early twentieth-century summer residences. A toponomastic survey was integrated with this archaeological work to facilitate the rapid exchange of information between these different fields of study. Place names can be studied from many different perspectives. During the Maritime Helsinki project, our focus was on etymological research.[1]

---

[1] The first major Finnish study of toponyms from an etymological point of view was Viljo Nissilä's doctoral thesis Vuoksen paikannimistö 1 ("The Toponomy of the Vuoksi Area") of 1939, which discussed place names in the area of Vuoksi in Karelia.

Background

Helsinki, the capital city of Finland, is located in the region of Uusimaa (Sw. *Nyland*) on the northern coast of the Gulf of Finland. The archipelago of Helsinki consists of ca 300 islands, ranging in size from rocky islets to islands large enough to support settlement. It extends ca 10 km seaward from the coastline, and ca 20 km along it. Most of the islands are small, being less than 0.5 hectares in area (Guide to the Archipelago 2009, 6). They can be divided into the outer archipelago, which is mainly characterised by barren cliffs, and the inner archipelago, which includes several large and more forested islands which have been inhabited in historical times.

The environmental conditions in the various parts of the archipelago have also influenced their land use: the outlying islands have mainly been used for fishing and the hunting of seal and waterfowl, while the inner islands have also periodically supported permanent human settlement. However, the border between the inner and outer archipelago has not been temporally permanent due to isostatic land uplift and changes in vegetation. Immediately after the last glacial period and during the consecutive periods of the Stone Age, the area of present-day southern coastal Finland began to gradually rise above sea level. Even the largest islands of the Helsinki archipelago thus started out as outer islets, and only later did they become large enough to support vegetation and settlement.

Based on the results of Hyvärinen (1999), Debenjak prepared a GIS-based shore displacement simulation of the research area to aid in the recognition of areas available for land use during different time periods. The simulation shows that the first isles in the current archipelago rose above sea level around 4000 BCE (see Fig. 2a, 2d). At the beginning of the Common Era, the larger islands were all above sea level, and their current form was already recognisable (Fig. 2b, 2e). In many cases, however, the impact of shore displacement can be seen even in relatively recent history. During the late Middle Ages, the sea level was still ca 1.5 m higher than at present (Fig. 2c, 2f), and especially in low-lying areas, a small land uplift can reveal wide stretches of new land.

The waterways and islands of the Helsinki archipelago have also been important for seafaring and military use, as testified by old navigation marks and numerous shipwrecks spanning several centuries, as well as the line of fortifications on the islands, constructed in several phases from the late 17th century onwards to protect Helsinki from attacks from the sea. A seafaring route along the southern coast of Finland is known to have existed as early as the Medieval Period, and ships also sailed between Finland and Tallinn (Reval) across the Finnish Gulf at least from the thirteenth century onwards (Kerkkonen 1959, 9–11). During the fifteenth and sixteenth centuries, an important part of this trade was handled by independent peasant sailors, and archival sources provide evidence that traders also set sail from the present-day Helsinki region, for example from the villages of Vik (Viikki) and Degerö (Laajasalo) (Kerkkonen 1959, 85–90; see also the map at the end of the book).

Toponyms and toponomastic research have long interested scholars of history, linguistics, and archaeology in the Nordic countries. Place names are still a popular area of interest, and works dealing with the origins of toponyms are published regularly; for example, in 2007, the Institute for the Languages in Finland, in collaboration with Karttakeskus,[2] published a massive toponomastic reference book, *Suomalainen paikannimikirja ("The Finnish Book of Toponyms")*. At the same time, knowledge of Finnish place names is increasing through information provided by various regional monographs (Ainiala *et al.* 2012, 45–46).

Research history

The archipelago of Helsinki has been a subject of archaeological research since the late nineteenth century, but the research has focused mainly on investigating and excavating prehistoric burial cairns which were discovered by the summer residents of the islands (e.g., Aspelin 1886; Appelgren-Kivalo 1910; Cleve 1931). Later, scientific research has mainly focused on the fortress of Suomenlinna (Sveaborg) and the wide chain of fortifications spanning multiple periods which was established on the islands along the coast of Helsinki. A construction project that begun under Swedish sovereignty, the fortifications were later expanded by the Russian Empire to protect the capital of the autonomous Grand Duchy of Finland (e.g. Gardberg & Palsila 1998; Löfgren 1972). During the late 20th and early 21st centuries, scholars and historians have also published local histories of individual islands (Sädevirta 1994; Nygård 2003; Enqvist & Eskola 2011). However, apart from continuing research on Suomenlinna, archaeological research has been sporadic, and there is a distinct lack of systematic research on the archipelago.

In 2002–03, the multidisciplinary Vårt Maritima Arv ("Our Maritime Heritage") research project carried out a large-scale archaeological survey of the coast of Uusimaa. A few sites in the coastal Helsinki area were investigated as part of this project. However, the large research area, and the emphasis of the research on western Uusimaa, did not allow for any detailed research on the individual islands (Jansson & Latikka 2008). Nevertheless, the research project laid a good foundation for further research in the coastal area.

During the project, an overview of the settlement history of coastal Helsinki was gathered from various sources. The location and research reports on already known ancient sites in the area were collected from the Registry of Ancient Monuments and Sites maintained by the National Board of Antiquities in Finland. GIS-based maps of the area were made showing the location of known settlements, the modelled shoreline at different times, soil types, and the location of fresh water springs, streams, and lakes to help visualise the conditions for settlement and natural conditions. In addition to archaeological sources, historical maps dated from the seventeenth to the nineteenth centuries from the collections of the Finnish National Archive were also used to gather information about settlement in the archipelago.

Toponyms in the coastal Uusimaa region have been studied by several scholars, including Åke Granlund (1956), Kurt Zilliacus (1994), Lars Huldén (2001), and Saulo Kepsu (2005), among others. Most of the earlier work focused on Swedish place names, since, in this region, the older toponyms are generally of Swedish origin, and the Finnish names used today are in many cases younger, having been translated or adapted from Swedish toponyms. Although some research on the

---

[2] Karttakeskus is a Finnish company specialising in the production and publication of maps and other geographic information.

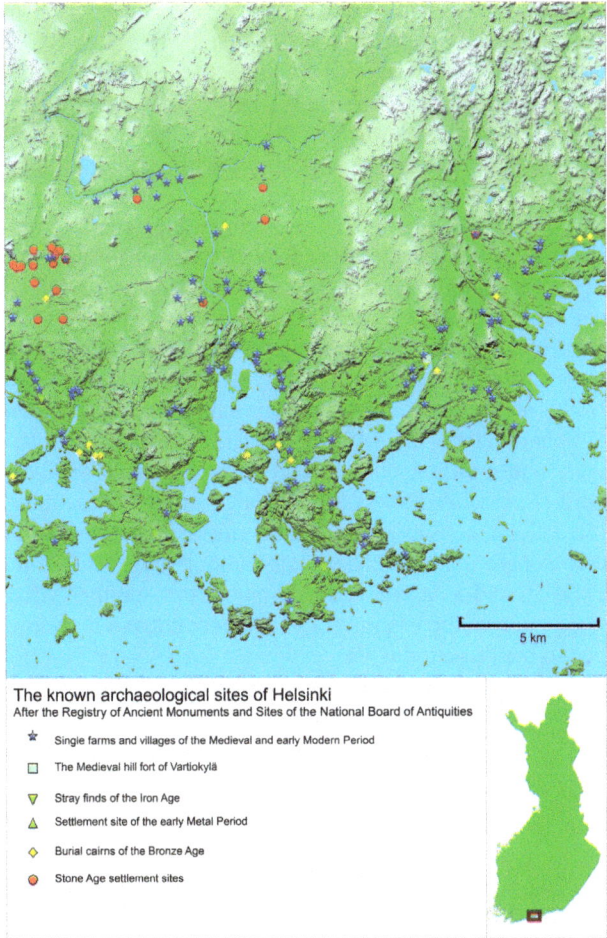

Fig. 3. Archaeological sites by type and period in the Helsinki area.

coastal Helsinki area had been done, more localized research was lacking.

During our research project, toponyms and information on their origins were gathered from multiple sources. Lars Huldén's (2001) work *Finlandssvenska bebyggelsenamn: namn på landskap, kommuner, byar i Finland av svenskt ursprung eller med särskild svensk form* ('Finnish-Swedish Settlement Names: Names for Provinces, Municipalities, and Villages in Finland of Swedish Origin or with a Specific Swedish Form') was a major literary source for toponomastic research. Saulo Kepsu's (2005) work *Uuteen maahan: Helsingin ja Vantaan vanha asutus ja nimistö* ('To the New Land: The Old Settlement and Toponymy of Helsinki and Vantaa') provided more information about the history of the area, as well as on the origins of the place names in focus. In addition, the reference book *Helsingin kadunnimet* ('The Street Names of Helsinki'), published by the City of Helsinki (1970), gave us much-needed information about place names. Toponyms were also tracked down from old maps in the Finnish National Archive, The Society of Swedish Literature in Finland, and The Onomastic Archive of the Institute for the Languages in Finland. The use of Swedish words in place names was investigated with the help of *Namnledslexicon*, an online database published by the Institute for the Languages in Finland and edited by Kurt Zilliacus in 1999.

The toponomastic reference book *Suomalainen paikannimikirja* ('The Finnish Book of Toponyms') was also used in our research.

The prehistory and history of coastal Helsinki: an overview

Settlement patterns and changes on islands are often related to those on the mainland since permanent maritime settlements are usually more or less dependent on the coast – although not necessarily the nearest one – for part of their subsistence (e.g. Kaukiainen 2006, 211–18, discussing the economy of island settlements in the eastern Gulf of Finland). Therefore, to understand the settlement processes of maritime Helsinki, we must provide a short overview of the known history and population fluctuations in the region.

Due to post-glacial developments in the Baltic Sea basin, most of the present-day Helsinki archipelago was below sea-level during the Stone Age (ca 8800–1800 BCE). As a result of the post-glacial shore displacement on the coast of Finland, the Stone Age dwelling sites that are known in the Helsinki region are now located inland, at a height of 20–32 metres above sea level, their elevation increasing with their age. Although many of these sites were originally in a maritime setting, even the closest Stone Age dwelling sites now lie more than two kilometres inland from the present-day coastline (Fig. 3).

During the Bronze Age, there was human activity in the areas that now form the coastal parts of Helsinki, as shown by the presence of Bronze Age cairns on the islands of Kulosaari and Lehtisaari. On the mainland, there are several more similarly dated cairns, and finds such as bronze axes (Cleve 1950). However, although the presence of burials makes it reasonable to presume the existence of settlements, no Bronze Age dwelling sites are known, probably due to the later intensive land use in these areas.

The matter of settlement during the Iron Age is likewise unclear. The main problem in researching the Iron Age in the Helsinki area is the paucity of archaeological material, both stray finds and settlement sites – a situation that is common to the whole of eastern Uusimaa. This has led to the common view that the region was only occasionally and sparsely settled (Tuovinen 2011). However, recent research has begun to change the idea of the Uusimaa region's supposed emptiness during the later Iron Age. Evidence of settlement can be found from the results of pollen analyses taken from bottom sediments of the Kangaslampi, Storträsk, and Haltingträsk lakes in Helsinki, which point towards slash-and-burn cultivation in the area since the 8th century (Alenius *et al.* 2014, 100). An Iron Age spearhead (no. 1000005715, Registry of Ancient Sites and Monuments), found on the island of Santahamina in Helsinki, proves that at least some human activity also took place in the archipelago.

The southwestern part of present-day Finland was gradually brought under Swedish rule starting from the late twelfth century. The establishment of a Swedish presence in Finland was accompanied by the colonisation of coastal areas by a Swedish population. Together with the development of cultivation techniques and an improvement in the climatic conditions, this resulted in an expansion of settlement in Uusimaa (Lillman 2014, 24–31). At the end of the Medieval Period, at least 22 hamlets existed in the Helsinki region (Suhonen & Heinonen 2011; see Fig. 3). During this period, many new Swedish toponyms were coined by the new settlers.

As the pollen analysis results prove, the Helsinki region was not uninhabited before the arrival of the Swedish settlers. A number of specific toponyms in the area suggest the same, and give us information about the cultural and ethnic origin of the earlier inhabitants. These place names were early loans into Swedish, and indicate that speakers of a Finnish dialect, the Tavastians, used the area as their hunting and fishing grounds. For example, the Finnish present-day name *Huopalahti* is a phonetic adaptation of an earlier Swedish name *Hoplax*; both names are used today for one of the city's districts. However, the Swedish alternant was in turn loaned and assimilated into the phonetic system of the Swedish language by the new settlers; it derives from the Proto-Finnic name *Haapalaksi (*haapa* 'aspen', *laksi 'bay') (Ainiala *et al.* 2012, 96). These kinds of Proto-Finnic names which at first sight may seem to be of Swedish origin can be found throughout a broad area across Southern Finland. For example, in Loviisa, a municipality situated roughly 80 kilometres to the east of the capital, the toponyms *Märlax* and *Påsalö* also derive from the time of an earlier Finnish population. *Märlax* likely derives from the name *Mertalaksi (*merta* 'fishing trap', *laksi 'bay'); while *Påsalö* contains the Swedish word *ö* 'an island' and the former Finnish name *Paasisalo (*paasi* 'flat rock', *salo* 'island') (Huldén 2001, 331–32).

During the late sixteenth and early seventeenth centuries, settlement in the Helsinki region decreased rapidly. This depopulation had many causes: a cooling of the climate, the spread of epidemics, and continuous attacks on the coastal hamlets by Russian Cossacks which resulted in the abandonment of many farms (Haggrén 2005, 2; Paikkala 1996, 18–19). For example several farms were abandoned in the hamlets of Degerö and Botby after the Cossacks invaded the coast of Helsinki at the end of the sixteenth century (Sädevirta 1994, 3, 138). Further depopulation was caused by years of famine at the end of the seventeenth century (Lönnqvist 1980), pestilence, and the Russian occupation of Helsinki during the early eighteenth century (Haggrén 2005, 2). The time of depopulation cannot have lasted very long, however, since some of the earlier toponyms have survived to our time. Even though settlement on the islands decreased, more widely known place names remained in use among the settlers in the wider Helsinki region, as well as people travelling in the archipelago.

A renewed settlement expansion began slowly during the latter half of the 18th century (Hornborg 1950). In the archipelago of Helsinki, this new period can be seen in the expansion of land use on the islands (Paikkala 1996, 3). One of the most influential factors influencing the archipelago of Helsinki at this time was the construction of Sveaborg (now known as Suomenlinna) – a huge fortress established to defend the town against military threats from the sea. The construction work began in 1741, and also involved the surrounding islands. Vallisaari and the neighbouring Kuninkaansaari formed part of the Sveaborg defence system, and stone was mined and shipped to Sveaborg from Vartiosaari (Salonen & Schalin 2013, 20). By the end of the 18th century, there were crofts (lease farms) of the hamlets of Degerö and Botby on the islands of Vartiosaari and Villinki (Salonen & Schalin 2013, 18), while Vallisaari and Kuninkaansaari were under military use as parts of the fortress of Sveaborg (Enqvist & Eskola 2011). Later, in the 19th century, recreational activity in the countryside and in the Helsinki archipelago increased, especially among more well-to-do citizens, and as a consequence, numerous summer villas were built on the islands – a phenomenon that has continued to the present day.

The case studies: Villinki and Vallisaari

Villinki

The first parts of the present-day island of Villinki emerged from the sea during the Bronze Age (ca 1500 BCE). By the beginning of the Common Era at the latest, the island was fully habitable and almost at its current area of 1.68 square kilometres. However, the first known settlement on the island only dates to post-Medieval times: the farmstead of Villinge and its owner, a peasant Lasse Nilsson, are mentioned in the tax lists of the Viipuri and Porvoo administrative districts in 1544 (KA 5003: 4). Five years later, another holder, Simon Villing, is mentioned, listed under the nearby village of Brändö (Kulosaari) (Suhonen 2010, 111). This evidence points towards Villinki having been a small settlement, likely a hamlet or just a single farmstead, and may give an indication as to the origins of the individuals living on the island in the sixteenth century.

Toponomastic evidence from Villinki sheds some light on the history of the island. A name beginning with *Villi-* appeared for the first time in historical documents in the 16th century, in the orthographic forms *Villingby, Villingh, Willing,* and *Willinge,* amongst others (Helsingin kadunnimet 1970, 227; Huldén 2001, 300; Kepsu 2005, 75). The etymology of the toponym is unclear, and there has been debate over its origins. It may derive from the Old Swedish word *vidher = *ved* 'forest' in modern Swedish (Helsingin kadunnimet 1970, 227). On the other hand, according to Kepsu (2005, 75), it is possible that the toponym was brought to the region by Swedish settlers: there was a settlement in the Danmark parish in the province of Uppland, the name of which was written in the forms *in Vilingi* and *in Villingi,* in 1291. In Finland, on the other hand, many names starting with *Villi-* are used for settlements, and usually include the personal name *Villi,* deriving from the names *Wilhelm, Willi, Willich,* and so on (SPK 2007, 508). Nevertheless, the name

Fig. 4. Villinki on Samuel Broterus' map from 1697 (National Archive of Finland).

appears to be older than the first archived sources mentioning Villinki.

The exact location of the sixteenth-century farmstead or hamlet on Villinki is unknown: the settlement was probably abandoned in the late sixteenth century when 25 years of warfare between Russia and Sweden resulted in the emptying out of most island settlements on the southern coast of Finland. In the first maps of the archipelago from the late seventeenth century, the island is uninhabited and unfortunately, there is a large hole in the map of Villinge, right in the Byvik area (Broterus 1697; see Fig. 4). Later, in a map of 1742, the island is shown to be devoid of settlement (Geographisk Charta öfwer Nyland 1742).

The toponomy can provide some information on 16th-century settlement, however. *Byvijk*, 'Village Bay', is marked already on Broterus' late-seventeenth-century map above the north-west coast of the island. Furthermore, the most fertile land on the island is located on the south-east side of the bay (Haavisto et al. 1974). This area was uplifted above sea level during the early Iron Age. Based on the GIS model of the ancient shoreline, there may have been a small freshwater pond to the east of Byvik that was separated from the sea due to land uplift (Fig. 2b). Both the toponomastic evidence and the natural environment therefore strongly indicate that the earliest settlement in Villinki was located in the area around *Byvijk*, where buildings of the late eighteenth-century settlement were also located (Winter 1798; see Fig. 5).

In the latter half of the seventeenth century, a *seat* farm (i.e., the permanent residence of a nobleman; Sw. *sätesgård* or *säteri*) was established on the nearby island of Degerö (Laajasalo), and Villinki was transferred to its possession. The island was mainly used as a supply of firewood. In 1764, Villinki was leased for 20 years. During that time, brick manufacture started on the island, most likely resulting from the need for building material in the construction of the fortress of Sveaborg. It is not known how long this brick manufacture continued, but usually this kind of small industry was temporary in nature. The brick manufacturing site is not marked on the late eighteenth-century map drawn by Timothy Winter (1798), but traces of the industry can be found on the map on the basis of the toponomy: there is a long, narrow meadow known as Lergropsängen; *lergrop* 'clay pit' *äng* 'meadow,' and two clay pits are drawn within the meadow. The larger of these clay pits can still be found, and its fine, blue-grey clay confirms that it could indeed have been a clay pit for brick manufacture.

At the end of the eighteenth century, the seat farm of Degerö was divided in the *Storskiftet*,[3] first into three, and later into four separate estates. (Nygård 2003, 10; Sädevirta 1994, 4). In this process, Villinki became an independent seat farm, which it remained until the beginning of the twentieth century (Nygård 2003, 11). A

---

[3] The Great Partition: an agricultural land reform started in Sweden (including Finland) in the mid-18th century. The new division of land transformed the medieval landholding system.

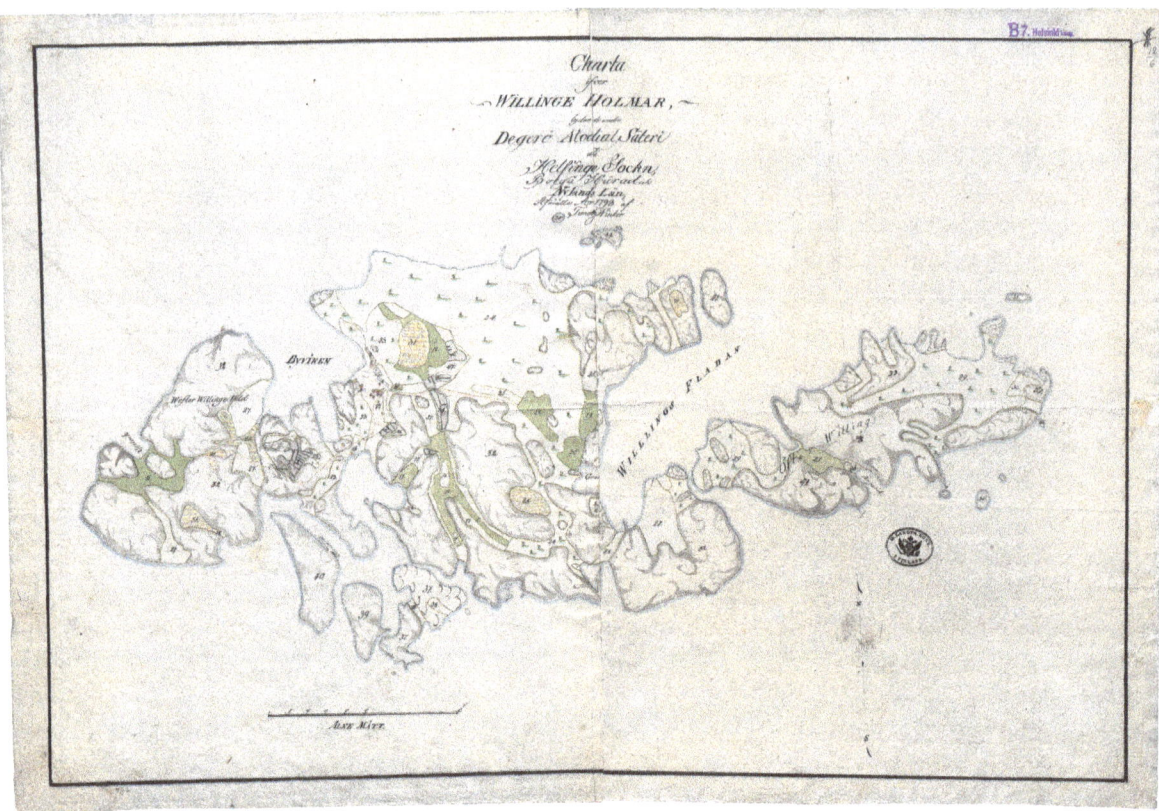

Fig. 5. Villinki in 1798 (National Archive of Finland).

new settlement was established on the island during the late 18th century, as can be seen on maps of Villinki (Fig. 5). The buildings and most of the cultivated land are clustered around Byvik. It is possible that the buildings of the seat farm were erected on the same site as the earlier sixteenth-century farmstead. In later nineteenth-century maps, a few crofts belonging to the seat farm can also be found in the southern part of the main island of Villinki, as well as in the eastern parts of the island (Itä-Villinki).

In addition to locating the settlement, the investigation of place names provides information about the economic life of the inhabitants of Villinki. The toponyms on Villinki and its nearby islets show that in the eighteenth and nineteenth centuries, the locals practiced small-scale farming and animal husbandry. Swedish names, such as *Oxhage* (*oxe* 'bull', *hage* 'fencing'), *Bastuåkern* (*bastu* 'sauna' or 'fishing hut', *åker* 'field' or 'farmland') and *Svinholmen* (*svin* 'pig', *holm* 'island'),[4] indicate this through their lexical components.

Fishing was another important means of livelihood for the residents of Villinki. *Torskholmen* (*torsk* 'codfish', *holm* 'island') was the name of a small island near Villinki (Alanen *et. al* 1989, 53); the location was known as a good place for fishing. The same stands for a nearby place called *Notgrundet* (*not* 'net', *grund* 'ground'). The names Viipurinkivi ('Viipuri's rock') and Viipurinkaita ('the straits of Viipuri') to the south of Villinki hint at a route used for sailing to the east as far as Viipuri (Viborg) at the eastern end of the Gulf of Finland. A combination of farming, fishing, and hunting of seal and waterfowl, often supplemented with small-scale shipping and marine piloting, were a common means of making a living for the people of the island settlements in Finland up until the early twentieth century (Talve 1990, 131–32; Kaukiainen 1970, Summary).

The construction of luxurious summer villas on the seaside – a phenomenon which first started among the wealthy inhabitants of Helsinki in the mid-nineteenth century – can be seen in the rapid division of new plots on Villinki at the end of the nineteenth century. The eastern part of Villinki (nowadays called *Itä-Villinki*, "East Villinki") was claimed as a military area in 1918 (Enqvist 2007, 164–65), and entrance to the island is still restricted. The fishing and farming villages of the Gulf of Finland largely disappeared after WWII, and the same happened in Villinki, but the villa community has lived on. The locations of the early twentieth-century crofts are now covered up by summer cottages.

During the spring of 2015, we spent two weeks surveying the island of Villinki. The goal of the archaeological

---

[4] It was common in the archipelago to take farm animals, especially the small cattle, but sometimes also cows and horses, out to the smaller islands to graze for the summer (Talve 1990: 81). However, it should be noted that sometimes *svin* may also refer to 'badger' or 'wild boar' (Namnledslexikon). Wild boar is unlikely, though, since this animal only appeared in Finland from the 1970s onwards.

survey was to search for traces of the early historical and possibly prehistoric settlement and land use. Our field methods were pedestrian survey, field walking, and the collection of finds from the ploughzone and soundings in the area of the oldest documented settlement. Most of the finds collected from the soundings and field walking date to the period of the seat farm from the latter half of the eighteenth to the mid-nineteenth century, and the period of the summer villas in the late nineteenth and twentieth centuries. However, some finds were also collected probably testifying to settlement in the sixteenth century or even earlier, and evidence of possible Bronze or Iron Age activity was also recognized.

Simultaneously with the archaeological survey, a collection of toponyms was carried out by Marika Luhtala, who interviewed the residents of the island. The interviews with the island's summer residents and a comparison with maps of various periods show that the present-day place names in Villinki are largely of recent, mostly Swedish origin, and have been given by the summer residents, while the names used by the earlier small farmers and fishermen are no longer known. Even names such as Pukkiluoto / *Bocksholm* and Tulisaari / *Kasaberget* (Sw *kasa* 'bonfire', *berg* 'high rock, mountain'), which could easily be interpreted as evidence of earlier land use methods, are actually recent and coined by the summer residents of the island. They reflect the landforms of these small, rocky islets, as well as perhaps romanticised ideas of the history of the archipelago, rather than the true past reality.

Vallisaari
The history of the island of Vallisaari offers a totally different perspective on the coastal settlement of Helsinki. Vallisaari is located near the fortress of Sveaborg and, consequently, military use had a significant impact on the history of the island. From the perspective of settlement study, Vallisaari appears to have been an ideal island to settle. For example, a small lake in the middle of the island provided fresh water, which was not only important for permanent settlement, but also for ships sailing along the southern coast of Finland. Located near the Helsinki mainland, the island, with its high cliffs, has played an important part in the defence of the capital since at least the eighteenth century (Enqvist & Eskola 2011, 46). This long period of military use has, however, practically destroyed the the island's ground layer: in almost every part of the island, the soil has been dug out, used for construction, or otherwise disturbed, making Vallisaari a challenging subject for archaeological research.

The toponomy of Vallisaari is temporally layered, and clearly illustrates how the use of the island has developed. In 1640, the traditional Swedish place name *Träsköön* appeared in maps and other historic documents. The name literally means 'Lake Island', which makes sense, given that Vallisaari was probably known among locals and sailors alike for its fresh water source. For the neighbouring *Kuninkaansaari*, *Kungholmen* in Swedish, the traditional place name *Bockholmen* was used in the same year. *Bock-* stands for 'billy goat', and has connections either to grazing activities, or to the rocky appearance of the place (Namnledslexikon; Helsingin kadunnimet 1970, 231).

The use of the island changed in the late seventeenth century as military activity increased in the area. The change is also reflected in the toponomy: the Swedish name *Skanslandet* appears on a map for the first time in 1696, in the orthographic form *Skantz Landhet* (Forssel 1696). As a modifier, the toponym contains the Swedish word *skans*, 'bulwark', indicating that the fortification of the island had already begun by the late seventeenth century. The old name, *Träsköön,* survived only in written form on maps, and its use was documented for the last time in 1755 (Helsingin kadunnimet 1970, 231). Any other place names on the island, presumably known and invented by the local population have been forgotten, since they were only used by a limited group of people.

In addition to the name of the main island, many other interesting toponyms are found in the neighbouring areas around Vallisaari during the seventeenth and eighteenth centuries. For example, the Swedish name *Kugghamnsundet* appeared on a map in the 1640s; later, the elliptical *Kugg-Sundet* (1778), *Kungssundet* (1816), and *Kuggsund* (1855) were recorded (Granlund 1956, 114; Helsingin kadunnimet 1970, 230). *Kuggsundet* is still used today in addition to the Finnish name *Kukisalmi*, and the referent lies to the east of Vallisaari. The toponym is a strong indication that shipping took place in the area, since *Kugg* = *kogg, kogger, koggi* means 'a high-edged ship used during the fifteenth and sixteenth centuries by the Hanseatic merchants' (Helsingin kadunnimet 1970, 230; Zilliacus 1994, 91). This location was probably used as a resting place when sailing the Gulf of Finland. Roughly 30 similar *Kugg-* names have been documented along the southern coast of Finland, in places where merchants used to stay during their sailing trips (Pitkänen & Zilliacus 1996, 52).

In the eighteenth and nineteenth centuries, military activity in the area increased as the fortress of Sveaborg was erected. Toponyms dating back to this period include, for example, Swedish *Hamnsundshällen* (1778) and *Båkholmen* (1774) (Helsingin kadunnimet 1970, 230–31). Both names have a close connection to the sea and sailing, since *Hamnsundshällen* (whose referent lies on the eastern side of Kuninkaansaari) is built from the words *hamn* 'harbour', *sund* 'strait', and *häll* 'stone' or 'brick', while *Båkholmen* (used of both Vallisaari and a smaller nearby island) contains an originally Old Saxon word *båk* 'beacon' (Namnledslexikon) and Swedish *holm* 'island'.

In the beginning of the nineteenth century, Finland came under Russian rule as an autonomous Grand Duchy. During this period of autonomy, place names appeared in the toponomy of Vallisaari honouring the Emperor, such as *Alexandersön* 'Island of Alexander' and *Alexanderön* 'Alexander Island' (see Fig. 6). These names can be found on maps dating to the beginning of the twentieth

Fig. 6. Vallisaari and the surrounding islands. Close-up from a late 19th–early 20th-century map (National Archive of Finland).

century, and they probably derive from *'Ostrov Aleksandrovskij'*, used for Vallisaari on Russian military maps in the late nineteenth century. The period of Russian rule ended in 1917 when Finland gained its independence. The old name *Skanslandet* again became relevant for use as the island's Swedish name, translated into *Vallisaari* for the Finnish speaking population. The names became official in 1918 (Helsingin kadunnimet 1970, 231).

The earliest known civilian settlement on the island of Vallisaari was a small village of marine pilots in the north-western part of the island. According to historical sources, the village continued to be occupied from the end of the eighteenth to the beginning of the twentieth century (Enqvist & Eskola 2011, 93–103, 131). Maps made of Vallisaari in the nineteenth century show small cottages clustered around the old dock in the northwestern part of the island.

During the autumn of 2014, an archaeological survey was carried out to search for the remains of the marine pilots' village. The remains of eight buildings, likely belonging to the pilot village, were found in the area indicated on nineteenth-century maps. Later, with the increasing military presence on the island, the civilian settlement became restricted and more closely regulated, and a guard house was built for the pilots. The remains of this building, which still existed in the beginning of the twentieth century, were also identified in the survey (Debenjak 2014, 10).

The military use of Vallisaari continued until the end of the twentieth century. On present-day maps of the island, names taken from the distinguished military dignitaries and major happenings of the period dominate the toponomastic field. One of the youngest names in Vallisaari is linked to a disastrous event in its twentieth-century history. The Finnish name *Kuolemanlaakso*, meaning 'Death Valley', commemorates the explosion of an ammunition workshop on 9 July 1937, which killed twelve people in a valley in the eastern part of the island (Enqvist & Eskola 2011, 143).

The settlement of marine pilots and their families can be reconstructed through archaeological evidence and historical sources, but it is not reflected in the toponymy of the island at all – an observation which illustrates the importance of cooperation between disciplines. The example of Vallisaari shows how the significance of a place on a map, and even its name, depended on the purpose for which the map was drawn. It can be assumed that the civilians living in Vallisaari had their own names for well-known places on the island – the few alleys and streets, the lake, the docks, and the surrounding hills and meadows. However, the only known toponymy from this period is preserved in military maps and reports of the island, where different names were used.

Discussion

The Maritime Helsinki project studied the development and fluctuation of settlement in the coastal area and archipelago of Helsinki with the help of interdisciplinary cooperation between archaeology and cultural historical onomastics.

Place names are often built in a certain way, and therefore the investigation of different structural types and their geographic distribution can help us to piece together the origins of settlement (Kiviniemi 1977, 6–7). The study of toponomastics in the Maritime Helsinki project was mainly based on the analysis of lexical elements in names, as there are usually signs in the toponomy left behind by the previous community of settlers: in this case, the earlier Tavastian and Swedish speaking populations. Good examples from the research area are the names *Tavastvarpet (tavast* 'dweller of Tavastia') and *Repox holmen (repo,* in Finnish, means 'fox'). Names can also contain clues as to the origin of settlement in a more localised way, as some are based on personal names. In our research area, for example, we find the names *Puuphsund* and *Maununkari, Månsholmen* in Swedish, that can be traced back to different periods of time. As mentioned below, *Puuphsund* may be connected to a certain Tavastian farmstead, while *Maununkari* is a translated form of a Swedish male name (Helsingin kadunnimet 1970, 227). *Måns* is a variant of the personal name *Magnus*, which has been used since the 15th century (Namnledslexikon). It thus seems clear that the name Månsholmen is connected to Swedish speaking settlers, perhaps as far back as the early Medieval period.

The study of toponomy can be applied to the investigation of the origins of settlement, but sometimes place names can also be useful in revealing old burial grounds or dwelling sites. In Finland, for example, there are toponyms starting with *Hiisi-*. These names are often connected to graves or graveyards dating back to the Iron Age in southwestern Finland (Pitkänen 1985, 272). *Hiisi* is a Finnish word that meant either 'sacred forest' or 'guardian spirit of the forest' for ancient Finns; in some cases, it also held the meaning 'distant woodland' or 'devil'. Nowadays, however, the word is used mainly as a curse word (SKP). Names connected with burial grounds did not come up during the investigation of the Helsinki archipelago, but the name *Byvijk* helped us to locate the probable site of the old hamlet in Villinki.

After exploring the place names in our research area, we can conclude that the toponyms which reveal information about the earlier stages of occupation can be divided into two main groups. Toponyms of the first type contain an appellative of ethnic identity, and were given by the Swedish speaking population. For example, the name *Tavastvarpet* was given to a place used by the people from Tavastia. The place was probably used as a hunting ground (Swedish *varp* 'trap'). *Lappvik* is another name which includes an appellative indicative of ethnicity, or at least some kind of cultural identity: *Lapp* 'person of Saami origin' or 'nomad'; *vik* 'bay'. The second major type of toponym are those that contain Finnish proper nouns or words. The toponym *Puuphsund* from 1678 may contain in its first part the personal name *Puuppo,* which at that period was also the name of an old Tavastian farmstead. As a different example, the toponym *Repox holmen,* documented in 1777, contains as its modifier a Finnish word, *repo* 'fox'. The latter part of the name is in Swedish: *holm* 'island' (Kepsu 2005, 62, 75).

The temporal layering of place names we have observed also indicates that caution must be executed when using them as archaeological indicators. As our case studies show, microtoponyms are especially subject to frequent changes which may happen in the course of a couple of generations, and as a rule, they tend to be fairly recent. As examples, most of the names now used in Villinki are datable to the summer villa period, which only began in the late nineteenth century, while the microtoponyms of Vallisaari mostly relate to its twentieth-century military use. For "archaeological toponomastics", historical maps are therefore generally more useful than the current toponomy, as they may contain old names that have been forgotten.

Conclusion

As it can be seen in our case studies, the toponomy of the archipelago is temporally layered. While the earliest place names indicate a Tavastian presence in the coastal parts of Helsinki, the earliest place names in the islands are of Medieval Swedish origin. The earliest names dating back to this period have connections to sailing on the Baltic Sea, or are otherwise traditionally inherited toponyms used by the local population. From the seventeenth century, the place names tell the story of the centuries-long military activity on Vallisaari, as the island became part of the defence line surrounding Helsinki from the sea. In eighteenth-century Villinki, on the other hand, we find place names related to subsistence activities such as fishing, animal husbandry, and small-scale farming. Thus, even though Vallisaari and Villinki lay close to each other, their different histories are reflected in the toponomastic data. Through a combination of archaeological methods and cultural historical onomastics, it was possible to construct a more comprehensive picture of the development of these islands.

Currently, there is an increasing amount of research being conducted on the Iron Age settlement of the whole Uusimaa region. Cultural historical onomastics also show that the degree of Iron-Age Finnish settlement and land use on the southern coast was more extensive than was previously thought. As the research in the archipelago shows, place names can not only contain information about the languages spoken by the inhabitants of the area, but also about past land-use practices and the locations of settlements and burial grounds. Therefore, the study of toponyms, especially when incorporating place names on the earliest historical maps, can be used to recognise and locate earlier settlements. In an ideal case, the existence of these settlements can then be confirmed by means of archaeology and other disciplines, such as palynology. On the other hand, new knowledge of the history of settlement in Uusimaa can also benefit research into the archipelago of Helsinki, since the settlement and land use of the islands has developed in close connection to the mainland.

Acknowledgements

The authors would like to thank the Faculty of Arts at the University of Helsinki for funding the research of the Maritime Helsinki project in 2014. The research on Villinki in 2015 was carried out through Docent Terhi Ainiala's personal funding.

Bibliography

Abbreviations
SKP = Suomen kielen perussanakirja
SPK = Suomalainen paikannimikirja.

Archive sources
Broterus, Samuel. 1697. Geo......a och Afritning uppå ..... belegit i Helssing .....Sibbo Sochns

Scerigårdar afmätt åhr 1697. ULM Hki 8:1.

Forssel, Lars. 1696. Geografisk Delineation Över Helsingfors Stadens Hörig Fiskevatten Och Tillhörig Holmar. Helsinki, Kaupunkisuunnitteluvirasto, Asemakaavaosasto. Kartat ja piirustukset. Yleiskartat. Ia:5. City of Helsinki.

Geographisk Charta öfwer Nyland... 1742. KA: Maanmittaushallitus. Maanmittaushallituksen kartat, Alue- ja rajakartat, MH MH 26/- -. The National Archives of Finland.

KA 5003. Viipurin ja Porvoon läänien maakirja (1544). (The tax lists of Viipuri and Porvoo [1544]). The National Archives of Finland.

Senaatin kartasto. KA: Maanmittaushallituksen historiallinen karttaarkisto (kokoelma). Senaatin kartasto VI 30 [Helsinki]. The National Archives of Finland.

Winter, Timothy. 1798. Charta öfver Willinge Holmar lydande under Degerö Alodial Säteri uti Helsinge Sockn, Borgå Härad och Nylands Län, Afmätte År 1798 af Timothy Winter. KA Maanmittaushallituksen uudistusarkisto, B7Helsinki:12/1-10 Laajasalo / Degerö; Isojako (1794). The National Archives of Finland.

Literature
Ainiala, Terhi, Minna Saarelma, Paula Sjöblom. *Names in focus: an introduction to Finnish onomastics.* Translated by Leonard Pearl. Helsinki: SKS, 2012.

Alanen, Timo & Saulo Kepsu *Kuninkaan kartasto Suomesta 1776–1805. (The Royal Atlas over Finland 1776–1805.)* Helsinki: SKS, 1989.

Alenius, Teija, Georg Haggren, Markku Oinonen, Antti Ojala, Ritva Liisa Pitkänen. The history of settlement on the coastal mainland in southern Finland. Palaeoecological, archaeological and etymological evidence from Lohjansaari island, Western Uusimaa, Finland. *Journal of Archaeological Science* 47 (2014): 99–112.

Appelgren-Kivalo, Hjalmar. *Helsinki Hertonäs Skepparberget Tarkastus 1910. ("The investigation of a cairn in Helsinki Hertonäs Skepparberget").* Unpublished research report no 128818. Helsinki, National Board of Antiquities, 1910.

Aspelin, J. R. *Helsinki Hertonäs Thorsnäs Brändö Grind Skepparudden. Kiviröykkiön kaivaus ("Helsinki Hertonäs Thorsnäs Brändö Grind Skepparudden. The excavation of a cairn").* Unpublished research report no 128773. Helsinki, National Board of Antiquities, 1886.

Cleve, Nils. *Helsinki Brändö Hertonäsboulevarden Kiviröykkiön kaivaus* ("*Helsinki Brändö Hertonäsboulevarden, the excavation of a cairn*"). Unpublished research report no 128780. Helsinki, National Board of Antiquities, 1931.

Cleve, Nils. Helsingin seutu esihistoriallisena aikana (The region of Helsinki during prehistoric times). In *Helsingin kaupungin historia* I (*History of the City of Helsinki* I), 57–78. Helsinki: SKS, 1950.

Debenjak, Annukka. *Vallisaaren Luotsilahden luotsimökkien jäänteet ("The remains of the maritime pilots houses in Luotsilahti, Vallisaari").* Unpublished research report no 146366. Helsinki, National Board of Antiquities, 2014.

Enqvist, Ove & Taneli Eskola. *Kruunun jalokivet: Vallisaari ja Kuninkaansaari (The Crown Jewels: Vallisaari and Kuninkaansaari).* Vantaa: Moreeni, 2011.

Enqvist, Ove. *Kellä saaret ja selät on hallussaan... Rannikkopuolustuksen aluekysymykset autonomisessa ja itsenäisessä Suomessa (Who owns the islands and the open seas... Regional questions of the coastal defence during Finland's autonomy period and independence).* Sotahistorian laitoksen julkaisuja (Publications of the Department of Military History) 1, no 9. Helsinki: Edita, 2007.

Finnish Ministry of Finance 2014. *Valtiovarainministeriön tiedote: valtion tavoitteena on avata puolustuskäytöstä vapautuvat Helsingin edustan saaret uuteen käyttöön.* <https://www.vm.fi/vm/fi/03_tiedotteet_ja_puheet/01_tiedotteet/20130304Valtio/name.jsp>. Accessed 12.6.2014.

Gardberg, C. J. & Kari Palsila. *Sveaborg.* Helsinki: Otava, 1998.

Granlund, Åke. *Studier över östnyländska ortnamn.* Skrifter utgivna av Svenska litteratursällskapet i Finland 358. Helsinki: Svenska litteratursällskapet. 1956.

Guide to the Archipelago 2009. Helsinki Sports Department, Maritime division, 2010. <http://www.hel.fi/hel2/Helsinginseutu/liitteet/Saaristo_opas.pdf> Accessed 2.12.2015.

Haavisto, Maija; Esa Kukkonen; Boris Winterhalter. Helsinki Soil Map 1:100000. Maps of Quaternary deposits. Vol. 2034. Map sheet 2034. 1974.

Haggrén, Georg. *Autioituneet kylätontit - kurkistusreikä Uudenmaan asutushistoriaan (Abandoned village sites – a peephole to the settlement history of Uusimaa).* CD-rom published by Vårt Maritima Arv ("Our maritime heritage" project) Helsinki: Department of Cultural Studies, University of Helsinki, 2005.

Helsingin kadunnimet ("Street names of Helsinki"). Publications of the City of Helsinki 24. Helsinki: City of Helsinki, 1970.

The Helsinki City Planning Department. 2014. Vartiosaari. <http://www.hel.fi/www/Helsinki/fi/asuminen-ja-ymparisto/kaavoitus/ajankohtaiset-kaavat/vartiosaari/>. Accessed 12.6.2014.

Hornborg, Eirik. *Helsingin kaupungin historia II: Ajanjakso 1721–1809 ("The history of the City of Helsinki II: Period 1721–1809").* Helsinki: SKS. 1950.

Huldén, Lars. *Finlandssvenska bebyggelsenamn: namn på landskap, kommuner, byar i Finland av svenskt ursprung eller med särskild svensk form.* Skrifter utgivna av Svenska litteratursällskapet i Finland 635. Helsinki: Svenska litteratursällskapet i Finland, 2001

Hyvärinen, Hannu. Shore displacement and Stone Age dwelling sites near Helsinki, southern coast of Finland. Huurre, M. (ed.), *Dig it all. Papers dedicated to Ari Siiriäinen.* Helsinki: The Finnish Antiquarian Society – The Archaeological Society of Finland, 1999.

Jansson, Henrik & Jaakko Latikka. *Länsi- ja Keski-Uudenmaan saariston ja rannikkoalueiden inventointi 2002–2003: Tammisaari, Hanko, Inkoo, Siuntio, Kirkkonummi, Espoo, Helsinki. ("The survey of the archipelago and coastal regions of western and middle Uusimaa.")* Vårt Maritima Arv ("Our maritime heritage" project). Department of Cultural Studies, Archaeology, University of Helsinki. Unpublished research report. National Board of Antiquities, Helsinki, 2008.

Kaukiainen, Yrjö. *Suomen talonpoikaispurjehdus 1800-luvun alkupuoliskolla ("Finnish peasant shipping in the first hald of the 19th century").* Helsinki: Suomen Historiallinen Seura, 1970.

Kaukiainen, Yrjö. *Rantarosvojen saaristo. Itäinen Suomenlahti 1700-luvulla ("The archipelago of ship robbers. Eastern Gulf of Finland in the 18th century").* Helsinki: SKS, 2006.

Kerkkonen, Gunvor. *Bondesegel på Finska viken.* Skifter utgivna av Svenska Litteratursällskapet i Finland 369. Helsinki: Svenska Litteratursällskapet I Finland, 1959.

Kepsu, Saulo. *Uuteen maahan: Helsingin ja Vantaan vanha asutus ja nimistö. (To the new land: the old settlements and onomastics of Helsinki and Vantaa).* Suomalaisen Kirjallisuuden Seuran Toimituksia 1027. Helsinki: SKS, 2005.

Kiviniemi, Eero. *Väärät vedet. Tutkimus mallien osuudesta nimenmuodostuksessa ("Wrong waters. A study on the influence of models on the formation of place names").* Publications of the Finnish Literature Society 337. Helsinki: SKS, 1977.

Lillman, Sanna. *Lohjanjärven alueen asutuksen kehitys rautakaudella ja varhaisella historiallisella ajalla (The development of settlement in the area of Lohjanjärvi during the Iron Age and early historical period.).* MA thesis in Archaeology, University of Helsinki. 2014.

Löfgren, Kaj-Erik. *Helsingin merilinnoitusten inventointi. (The survey of the maritime fortifications in Helsinki.)* Unpublished research report no. 749. National Board of Antiquities, Helsinki, 1972.

Lönnqvist, Bo. *Skärgårdsbebyggelse och skärgårdskultur i Nyland.* Kustbygd Folklivsstudier XIII, Svenska Litteratursällskapet 489, 127–204. Helsinki: Svenska Litteratursällskapet i Finland, 1980.

Namnledslexikon. The Institute for the Languages in Finland, 1999. Updated 2007. <http://kaino.kotus.fi/svenska/ledlex/>. Accessed 9.6.2014.

Nygård, Stefan. *Villinki – saariston huvilayhteisö ("Villinki – the summer villa community in the archipelago").* Memoria – the publications of the Helsinki City Museum. Helsinki: Helsinki City Museum, 2003.

Paikkala, Sirkka. *Saaristo-Espoo: nimistöä, luontoa, historiaa ja tulevaisuutta ("Archipelago-Espoo: toponyms, nature, history and future").* Espoon kaupunkisuunnittelukeskus, nimistöryhmä. Espoo: City of Espoo, 1996.

Pitkänen, Ritva Liisa. *Turunmaan saariston suomalainen lainanimistö ("The Finnish loan names in the Turunmaa archipelago").* Publications of the Finnish Literature Society 418. Helsinki: SKS, 1985.

Pitkänen, Ritva Liisa & Kurt Zilliacus. Paikat ja niiden nimet ("Places and their names"). In Paikkala (ed.) 1996, 31–116.

Salonen, Kati & Mona Schalin. *Vartiosaaren kulttuuriympäristöselvitys – historia, ominaispiirteet, arvot ja merkitys ("The cultural landscape of Vartiosaari – history, characteristics, values and significance").* Helsingin kaupunkisuunnitteluviraston julkaisuja 2013: 2. Helsinki: City of Helsinki, 2013.

Suhonen, Veli-Pekka. Helsingin keskiaikaiset ja uuden ajan alun kylänpaikat. Arkistoselvitys ('The medieval and early modern villages in Helsinki. Archive research'). Unpublished research report. National Board of Antiquities, Helsinki, 2010.

Suhonen, Veli-Pekka & Janne Heinonen. *Helsingin keskiaikaiset ja uuden ajan alun kylänpaikat ('Sites of medieval and early modern villages in Helsinki').* Unpublished research report. National Board of Antiquities, Helsinki, 2011.

Suomen kielen perussanakirja 1, *A–K.* ('A basic dictionary of Finnish 1, A-K'). Kotimaisten kielten tutkimuskeskuksen julkaisuja 55. Helsinki: The Institute for the Languages in Finland, 1990.

Suomalainen paikannimikirja ('The Finnish Book on Toponyms'). Kotimaisten kielten tutkimuskeskuksen julkaisuja 146. Helsinki: Karttakeskus and The Institute for the Languages in Finland, 2007.

Sädevirta, Sirkka. *Laajasalon, Villingin ja Santahaminan historiaa ('On the history of Laajasalo, Villinki and Santahamina').* Helsinki: City of Helsinki, 1994.

Talve, Ilmar. *Suomen kansankulttuuri ("The peasant culture of Finland").* Helsinki: SKS, 1990.

Tuovinen, Tapani. The Finnish archipelago coast from AD 500 to 1550 – a zone of interaction. *Maritime Landscape in Change: Archaeological, Historical, Palaeoecological and Geological Studies on Western Uusimaa. Results of the research project "SEAS - Settlements and Economies around the Sea -Maritime settlement, subsistence and economic histories around the Baltic Sea 500-1700 AD.* Iskos 19: 10-60. Helsinki: The Archaeological Society of Finland, 2011.

Zilliacus, Kurt. *Orter och namn i "Finska skären".* Söreningen Konstsamfundets publikationsserie XV. Helsinki: Konstsamfundet, 1994.

Vectors of Language Spread at the Central Steppe Periphery: Finno-Ugric as a Catalyst Language

Johanna Nichols and Richard A. Rhodes, UC Berkeley

1. Introduction

An unexpected event occurred somewhere between approximately 4500 and 6000 years ago in the vicinity of the central steppe: the Proto-Uralic language family began its spread, eventually to cover half of northernmost Eurasia. More definitively, about 4000 years ago its Finno-Ugric component began its rapid spread over most of that range. The speakers of Uralic/Finno-Ugric were hunter-gatherers, their technology at most barely Neolithic, yet they exerienced a language spread of a magnitude usually associated only with food-producing cultures, and one that produced a Uralic monoculture across most of northern Eurasia from the forest-steppe ecotone north (i.e. above about 50°).[1]

The Finno-Ugric/Uralic spread is unexpected, even anomalous, if it is seen as an ordinary expansion of the language range and speech community size of an ordinary hunter-gatherer population. There is nothing in the archaeological record or what can be reconstructed of Proto-Uralic material culture to explain the advantage that early Uralic must have acquired over neighboring hunter-gatherer societies. This chapter aims to reconstruct for early Uralic a geolinguistic, sociolinguistic, and economic position vis-à-vis neighboring societies that explains the spread, and in fact makes it almost inevitable. We adopt the theoretical position advocated by Saarikivi and Lavento 2012: that historical linguistic-archaeological work needs to shift focus away from identifying protolanguages with archaeological cultures and toward identifying forces (economic, environmental, etc.) that have shaped areas (which consist of societies, languages, and cultural elements in some geographical context).

We use the following geographical terminology. The *central steppe* is today's central and northern Kazakhstan, i.e. from the Urals to the Altai Mountains; the *western steppe* runs from the Urals west to Eastern Europe; the *eastern steppe* (a.k.a. Mongolian steppe) is today's Mongolia plus Inner Mongolia and northern Xinjiang. Immediately to the north of the steppe runs the narrow band of the forest-steppe zone, an ecotone of transitional patchy grassland and forest; to its north is the forest (or taiga), chiefly coniferous; and north of that, tundra extending to the Arctic Ocean. The main concern here is the central steppe and the forest-steppe zone to its north.

Western Steppe	Central Steppe
PIE first split (4000) (horse)	
	Botai (3600-) (horse)
PIE dispersal (3500) (wheel)	
Yamnaya culture (3200-) (nomadic pastoralism)	
Abashevo (2500-)	
	Sintashta (2300-)
	Andronovo (bronze; chariot)

Table 1. Neolithic to Bronze Age on the western and central steppes. (Sources for dates: Anthony 2007, Frachetti 2012, Svyatko et al. 2009.) Dates are in calibrated years BCE (= calendar years, approximately) and are rounded to the nearest hundred years.

The essential archaeological developments from the Neolithic to the Bronze Age are shown in Table 1.[2] The initial split of Proto-Indo-European (PIE) sent the Anatolian branch off in some direction eventually to enter history in central and western Anatolia, probably via the Balkan Peninsula, though there is no archaeological or linguistic evidence linking specifically Anatolian with the Balkan Peninsula. At this time, the Indo-European speakers, one of probably numerous Copper Age cattle-herding tribes on the westernmost steppe, were familiar with wool and animal traction, but not wheeled transport. They appear to have been early domesticators of the horse some time before 3500 BCE. By about 3500 BCE, they became familiar with wheeled transport, as is well reflected in the vocabularies of all non-Anatolian branches, and by c. 3200 BCE, the non-Anatolian clade, probably a dialect continuum at the time, had evolved into a nomadic pastoral society using wheeled carts and domesticated horses, and expanded to cover most of the western steppe in the form of the Yamnaya archaeological culture. (Anthony 2007, Darden 2001, Anthony & Ringe 2015.)

On the central steppe, independently[3] of and simultaneously to the IE domestication of the horse, the distinctive Botai-Tersek culture of today's northern Kazakhstan also domesticated the horse, but apparently used horses only for hunting and/or luring wild horses; the staple of their diet was wild horsemeat. They also used dairy products.[4] (Outram et al. 2009, Anthony 2007:216-220.)

---

[1] The east-west range of Uralic, from Saami in western Norway to Nganasan on the Taimyr Peninsula in north central Siberia, occupies nearly as many degrees of longitude as the pre-1492 range of Indo-European (a degree of longitude is of course narrower at 60°N than at the lower latitudes where most Indo-European languages have been spoken).

[2] Here and below, all dates are expressed in calibrated years BCE (approximately equal to calendar years). Most dates are rounded to the nearest hundred or thousand.

[3] Or by stimulus diffusion; communication between the western and central steppes was evidently well developed, as indicated by the gradual subsequent diffusion of cattle and sheep pastoralism into the indigenous central steppe cultures including Botai-Tersek, and the beeline migration of what appears to have been ancestral Tocharian from the western steppe to the Minusinsk Basin and Altai foothills, giving rise to the Afanasievo culture, at the very dawn of bronze technology and before other Indo-European groups took control of the mining and bronze production centers of the eastern Urals (see below in text).

[4] Lactose tolerance had not yet evolved in the western Eurasian population (Allentoft et al. 2015), so the dairy products consumed must have been soured or fermented (both yogurt-like products and fermented kumyss have most of their lactase converted to acid and/or alcohol). Butter is a possibility, though horse milk contains considerably less fat then cow's milk, so it would have been a less efficient use of milk. Cheese is a distant possibility, again because

A descendent of the Yamnaya culture, the Abashevo culture of the northeastern part of the western steppe and adjacent to the western flanks of the Ural Mountains, appears to have been a more militarized culture than its ancestors or predecessors and to have been directly ancestral to the slightly later Sintashta culture and its Andronovo[5] variant of the northwestern central steppe and eastern Ural flanks. These cultures developed bronze technology, both the production of bronze and manufacture of bronze tools and weapons, into a flourishing industry and also invented the chariot, developed chariot warfare, and spread rapidly over the central and then western steppes, and southward to absorb and dominate the Bactria-Margiana archaeological complex of urban west Central Asia. This expansion brought Indo-Iranian speech across the central and western steppes and southward to Iran, Afghanistan, and eventually India, and this distribution, together with the post-Yamnana origin and resemblances between Andronovo ritual and symbolism (evident in burials and military technology), and those attested in Sanskrit and early Iranian civilization make it clear that the dominant language of the Andronovo culture was ancestral Indo-Iranian. The expansion also spurred economic development and trade to the east (the Altai-Sayan area, another source of minerals) and southeast (Frachetti 2008), and in the forest-steppe zone to the north (Anthony 2007:Ch. 16), where indigenous hunter-gatherers did some bronze production and manufacture and traded bronze along an east-west trade route that eventually led to the eastern Baltic area. Marked economic differences and an evident military nobility characterized the Andronovo culture (Anthony 2007:Chs. 15-16), and it is probably safe to assume that the new levels of wealth triggered the growth of trade and the production of bronze even in the forest-steppe to the north. The major likely product of the northern forests that could have been traded for bronze, dairy products, and horsehides was furs, a high-value trade item to this day.[6] The next section proposes a model for this role and identifies Finno-Ugric as the language of the primary traders in the Bronze Age forest-steppe and forest zones.

2. Finno-Ugric as catalyst to the Iranian expansion

A language spread has a center, a trajectory or directionality, a range (which expands), and a frontier (Nichols 1998). The frontier, the edge of the range where the spreading language abuts other languages, is an interesting place: speakers of the expanding language and representatives of its institutions or influential groups meet and interact with speakers of other languages; the political, economic, and/or social institutions of the expanding society begin extending into surrounding groups; the meeting of very different economies, social structures, etc. creates risks and opportunities; and there are openings for entrepreneurs, traders, translators, bilingual and bicultural individuals to mediate between expanding and shifting societies and serve as intermediaries, facilitators recruiters, marketers, and representatives of neighboring societies. In short, it is a place of economic opportunity, not only for members of the spreading group, but also for those of the societies being absorbed, displaced, etc.

Especially where there is a marked economic or political difference between the society of the spreading language and its neighbors, an enterprising society near the frontier may seize (or be granted) the opportunity to function as intermediary, marketer, etc. Its language can then spread out in advance of the main spread, absorbing other languages from the periphery, and ending up with an arc-like distribution around part of the frontier. In its original homeland, its speakers shift to the language of the main spread, so it survives only in the far-flung arc, where its speakers are genetically and probably also culturally different from the original speakers. Though at some distance from the main spread, these surviving arc languages may have typological properties in common with the spreading language, reflecting contact at the frontier. Such a society is a *catalyst* society and its language is a catalyst language.

2.1. Some catalyst languages

Not every language spread has a catalyst language, but they are common enough to warrant a term and a place in linguistic-geography theory. Well-known cases of languages filling the role of catalyst to other spreads include the following (Nichols & Rhodes, in prep.):

A well-described example is Ainu, the sole survivor of what must once have been a diverse population of languages representing the prehistoric Jomon culture of Japan. When the Yayoi culture entered southern Japan from the Korean mainland around 300 BCE-300 CE, bringing with it the Japanese language, wet rice farming, state-level political organization, and a more rapidly increasing population, the Jomon languages began to go extinct. Ancestral Ainu, however, was a catalyst language, its society functioning as intermediary and transmission vehicle between the Yayoi culture and the north. Buttressed by this economic and cultural importance, ancestral Ainu spread across northern Honshu, then to Hokkaido, and even to Sakhalin. It survived longest only on Hokkaido, where it is recently extinct (this analysis of the prehistory of Ainu is from Janhunen 2002). Its attested distribution is an arc over the far frontier of the northward spread of Japanese, though, confined to the mostly north-south shape of Japan, it is a very narrow arc.

To the north of China, various ethnic groups probably played the catalyst role to the emerging Chinese state.

---

of the lower fat content, and because cheesemaking is a more complex process. All of these products keep well and transport well (yogurt is dried to produce a lightweight chewy substance which also doubles as yogurt culture), making them valuable in trade (valuable especially for their fat content).

[5] Henceforth simply Andronovo.

[6] We assume the bronze production in the forest-steppe zone was not an innovation or import from the steppe so much as a retention and elaboration of a prior technology. Indigenous non-IE-speaking people of the north central steppe and forest-steppe zone, including the Ural Mountains, must have owned the land with mineral deposits, known about metals, and begun to extract them as metallurgy advanced on the western steppe. They probably remained as miners, small-scale bronze manufacturers, traders, and entrepreneurs after the Andronovo people came to dominate mining, bronze production, and the manufacture of bronze items. See the next section.

The first clear example is the Xiongnu (or eastern Huns) (209 BCE-155 CE), who initiated the long-standing relationship whereby steppe pastoral nomads controlled trade and protection payments between other nomads, hunters and reindeer herders of the northern forest, and imperial China. The language of the Xiongnu is unknown; Bulgar Turkic appears to have been one of the languages spoken in their state, and may have been a *lingua franca* even then (Janhunen 1996:186-7, Schönig 2003:405; Pritsak 1982, Golden 2010, Maenchen-Helfen 1973:376-443).[7] The Xianbei successors to the Xiongnu (130-180) may have spoken a Para-Mongolic language (Schönig 2003:405), but Bulgar Turkic was clearly in use as a lingua franca during their reign (Werner 2014:49). Turkic spread across the entire eastern steppe by language shift (i.e. taking root as native language) under the Zhuan-Zhuan (a.k.a. Ruan-Ruan, Jou-jan, eastern Avar) in the early centuries CE, gaining a large demographic presence that dominates interior eastern Eurasia to this day.[8] The subsequent Turkic khanates (552-630; 683-840) spread Turkic speech beyond the eastern steppe to the central steppe and part of the western steppe. The central steppe remains largely Turkic-speaking now; the Russian conquest of the steppe beginning in the 16th century replaced most of the Turkic speech from the western steppe except around the periphery (Chuvash and Tatar to the north; Kumyk, Noghai, Karachay-Balkar, and Gagauz to the south).

The last steppe catalyst to Chinese empire was Mongolian (for the history of this spread, see Janhunen 2008). Ancestral Mongolic had begun to spread on the eastward steppe before Genghis Khan united the Mongolian-speaking nomads, defeating the (possibly also Mongolic-speaking) Tatars to gain control of the catalyst status. The political and economic strength of China at the time brought wealth and power to the Mongols, making possible the development of the catalyst state into the largest empire on earth to that date.[9] Mongolic speech spread to some extent with the empire, and now survives not only in Mongolia (including Inner Mongolia) but also in enclaves in southeastern Siberia, northwestern China, and Afghanistan (Kalmuck on the lower Volga in Russia is a later emigrant from eastern Central Asia). Most of these enclaves represent former military garrisons; the great demographic advantage of Turkic speakers in Central Asia and the central and western steppe meant that outside of Mongolia, the Mongol army spoke mostly Turkic, and the spread of Mongol rule brought Turkic speech to the cities of Central Asia.

Roughly contemporary to the spread of Mongolic was the spread of the Tungusic family to the north, a catalyst of sorts expanding from a homeland in Manchuria or northern Korea (the vicinity of the Jurchen and later Manchu later spread centers), in which Tungusic speech was catalyst between the various states of Manchuria and Korea on the one hand, and the reindeer herders and fur trappers of the Siberian forest on the other (for this history see Janhunen 2012). As a result, interior central and eastern Siberia have been mostly Tungusic-speaking in historical times (now shifting to Russian), with previous languages either absorbed or reduced to peripheral enclaves: Yukagir in the northeast, Yeniseian to the west; Yakut (Turkic) and Buriat (Mongolic) underwent spreads later than this, during the time of the Mongol empire.

The Germanic tribes, and especially those known as Goths, in late Roman and early post-Roman times, played an economic and military role in some ways analogous to that of the Mongolic and Turkic peoples in the east, with warlords profiting from both looting and protection money, and expanding into states and military powers competing with Rome. Perhaps their role could be seen as catalyst and as triggering the Germanic expansions across Europe; we leave this question for experts on Roman and Germanic history.

An example from the Americas is Quechua,[10] originally a language of the Peruvian coast and highlands which had undergone a spread into the Peruvian highlands before the rise of the Inka Empire, and in view of its wide use, was adopted as administrative language by the Inka. (The Inka ruling elite spoke another language, probably Aymara or extinct Puquina.) After the Spanish conquest, Quechua was used by the Spanish as official indigenous language for purposes of administration and religious proselytizing, giving it a wider spread and a larger speech community than it is likely to have achieved otherwise, and in particular, triggering a sizable southward Quechuan spread which absorbed much of the previously extensive Aymara language. In this post-Inka spread, Quechua functioned as catalyst language to the Spanish rulers (see D'Altroy 2015:5-62, Cerrón-Palomino 2015, DeMarrais 2012, Adelaar & Muysken 2004:182-183, Mannheim 1991).

Another, and similar, example is Aztec. Classical Aztec (i.e. its vernacular antecedent) was the spoken language of the rulers of the Aztec Empire and their ethnic group, but it was by no means a *lingua franca* throughout the Aztec Empire. To a lesser extent than was the case for

---

[7] Confederates of the Xiongnu evidently included some speakers of Yeniseian languages (Vajda 2012, in press, Vajda et al. in press, Werner 2014:Chs. 2-3, Vovin 2004). Early Yeniseian may have been a mini-catalyst for the Xiongnu state, consequently undergoing a modest spread from the northern periphery of the eastern steppe and the southern Altai foothills down the Yenisei to central Siberia where its sole survivor Ket is now spoken.

[8] The Zhuan-Zhuan themselves may have spoken some other language originally, neither Mongolic, Turkic, nor Iranian (Vovin 2011, 2004).

[9] Another factor may have been a short-term climate change bringing increased rainfall that expanded the yield and extent of the Mongolian grasslands and made possible substantial demographic growth of the Mongols and their livestock, powering the Mongol army (Hvistendahl 2012).

[32] We use this term for the language of the Inka Empire and early Spanish rule. What was probably a single language with clear dialect differences in the fifteenth century is by now a young language family usually referred to as Quechuan. As of the fifteenth century, ancestral Quechuan had undergone a spread from the coast into the Peruvian highlands and a secondary radial spread of a central Peruvian dialect, peripheralizing the more conservative varieties to the north and south.

Quechua, but still enough to create a catalyst situation, the Spanish treated it as *lingua franca* and official language, promoting its use in religion and official functions, so that by now, Aztecan varieties are in fact the main indigenous languages throughout the former Aztec Empire (see Suárez 1983:163-165).

Another likely example is Proto-Uto-Aztecan. Hill 2001 reconstructs terminology for maize agriculture and other Mesoamerican farming elements to Proto-Uto-Aztecan. Merrill 2012 argues that these are only Proto-Southern Uto-Aztecan (see also Kaufman & Justeson 2009). Either way, early Uto-Aztecan had close contact with Mesoamerican domestication. It then spread far to the north, where its modern daughters include agricultural Tohono O'odham and Hopi, and an arc of languages farther north in California, Nevada, Oregon, and Idaho spoken by foragers who had intensified plant-based economies, some management and improvement of wild plant stands with but no domestication per se (see various chapters in Madsen & Rhode 1994).

A complex example comes from the interaction of Cree and Ojibwe (both Algonquin) in the western Great Lakes region and beyond (Rhodes in press; Rhodes 1982, 1992, 2008, 2009, 2012; for Métchif in social context, Bakker 1997). Every kind of spread occurred in this area during the historical period, including one case of a catalyst language. Prior to about 1600 CE, Ojibwe was spoken in the vicinity of Sault Ste. Marie (the intersection of Lakes Superior, Michigan, and Huron) and Cree was spoken over a larger area to the north, west, and east. Sault Ste. Marie was the main nexus in a trade network and Ojibwe spread as an economically important language. The spread was in part by language shift, and as a result, some varieties of Ojibwe have Cree substratal effects. Cree was also spreading outward at contact, probably pushed by the pressures of war and dislocation caused by European settlement to the east; its westward expansion across the Great Plains pushed Athabaskan languages west and north (by this time the Cree had firearms, while their western neighbors did not, and retreated before the Cree expansion). The fur trade, run by European settlers, gave rise to a catalyst situation. The Hudson Bay Company, with its network of trading posts in indigenous communities, created wealth at least for the trading post operator and his family (usually a high-status native family, since the best families strove to marry their daughters to the wealthy traders). A network of trappers and traders formed and enabled both Cree and Ojibwe to profit and expand as catalyst languages.[11]

2.2. Proto-Finno-Ugric as a catalyst language

In the traditional Uralicist view, Proto-Uralic split into two branches, Finno-Ugric (the western branch) and Samoyedic (eastern), after which Finno-Ugric underwent a series of splits during a gradual westward spread, while Samoyedic diverged only much later, from a homeland in the east of the range, into daughter languages which are now of only Romance-like divergence. The primary split into Samoyedic vs. Finno-Ugric is based primarily on lexical divergence: Proto-Samoyedic has surprisingly few lexical cognates with the rest of Uralic, while its inflectional paradigms and other grammatical elements are largely shared. Consequently, Proto-Uralic has often been seen as very old, much older than Indo-European (which preserves a larger lexical stock across the family). The last two decades have seen a modest increase in the number of Uralic cognates in Samoyedic and recognition that Finno-Ugric has few, if any, solid non-lexical innovations that can firmly identify it as a unified clade, and the family tree structure is often viewed as flatter. (For overviews of the chronology and family tree, see Janhunen 2009, Abondolo 1998:1-42, Salminen 2001, Aikio 2006. Lehtinen et al 2014, a computational study notable for careful vetting of lexical data, find good evidence for early divergence of Samoyedic.) What is important to the present paper is the lexical divergence of Samoyedic, whatever the status of that branch in the family tree, and the fact that Finno-Ugric, more or less unified and separate from Samoyedic, experienced a sizable influx of loan vocabulary from Proto-Indo-Iranian and/or early Iranian, an episode we regard as a lexical analog to a clade-defining innovation in grammar or phonology, and as setting Finno-Ugric apart from Samoyedic. We therefore speak of Proto-Finno-Ugric below, without implying any claim about shared internal innovations.

The history and geography of the Finno-Ugric branch match closely what we have defined as the catalyst role. Proto-Finno-Ugric is traditionally located in the forest-steppe zone just east of the Urals, north of the central steppe (today's Kazakhstan), at about 4000 BP. New proposals put it variously farther east or farther west, but the traditional homeland represents an average of proposals; the exact location is not essential here, as long as the homeland is close to the Urals, and this is the only location that finds more or less independent evidence in the distribution of Indo-Iranian loanwords (Finno-Ugric must be close to the known Indo-Iranian homeland, Samoyedic farther east) and phylogenetic center of gravity (which runs either just north of Kazakhstan, if an initial Samoyedic/Finno-Ugric split is recognized; or approximately along the Urals, if Khanty, with or without Mansi and Hungarian, is grouped with Samoyedic in an earliest eastern branch). As the Indo-Iranian-speaking Sintashta and then Andronovo cultures took over and expanded the mines and metallurgy in the southern Urals and came to dominate the eastern steppe militarily, economically, and politically, the Proto-Finno-Ugric speakers (who may well have been the previous exploiters of the mines) produced much of the metalwork and facilitated and managed the trade in steppe artifacts with the hunter-gatherers to the north and along what must have been a pre-existent trade route connecting to the Baltic coast. They may or may not have been traders and managers before the Indo-Iranian spread. The steppe-forest interface was an important route for trade, especially in fur, where furs were a luxury item that could bring considerable wealth to small foraging societies including those at

---

[11] The French fur trade, in contrast, was carried out not by native Americans, but by French, and did not trigger a comparable catalyst spread.

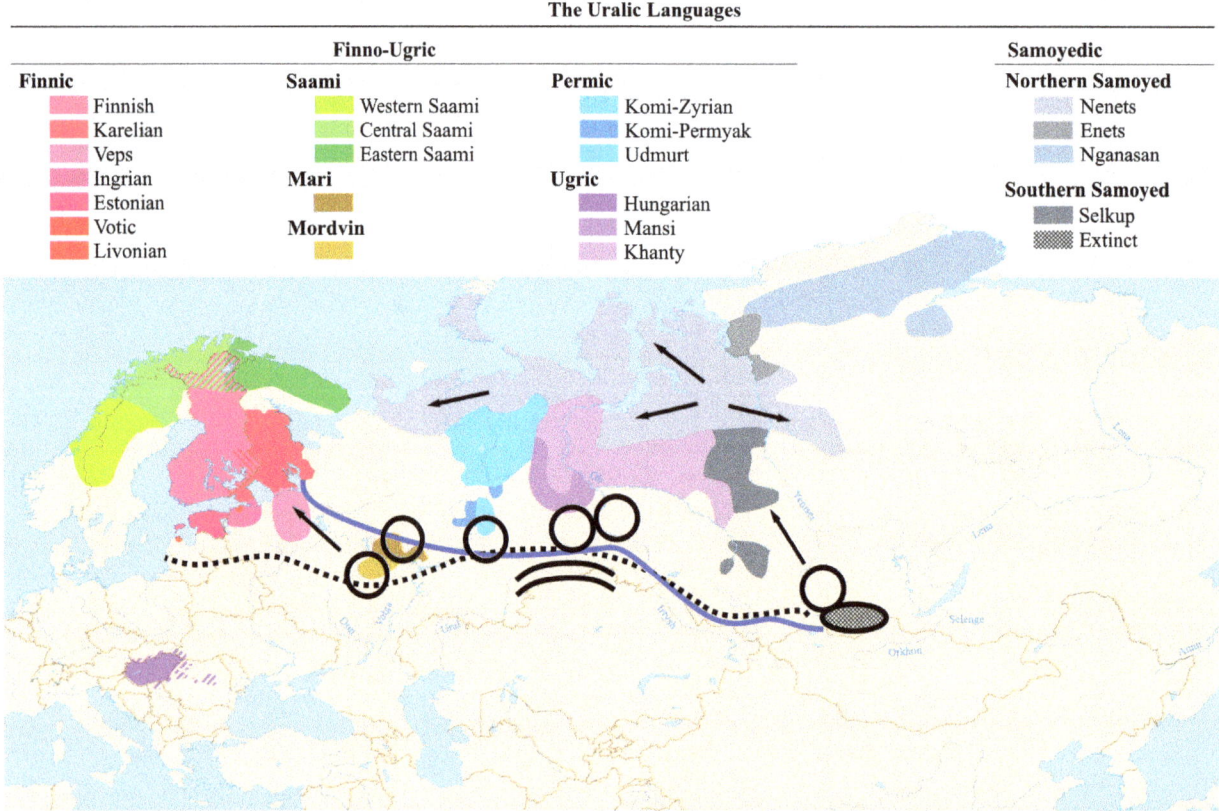

Fig. 1: The Uralic range. Base map with modern ranges (adapted from Wikimedia Commons). Stippled oval: extinct southern Samoyedic languages. Dotted line: approximate southern range of Uralic prior to the Russian expansion in the late middle ages (at that time the entire area north of the line was Uralic-speaking). Blue line: approximate central trajectory of the Fur Road. Double black arc: northern edge of central steppe and of Andronovo culture. Circles: approximate homelands of daughter branch proto-languages (the leftmost one is Saamic-Finnic-Mordvin). Arrows: directions of known recent spread (from branch homelands).

long distances from steppe centers of production; the trade is likely to have been waterborne and was archaeologically invisible until revealed by bronze artifacts (Barfield 2009:237). Linguistic diversity in the forest belt may have been preserved under this kind of trade system, but at the interface itself, one can assume the actual trade connections soon came to be dominated by a single society and language. We will call this interface the Fur Road,[12] and assume it fostered east-west language spreads (the spreading varieties eventually spread gradually northward, following the standing pattern in interior Eurasia). On this analysis, Proto-Finno-Ugric expanded along the Fur Road as catalyst far to the west of its homeland, and north all along this route. It also acquired a sizable stock of early Indo-Iranian loan vocabulary (Joki 1973, Koivulehto 1999, 2000; Holopainen in progress is a current overview and critique; for the Indo-Iranian spread and its involvement with Finno-Ugric see Anthony 2007: Chapters 15-16). Only something like long-term dominance of an east-west trade network would seem to be able to explain the sizable spread of Finno-Ugric and the continued momentum that brought Saami and then Finnic to Fenno-Scandia in a process completed only in the late middle ages (overviews of the Saami and Finnic spreads: Aikio 2012, Saarikivi & Lavento 2012). In the linguistic geography of Uralic, the deepest branching is to the east (Samoyedic vs. Finno-Ugric or Samoyedic-Ugric vs. the rest, depending on one's stance on phylogeny: see Fig. 1, where Samoyedic languages are gray and Finno-Ugric in other colors). Successive leftward branches are successively shallower, beginning with the split of Ugric (possibly a clade or possibly two clades, Khanty vs. Hungarian plus Mansi) early in the family history and ending with the much more recent divergence of Saami-Finnic-Mordvin (the rest of the higher-level branching of Finno-Ugric is not well resolved: see Lehtinen et al. 2014). This branching history bespeaks an origin to the east, perhaps somewhere between the Khanty (lavender) and Samoyedic (gray) homelands, and successive westward movement. Note that the branch homelands form an arc over the central steppe (for branch homelands see also Salminen 2013).

3. Modeling the Samoyedic divergence

Samoyedic, the easternmost branch of Uralic, has an internal age of only about 2000 years, but was the first to diverge from the rest of Uralic. Its prehistory is mysterious: its morphological paradigms show many resemblances to those of the Finno-Ugric languages, but it has rather few lexical cognates (and distinctly fewer than would be consistent with the close resemblances in morphology). It lacks entirely the Indo-Iranian vocabulary that marks Proto-Finno-Ugric as involved with the Sintashta-Andronovo culture and must therefore have diverged and moved out of the cultural reach of the cen-

---

[12] Adapting Barfield's term *Fur Route*, to make it parallel *Silk Road*, the major trade route south of the steppe.

tral steppe before that — how long before is difficult to say, given that Samoyedic morphology suggests divergence not long before the Finno-Ugric spread while the small number of lexical cognates suggests a longer independent development.

There are two possible scenarios that could explain the discrepancy. Both use the catalyst status of Finno-Ugric to suggest and narrow down hypotheses. The first scenario posits a Proto-Uralic homeland in the easternmost range of the attested Uralic territory, perhaps near the Minusinsk Basin along the mid to upper Yenisei in the Altai lowlands. Pre-Proto-Samoyedic[13] stayed near the homeland (the Samoyedic homeland is probably in the attested southern Samoyedic range in the Altai-Sayan area, between the upper Ob' and upper Yenisei: Janhunen 1998:457, 2012); Proto-Finno-Ugric moved westward, presumably along the Ob', entered the Fur Road traffic, and ended up in the right place at the right time to function as catalyst to the Andronovo expansion and undergo a rapid westward spurt. Since movements along trade routes can be rapid, the time between the initial westward drift of Proto-Finno-Ugric into the Fur Road and its dominance of trade during the rise of the Andronovo culture need not have been long, which fits the morphological picture well. On this scenario the low count of Uralic cognates in Samoyedic is due not to losses of native vocabulary in Samoyedic, but to losses in Finno-Ugric, which presumably acquired new vocabulary in the course of contacts and language shift during its spread as a trade language, and especially as Andronovo catalyst. Then Samoyedic is lexically conservative and Finno-Ugric innovative, most of its internal (non-Samoyedic) cognates actually being loans from one or more unknown sources. The Iranian loans are the ones we can actually identify, because Iranian languages have survived; all other sources have gone extinct, absorbed by Finno-Ugric and/or Iranian.

An open question in this scenario is who dominated the Fur Road before Finno-Ugric stepped in, and why they lost dominance. A possible problem is that the Altai foothills, upper Yenisei, and Minusinsk Basin have generally been a language sink rather than a source of spreads (see Janhunen 2012 for the history), so Finno-Ugric departs from the usual situation.[14]

The other scenario posits a Uralic homeland on the northern central steppe or the forest-steppe zone, just to the north (this is the traditional Finno-Ugric homeland, just east of the Urals), and a gradual spread along the Fur Road that brought Proto-Samoyedic eastward along the Ob'. Equally early branches could also have moved west, but if so, they went extinct as the trade spurt occasioned by Andronovo economic expansion overtook the near neighbors of expanding Finno-Ugric. Samoyedic, meanwhile, had moved far to the east and out of the Andronovo cultural and economic sphere. Spreading as trade language, it lost much native vocabulary in contact episodes and language shifts; what we know now as Samoyedic is the surviving enclave in some far outpost of the eastern Fur Road. In this scenario, then, Finno-Ugric is lexically conservative and Samoyedic has replaced much Uralic native vocabulary with loans from unknown sources (this is the traditional view).

A possible difficulty with this scenario is that language shifts and substratal effects should cause changes in grammar but not lexical losses, while in Samoyedic the outcome is the reverse. Another is that while the upper Ob' and Minusinsk Basin region has been an attractor ever since bronze production began, the attraction has been the Altai and Sayan mineral deposits, but the Samoyedic spread may have been earlier than that. Alternatively, Samoyedic could have moved to the Altai area very soon after the invention of bronze technology – a risky hypothesis, as the time between the first bronze and the rise of the Andronovo culture is very short.[15]

Trade between steppe and forest peoples is likely to have existed ever since both ecologies were inhabited. Furs from forest animals and horse hides and horsehair from the steppe would have been valuable to hunter-gatherers in the opposite ecologies. The magnitude and geographical range of trade must have increased incrementally with the domestication of the horse by the Botai culture, as dairy products would have been valued trade items and the more efficient hunting made possible by horse domestication could have created a tradable surplus of meat. The magnitude and range of trade increased substantially with bronze production and the rise of large wealth discrepancies in the Andronovo culture. Samoyedic would then have spread with the earlier trade, and Finno-Ugric with the later, wealthier phase.

Note that Samoyedic and eastern Finno-Ugric (especially Khanty) are grammatically conservative and typologically match the Trans-Pacific macroarea rather well (especially as regards their person categories and noun-verb part-of-speech flexibility; for the former see Nichols 2012; for Trans-Pacific see Bickel & Nichols 2006). The western branches (especially Saamic, Finnic, and Mari) have undergone grammatical changes as they moved westward into the northern European typological sphere.[16] The distribution of conservative languages sup-

---

[13] For the rest of this section we omit the *Pre-* and speak simply of Proto-Samoyedic or (omitting the *Proto-*) simply Samoyedic.
[14] Yeniseian is an exception; it evidently originated on the upper Yenisei and the Altai south slope, and spread down the Yenisei. But this spread was driven by the Xiongnu expansion on the eastern steppe (see §2.1), and economic forces of that magnitude did not exist there at the time of the Proto-Uralic breakup.

[15] There is a Proto-Uralic word for 'metal', in Samoyedic reshaped under the influence of a similar Tocharian word or replaced whole cloth by that Tocharian word (see Janhunen 1983). Assuming Samoyedic inherited the original word and only later changed it, it is possible that Pre-Proto-Uralic speakers dominated the trade routes north of the central steppe during the Copper Age, were aware of mineral deposits to the east, and rapidly developed trade in metals once bronze technology made the Altai deposits valuable.
[16] Mari and Mordvin are neighbors on the middle Volga, but Mari is innovative and Mordvin conservative in the same aspects of typology. Mordvin is phylogenetically close to Finnic and Saami (which are innovative in the relevant respects); Mari is not phylogenetically close, but has innovated in much the same ways.

ports an origin in the easterly part of the Uralic range (or farther east) but cannot discriminate between the central steppe and Minusinsk Basin origins.

So far there is no known linguistic evidence that would indicate whether it is Samoyedic or Finno-Ugric that is lexically conservative. The best such evidence would be finding an external source for either the non-Samoyedic vocabulary of Finno-Ugric or the non-Finno-Ugric vocabulary of Samoyedic. No such source can exist in principle if it is Finno-Ugric that has borrowed, since the spreads of Iranian (and later Turkic) on the steppe and Finno-Ugric to the north have obliterated all traces of previous languages. Conceivably a source for Samoyedic borrowed vocabulary, if it is Samoyedic that has borrowed, may survive to the east of Uralic, though it is hard to believe that two centuries of close comparative lexical work have not revealed it. The most parsimonious assumption is that whatever language or languages contributed vocabulary to one of the initial Uralic branches has gone extinct.

Pondering the two scenarios for the Uralic breakup and the origin of Samoyedic is a thought experiment. It does not tell us whether it was Samoyedic or Finno-Ugric that borrowed a good deal of its vocabulary, but it does show that at least one language on or near the north central steppe periphery has gone extinct.

A last consideration in deliberating the Uralic homeland and Samoyedic origins is whether the Minusinsk Basin is a language sink because it is an attractor, or because it is what can be called a *draw*. An attractor, in the technical sense taken from complex systems theory, is a state (or in this case a location) that has more ways in than out, or that is easier to enter than to leave. In some sense, it is not just the Minusinsk Basin, but the entire Altai system that acts as sink and attractor, and this may be because of the foothill and mountain geography. In mountains, languages tend to spread uphill, but not downhill (Nichols 2015, 2013, 2005), so languages should naturally spread into the upper Yenisei area but rarely out of it. Another reason may be that both eastward and westward migration and trade networks meet at the Minusinsk Basin, so two trajectories lead in. A draw, on the other hand, is a magnet: a place that people chose to move into because they are aware of its advantages, its better resources, etc.

At least since the beginning of the Bronze Age, the Minusinsk Basin has been a draw to people aware of its mineral deposits, and perhaps also to pastoralists aware of its mixed grassland vegetation and slightly milder climate than nearby. See again note 3: the early presence of the Afanasievo Culture, an evident immigrant from the western steppe, at the very dawn of the Bronze Age suggests strongly that the Minusinsk Basin was a draw at the time (and that information was efficiently communicated over the western and central steppes). If the Minusinsk Basin is an attractor, but not a draw, an easterly origin for Uralic is supported (then Samoyedic, remaining behind in or near the homeland, once in the Minusinsk Basin, naturally remained there). If it is a draw, an origin north of the central steppe is supported (then Samoyedic moved with the trade routes from where there was interest in mineral resources to where they could be found).

4. Uralic and Indo-European

It has long been thought that Proto-Uralic and Proto-Indo-European were sisters or neighbors or both, though just beyond the horizon of detectability by the ordinary comparative method (e.g. Campbell 1990, Ringe 1998, Helimski 2001, Anthony 2007:93-97). The best of the lexical comparisons is Koivulehto 2001 (also 1999b, 2000). Arguing on the basis of close knowledge of Uralic and close and sophisticated reading of the Indo-European literature, Koivulehto identifies the best of the possible PIE-PU sharings and states that they cannot be shared inheritances because the phonological properties of the Uralic words cannot have been inherited from a Pre-PIE ancestor. For example, the treatment of PIE laryngeals in PU is not what should have been expected from inheritance but is a plausible rendition of the phonetics of late PIE forms in the sound system of PU. Therefore, the sharings must be loans (from PIE into PU). Table 2 shows his 11 PIE-PU resemblant sets, marking those that are on the Swadesh 200-word list. Those are lexical stems; we also considered the personal pronoun roots, variously reconstructed as PU 1sg *mon- and 2sg *ton- or *me- and *te- (cf. IE nominative *eĝʰō, oblique *me-, 2sg *tu, *te-).

Out of a pre-set wordlist of 200 items, 8 matches with identical semantics are required to exceed chance; out of 1000 items (an estimate of the total number of roots likely to be reconstructed for a well-described protolanguage

	Proto-Uralic	**Proto-Indo-European**
1.	†*pele- 'fear'	*pelh$_1$- ['fear, frighten']
2.	*puna- 'plait, spin'	*pnH-e/o- ['spin, plait']
3.	PFU *kelke- 'shall, must'	*skelH- / *sklH- ['be guilty, shall, must']
4.	PFU *kulke- 'go, wander'	*kʷelH-e/o- in Skt. 'go, wander'
5.	††*mexe- 'sell, give'	*h$_2$mey-gʷ- 'change, exchange'
6.	†*mośke- 'wash'	*mozg-eh$_2$ye/o- ['wash, submerge']
7.	*pura(-) 'borer; bore'	*bʰr(H) 'bore'
8.	*śalka 'long thin pole'	*ĝʰalgʰo- / *ĝʰalgʰa: ['pole']
9.	*wosa 'merchandise'	*wosa: ['product, merchandise']
10.	†*wete 'water'	*wed-(er/en-) 'water'
11.	††*wetä- 'lead, draw'	*wedʰ-e/o- 'lead, marry'

Table 2. PU and PIE lexical sharings (Koivulehto 2001). † = on Swadesh 200-item wordlist with same meaning; †† = with similar meaning. (Item 11 is taken to match the gloss 'pull' on the Swadesh list.) Square brackets: Gloss partly based on Rix ed. 2001.

	2001 (PU)	1999b / 2000 (PFU)	Needed (PY+PFU)	Total
Semantic identity	**3**	3	6	8
Identity & pronouns	**5**	3	8	9+
Semantic similarity	**5**	7	12	19

Table 3. Total matches from Koivulehto 2001 (PIE-PU), 1999b, 2000 (NW IE loans into Finno-Ugric) that are on the Swadesh 200-word list in the same meaning (see Table 2), those plus personal pronouns, those plus items on the with similar meanings (see Table 2), and the total needed to exceed chance at $p < 0.05$ (calculation: Nichols 2010). Properly, only the 2001 words (bold) should be counted. The number required for semantic identity plus 1sg and 2sg pronouns is over 8 because the match for 1sg searches through the nominative and oblique stems and finds the match only in the oblique stem, allowing an additional degree of freedom for just the pronouns; also, the pronouns have one stem consonant each, a looser match (the calculation assumes two-consonant roots).

in the best cases), 28; (out of 2000 items (the typical number of elementary roots found in a well-described non-reconstructed language), 51; with similar but not necessary identical semantics, the numbers required are 19, 73, and 121 (for these calculations see Nichols 2010).[17] We use the Swadesh wordlist as a convenient pre-set wordlist, though of course it is a better comparison for hypotheses of shared descent than for loan vocabulary. Table 3 shows these frequencies and the frequencies needed to exceed chance. Koivulehto's words, though excellent matches taken individually, are not numerous enough to exceed chance.[18]

Koivulehto notes that the glosses in the list are not those of stable lexemes (as they should be if they are cognates and the relationship is as distant as this small number of cognates would suggest), so they must be loans, showing that PU and PIE were neighbors (and not sisters). But semantically, as a set, they are not obviously strong candidates for loans either; especially when there are only 11 loans from a given source, those loans are expected to mostly refer to concrete objects and especially objects likely to spread through trade or technological diffusion.

The needed numbers specified in Table 3 are those required to prove that the similarities are not due to chance, and they are the same for counting loans as for counting cognates. If PU and PIE were known to have been early neighbors, of course, the number of putative loans would not be required to exceed chance, as they would not be the sole proof that the languages were neighbors; but in this case, it is not known that PU and PIE were neighbors, so the putative loans are the only proof and their number needs to exceed chance. (Similarly, if they were known to be ancient sisters, cognates would be expected, and these words would be the best candidates.)

Helimski 2001 notes that in a list of 18 Proto-Uralic roots shown by Häkkinen 2001 to occur in every branch of Uralic, half resemble Indo-European roots (not all of those IE resemblants are in Koivulehto's list). Roots found in every branch are of course Proto-Uralic, but not all Proto-Uralic words are found in every branch (the minimum requirement is one Samoyedic and one non-Samoyedic attestation, i.e. one in each of the two initial branches). The pan-Uralic words are not just Proto-Uralic but also very stable, and Helimski's argument is that if half of the most stable vocabulary is Indo-European-looking, that suggests that if there is a PU-PIE relationship, it is one of descent and not contact. The difference between Koivulehto's and Helimski's analyses may be due in part to differently defined sets (PU and PIE for Koivulehto; PU and in all branches for Häkkinen and Helimski), but apart from that such radical inconsistencies are not surprising in a wordlist too small to exceed chance.[19]

5. Discussion and conclusions

The problem of Indo-European and Uralic connections remains a problem; there are some striking resemblances in word roots, but not enough to exceed chance. On the other hand, numbers of resemblances in the chance range is exactly what should be expected of a family as old as the putative ancestor of Indo-European and Uralic or in ancient neighbors from that time frame. Unless additional criteria for relatedness are applied, the search for evidence for Indo-Uralic leads to a dead end.

Possible Uralic homelands, however, have been narrowed down by the analyses given here. From the Neolithic on, cultures of the steppe and the forest to the north have interacted closely (Kosinskaya 2001, for the central

---

[17] A larger problem is that this method was designed to be applied to modern or attested languages. For protolanguages, the segments are not phonetically characterizable phonemes but labels for reconstructions, and the glosses are also a different and looser kind of entity than glosses of attested words. Therefore, the close phonological and close or identical semantic resemblance we have attributed to the IE-Uralic material are probably incorrect in reality and should be downgraded by one notch, which greatly increases the number of matches required to exceed chance (from 8 to 19 matches on a 200-word list for just the semantic broadening, shown in Table 3, and a similar increment for the phonological broadening).

[18] A recent contribution on IE-Uralic by Kassian et al. (2015), though computationally sound, has similar shortcomings of phonological and semantic breadth and other problems involving multiple choices from which to select a potential match; see the responses of Kallio 2015, Kessler 2015, and Ringe 2015.

[19] We did a similar analysis of the proposed ancient loans between PIE and Proto-Kartvelian of Klimov 1994:49-83. Klimov's expertise in Kartvelian and sophisticated use of IE materials are comparable to Koivulehto's for Uralic. Klimov, like Koivulehto, finds the words unlikely candidates for cognates (formally and semantically) and considers them loans. He found a total of 15 putative lexical loans, to which we add the first and second person singular pronouns, out of a Common Kartvelian wordlist that we estimate at 500-1000 roots; three of his roots and three roots for the pronouns are on the Swadesh 100-word list and one more on the 200-word list. (The Kartvelian first person singular pronoun has suppletive roots (nom. *men, gen. *č(w)em- that match PIE oblique *me-, nom. *eĝhō reasonably well in form.) The number of matches is very similar to that for Uralic, and as for Uralic, are not enough to exceed chance and therefore not enough to establish that PIE and PK were sisters, or that they were neighbors. Kartvelian and Uralic are both put in the Nostratic macrogroup by its proponents, but recent discussions of the homeland have mostly mentioned the Uralic connection, and not the Kartvelian one.

steppe), and if Proto-Uralic (or for that matter early Proto-Finno-Ugric and Pre-Proto-Samoyedic) had been spoken north of the western steppe, where the Yamnaya culture is found (Yamnaya is believed to represent core Indo-European after the departure of Proto-Anatolian), it seems inevitable that there would have been a good number of recognizably PIE words in Proto-Uralic (or separately in early Proto-Finno-Ugric and Pre-Proto-Samoyedic), and they would include many cultural terms such as a word for 'wheel'. This is not the case however; Koivulehto's resemblant sets are mostly not cutural artifacts.

Historical linguistics cannot identify an exact homeland for Proto-Uralic or an archaeological culture where it is likely to have been spoken; nor can we tell if Indo-European and Uralic are ultimately related, whether by descent or adjacency, at some great time depth. What the approach taken here has been able to do is identify causes and means of the Proto-Finno-Ugric and perhaps Proto-Uralic spreads – a more modest goal, but probably a more fruitful one in the long run.

References

Abondolo, Daniel. 1998. Introduction. Daniel Abondolo, ed., *The Uralic Languages*: 1-42. London-New York: Routledge.

Adelaar, Willem F. H. and Pieter C. Muysken. 2004. *The Languages of the Andes*. Cambridge: Cambridge University Press.

Aikio, Ante. 2012. An essay on Saami ethnolinguistic prehistory. Riho Grünthal and Kallio, Petri, ed., *A Linguistic Map of Prehistoric Northern Europe*: 63-117. Helsinki: Société Finno-Ougrienne.

Aikio, Ante. 2006. New and old Samoyed etymologies, 2. *Finnisch-Ugrische Forschungen* 59:1-3: 9-34.

Allentoft, Morton E. et al. 2015. Population genomics of Bronze Age Eurasia. *Nature* 522.167-172.

Anthony, David W. 2007. *The Horse, the Wheel, and Language: How Bronze Age riders from the Eurasian steppes shaped the modern world*. Princeton, NJ: Princeton University Press.

Anthony, David, and Don Ringe. 2015. The Indo-European homeland from linguistic and archaeological perspectives. *Annual Review of Linguistics* 1.199-219.

Bakker, Peter. 1997. *A Language of our Own: The Genisis of Michif, the Mixed Cree-French Language of the Canadian Métis*. Oxford: Oxford University Press.

Barfield, Thomas. 2009. Introduction: Frontiers and border dynamics. In Bryan K. Hanks and Katheryn M. Linduff, eds., *Social Complexity in Prehistoric Eurasia: Monuments, Metals, and Mobility*, 235-240. Cambridge: Cambridge University Press.

Barfield, Thomas. 1989. *The Perilous Frontier: Nomadic Empires and China, 221 BC to AD 1757*. London: Blackwell.

Bickel, Balthasar and Johanna Nichols. 2006. Oceania, the Pacific Rim, and the theory of linguistic areas. Zhenya Antić, Charles B. Chang, Clare S. Sandy, and Maziar Toosarvandani, eds., *Proceedings of the 32nd Annual Meeting: Special Session on the Languages and Linguistics of Oceania*: 3-15. Berkeley: Berkeley Linguistics Society.

Campbell, Lyle. 1990. Indo-European and Uralic trees. *Diachronica* 7.149-180.

Carpelan, Christian, Asko Parpola and Petteri Koskikallio, eds., *Early Contacts between Uralic and Indo-European: Linguistic and Archaeological considerations*. Helsinki: Suomalais-Ugrilainen Seura.

Cerrón-Palomino, Rodolfo. The languages of the Inkas. In *The Inka Empire: A Multidsciplinary Approach*, edited by Izumi Shimada, 39–53. Austin: University of Texas Press, 2015

D'Altroy, Terence N. 2015. *The Incas (Second edition)*. Malden, MA and Oxford: Wiley/Blackwell.

Darden, Bill J. 2001. On the question of the Anatolian origin of Indo-Hittite. In Robert Drews, ed., *Greater Anatolia and The Indo-Hittite Language Family*, 184-228. Washington, DC: Institute for the Study of Man.

DeMarrais, Elizabeth. Quechua's southern boundary: The case of Santiago del Estero, Argentina. In *Language and Archaeology in the Andes: A cross-disciplinary exploration of prehistory*, edited by Paul Heggarty and David G. Beresford Jones, 373–406. Oxford: Oxford University Press, 2012.

Dörrbecker, Maximilian (Chumwa). 2008. Uralische Sprachen. https://en.wikipedia.org/wiki/File:Linguistic_map_of_the_Uralic_languages.png.

Frachetti, Michael D. 2012. Multiegional emergence of mobile pastoralism and nonuniform institutional complexity across Eurasia. *Current Anthropology* 53:1.2-38.

Golden, Peter B., 2010. *Turks and Khazars: Origins, Institutions, and Interactions in Pre-Mongol Eurasia*. Farnham, Surrey: Ashgate.

Güldemann, Tom, Patrick McConvell, and Richard A. Rhodes, eds. In press. *Hunter-Gatherer Languages in Global Perspective*. Cambridge: Cambridge University Press.

Haak, Wolfgang, Iosif Lazaridis et al. 2015. Massive migration from the steppe was a source for Indo-European languages in Europe. *Nature* 522.207-211.

Häkkinen, Kaisa. 2001. Prehistoric Finno-Ugric culture in the light of historical lexicology. Christian Carpelan, Asko Parpola, and Petteri Koskikallio, eds., *Early Contacts between Uralic and Indo-European: Linguistic and Archaeological considerations*, 169-186. Helsinki: Suomalais-Ugrilainen Seura.

Helimski, Eugene. 2001. Early Indo-Uralic linguistic relationship: Real kinship and imagined contacts. Carpelan et al. eds. 187-205.

Holopainen, Sampsa. In progress. Indo-Iranian loanwords in Uralic. Ph.D. dissertation, Helsinki University.

Hvistendahl, Mara, 2012. Roots of empire. *Science* 337: 1596-1599.

Janhunen, Juha. 2014. *A Legkeletibb Uráliak*. Budapest: Magyar Tudományos Akadémia.

Janhunen, Juha. 2012. Etymological and ethnohistorical aspects of the Yenisei. *Studia Etymologica Cracoviensia* 17.67-87.

Janhunen, Juha. 2012. The expansion of Tungusic as an ethnic and linguistic process. In Andrej L. Malchukov and Lindsay J. Whaley, eds., *Recent Advances in Tungusic Linguistics*, 5-16. Harrassowitz: Wiesbaden.

Janhunen, Juha. 2008. Mongolic as an expansive language family. Tokusu Kurebito, ed., Past and Present Dynamics: The Great Mongolian State, 127-137. Tokyo: Tokyo University of Foreign Studies, Research Institute for Languages and Cultures of Asia and Africa.

Janhunen, Juha. 2002. On the chronology of the Ainu ethnic complex. *Bulletin of the Hokkaido Museum of Northern Peoples* 11.1-20.

Janhunen, Juha. 1998. Samoyedic. Daniel Abondolo, ed., *The Uralic Languages*: 457-479. London: Routledge.

Janhunen, Juha, 1996. *Manchuria: An Ethnic History*. Helsinki: Suomalais-Ugrilainen Seura.

Janhunen, Juha. 1983. On early Indo-European-Samoyed contacts. *Symposium saeculare Societatis fenno-ugricae,* 115-128. Helsinki: Finno-Ugric Society.

Joki, Aulis J. 1973. *Uralier und Indogermanen: Die älteren Berührungen zwischen den uralischen und indogermanischen Sprachen.* Helsinki: Société Finno-Ougrienne.

Kallio, Petri. 2015. Nugae indo-uralicae. *JIES* 43:3-4368-75.

Kassian, Alexei, Mikhail Zhivlov, and George Starostin. 2015. Proto-Indo-European-Uralic comparison from the probabilistic point of view. *JIES* 43:3-4301-47.

Kaufman, Terrence and John S. Justeson. 2009. Historical linguistics and Pre-Columbian Mesoamerica. *Ancient Mesoamerica* 20.221-231.

Kessler, Brett. 2015. Response to Kassian et al., Proto-Indo-European-Uralic comparison from the probabilistic point of view. *JIES* 43:3-4357-67.

Klimov, G. A. 1998. *Etymological Dictionary of the Kartvelian Languages.* Berlin: Mouton de Gruyter.

Klimov, G. A. 1994. *Drevnejshie indoevropeizmy kartvel'skix jazykov.* Moscow: RAN.

Koivulehto, Jorma. 2001. The earliest contacts between Indo-European and Uralic speakers in the light of lexical loans. Carpelan et al. eds., 235-263.

Koivulehto, Jorma. 2000. Finno-Ugric reflexes of Northwest Indo-European and early stages of Indo-Iranian. In Karlene Jones-Bley, Martin E. Huld and Angela Della Volpe, eds., *Proceedings of the Eleventh Annual UCLA Indo-European Conference,* 21-44. Washington, DC: Institute for the Study of Man.

Koivulehto, Jorma. 1999. *Verba Mutuata.* (SUST 237.) Helsinki: Suomalais-ugrilainen Seura.

Kosinskaya, L. L. 2001. The Neolithic period of northwestern Siberia: The question of southern connections. Carpelan et al. eds. 265-287.

Lehtinen, Jyri, Terhi Honkola, Kalle Korhonen, Kai Syrjänen, Niklas Wahlberg, and Outi Vesakoski. 2014. Behind family trees: Secondary connections in Uralic language networks. *Language Dynamics and Change* 4.189-221.

Madsen, David and David Rhode. 1994. *Across the West: Human Population Movement and the Expansion of the Numa.* Salt Lake City: University of Utah Press.

Maenchen-Helfen, Otto J., 1973. *The World of the Huns: Studies in their history and culture.* Berkeley-Los Angeles: University of California Press.

Mannheim, Bruce. 1991. *The Language of the Inka since the European Invasian.* Austin: University of Texas Press.

Nakhleh, Luay, Don Ringe, and Tandy Warnow. 2005. Perfect phylogenetic networks: A new methodology for reconstructing the evolutionary history of natural languages. *Language* 81.382-420.

Nichols, Johanna. 2015. Types of spread zones: Open and closed, horizontal and vertical. In Rik De Busser and Randy La Polla, eds., *Language Structure and Environment: Social Cultural, and Natural Factors,* Amsterdam: Benjamins.

Nichols, Johanna. 2013. The vertical archipelago: Adding the third dimension to linguistic geography. Peter Auer, Hilpert, Martin, Stukenbrock, Anja and Szmrecsanyi, Benedikt, ed., *Space in Language and Linguistics*: 38-60. Berlin: Mouton de Gruyter.

Nichols, Johanna. 2012. Selection for *m : T* pronominals in Eurasia. Lars Johanson and Robbeets, Martine, ed., *Copies vs. Cognates in Bound Morphology*: 47-70. Leiden: Brill.

Nichols, Johanna. 2010. Proof of Dene-Yeniseian relatedness. In James Kari and Ben A. Potter, eds., *The Dene-Yeiseian Connection,* 266-278. Fairbanks: Alaska Native Language Center.

Nichols, Johanna, 2005. The origin of the Chechen and Ingush: A study in alpine linguistic and ethnic geography. *Anthropological Linguistics* 46: 129-155.

Nichols, Johanna, and Richard A. Rhodes. In preparation. *Language Spreads.*

Outram, Alan K. et al. 2009. The earliest horse harnessing and milking. *Science* 323.1332-1335.

Pritsak, Omeljan, 1982. The Slavs and the Avars. *Settimane di studio del Centro italiano di studi sull'alto medioevo XXX: Gli Slavi occidentali e meridionali nell'alto medioevo* 353-435.

Rhodes, Richard A. In press. Ojibwe language shift: 1600-present. Güldemann et al. eds.

Rhodes, Richard A. 2012. Algonquian trade languages revisited. Karl S. Hele and J. R. Valentine, eds, *Papers of the Fortieth Algonquian Conference,* 358-369. Albany: SUNY Press.

Rhodes, Richard A. 2009. The phonological history of Métchif. In F. Martineau and L. Baronian, eds., *Le Français d'un continent à l'autre. Mélanges offerts à Yves-Charles Morin,* 423-442. Québec: Presses de l'Université Laval.

Rhodes, Richard A. 2008. Ojibwe in the Cree of Métchif. In Karl S. Hele and Regna Darnell, eds., *Papers of the Thirty-Ninth Algonquian Conference,* 569-580. London, Ontario: University of Western Ontario.

Rhodes, Richard A. 1992. Language shift in Algonquian. *International Journal of Society and Language* 93.87-92.

Rhodes, Richard A. 1982. Algonquian trade languages. In William Cowan, ed., *Papers of the Thirteenth Algonquian Conference,* 1-10. Ottawa: Carleton University.

Ringe, Don. 2015. Response to Kassian et al., Proto-Indo-European-Uralic comparison from the probabilistic point of view. *JIES* 43:3-4348-56.

Ringe, Don. 1998. A probabilistic evaluation of Indo-Uralic. In Joseph C. Salmons and Brian D. Joseph, eds., *Nostratic: sifting the evidence,* 154-198. Amsterdam-Philadelphia: Benjamins.

Ringe, Don, Tandy Warnow, and Ann Taylor. 2002. Indo-European and computational cladistics. *Transactions of the Philological Society* 100.1.59-129.

Rix, Helmut, ed. 2001. *Lexikon der indogermanischen Verben. Die Wurzeln und ihre Primärstammbildungen.* Wiesbaden: Reichert.

Saarikivi, Janne and Mika Lavento. 2012. Linguistics and archaeology: A critical view of an interdisciplinary approach with reference to the prehistory of northern Scandinavia. In Charlotte Damm and Janne Saarikivi, eds., *Networks, Interaction, and Emerging Identities in Fennoscandia and Beyond,* 177-216. Helsinki: Suomalais-Ugrilainen Seura.

Salminen, Tapani. 2013. Map of the Uralic languages (based on the 1993 map with the same title by Riho Grünthal and Tapani Salminen). http://www.helsinki.fi/~tasalmin/Uralic.jpg

Salminen, Tapani. 2001. The rise of the Finno-Ugric language family. Carpelan et al. eds., 385-396.

Schönig, Claus. 2003. Turko-Mongolic relations. Juha Janhunen, ed., *The Mongolic Languages*: 403-419. London: Routledge.

Suárez, Jorge A. 1983. *The Mesoamerican Indian languages.* Cambridge: Cambridge University Press.

Svyatko, Svetlana V., James P. Mallory, Eileen M. Murphy, Andrey V. Polyakov, Paula J. Reimer and Rick J. Schulting. 2009. New radiocarbon dates and a review of the chronology of prehistoric populations from the Minusinsk Basin, southern Siberia, Russia. *Radiocarbon* 51:1.243-273.

Vajda, Edward, 2012. Between forest and steppe: Language and ethnicity in early Inner Asia. Presented at *The Steppes: Crucible of Eurasia,* Havighurst Center, Miami University.

Vajda, Edward. In press. Yeniseian substrates and typological accommodation in central Siberia. Güldemann et al. eds.

Vajda, Edward, Alexander Vovin and Étienne de la Vaissière, In press. Who were the *Kjet (羯) and what language did they speak? *Journal Asiatique.*

Vovin, Alexander. 2011. Once again on the Ruan-ruan language. Mehmet Ölmez, ed., *From Ötüken to Istanbul, 1290 years of Turkish (720-2010)*: 27-36. Istanbul: Istanbul Büyükşehir Belediyesi.

Vovin, Alexander, 2004. Some thoughts on the origins of the Old Turkic 12-year animal cycle. *Central Asiatic Journal* 48:1: 118-132.

Werner, Heinrich, 2014. *Die Jenissejer unter den frühen Völkern Zentralasiens*. Munich: Lincom Europa.

Notes on the Indo-European Vocabulary of Sheep, Wool and Textile Production

Birgit Anette Olsen, University of Copenhagen

Introduction
The identification of the Indo-European homeland in time and space has been a matter of controversy almost since the beginning of Indo-European studies. Leaving aside untenable claims such as Demoule's deconstruction of the Indo-European concept (2014), two competing theories dominate the current discussion: the Anatolian and the Pontic-Caspian model.

In an influential monograph from the late eighties, Colin Renfrew (1987)[1] introduced his "wave of advance" model, connecting the Indo-Europeans with the first agriculturalists and situating the homeland in Anatolia around 7000 BC. More recently, a number of scholars have backed up the out-of-Anatolia model and early dating through phylogenetic methods originally derived from studies of the spread of viruses (e.g. Gray and Atkinson: 2003; Nicholls & Gray: 2008; Bouckaert et al.: 2012). However, as maintained by Pereltsvaig and Lewis in a recent monograph (2015), sound linguistic analysis will always be a safer way to the knowledge of Indo-European origins than evolutionary biology, and moreover, even if the basic method is accepted, the results may differ according to the character of the data. Thus Chang et al. (2015), applying different principles for the linguistic input, arrive at a date of about 4000 BC and consider their results to strongly support the alternative theory: the steppe or Pontic-Caspian hypothesis.

This model was famously propagated in the works of Marija Gimbutas (e.g. 1973 and 1997), who assumed that the Indo-European homeland was situated in the south Russian and Ukrainian steppes about 4500 BC, from which Indo-European speaking pastoralists spread over vast areas to Europe in the west and parts of Asia in the east, bringing with them their language and culture. Variations on this view are held by the majority of linguists (e.g. Fortson 2010; Beekes 2011) and a number of archaeologists, such as Mallory (1989 and later), Anthony (2007 and 2013) and Kristiansen (e.g. 2012; also Kristiansen and Larsson 2005). Recently, two independent studies of ancient DNA (Allentoft et al. 2015; Haak et al. 2015) suggesting massive migrations from the steppes into Europe at about the same time have also been interpreted as supporting the steppe hypothesis.

The obvious way to solve the Indo-European problem is to combine archaeological and linguistic evidence by means of the so-called palaeolinguistic method: if a word for a certain cultural feature, object, plant or creature is attested with regular sound correspondences throughout the Indo-European family, we must conclude that the corresponding concept existed before the dispersal of the proto-language. In all their details, our linguistic observations have to be compatible with the archaeological culture(s) we associate with the Indo-Europeans. This is the approach systematically used by Mallory and Adams in their encyclopaedic treatments of Indo-European language and culture (1997 and 2006) and in Anthony's archaeological-linguistic synthesis (2007). Extreme scepticists tend to reject palaeolinguistic evidence as a matter of principle, interpreting some of the most striking lexical correspondences as potential cases of secondary semantic development. Thus, e.g. Heggarty (2006: 189) tries to explain away the Indo-European word for 'axle' as originally having the less precise meaning of 'pole', despite the unanimous testimony of Sanskrit, Greek, Baltic, Slavic, Italic and Germanic (cf. the justified criticism in Anthony 2013). This would be unlikely, if perhaps not exactly impossible, if we were dealing with an isolated term, but what tips the scales is the cumulative effect of a complete semantic field with corresponding vocabulary including 'wheel', 'thill', 'nave' and 'convey (in a wagon)', all pointing to one conclusion: wagon technology was an integrated part of Indo-European society, or at least the group of Indo-European minus Anatolian, which is agreed by propagators of both the Anatolian and the steppe hypothesis to be the first branch to break away from the rest of the family. In the following, we will distinguish between *Proto-Indo-European* = Indo-European proper, including Anatolian, and *Core Indo-European*, defined as Indo-European excluding Anatolian.

The terminology for wheeled vehicles is the most impressive indication for an approximate dating of Core Indo-European culture to a time after the invention of the wagon. This means a time frame from around 4000-3500 BC which is incompatible with the Anatolian hypothesis, but perfectly suited to the idea of a homeland on the steppes.[2]

Another cultural achievement that is important for the chronological determination of Indo-European culture is the utilization of sheep's wool in the sense of long fibres which may be used for spinning and weaving. While sheep were probably domesticated as early 8000-7500 BC in Anatolia, the matted "wool" of wild and early domesticated sheep was "virtually unspinnable" (Barber 1991: 24). These sheep shed their coats annually, and the shedding is very useful for the production of felt, but the spinning and weaving of wool presupposes wool sheep, for which there is no solid evidence until after 4000 BC.

As summarized by Anthony 2007: 59: "Sheep with long wooly coats are genetic mutants bred for just that trait. If Proto-Indo-European contained words referring unequivocally to woven woolen textiles, then those words have to

---

[1] Later modified in e.g. Renfrew 1999 and 2003.

[2] The Anatolian branch only shares one of the inherited terms associated with potential wagon technology, viz. *ḫišša-* 'carriage pole', with cognates in Vedic *īṣā́-* 'pole, shaft', Slovene *ojȩ́* 'carriage pole', Greek *oíax* 'handle of a rudder, tiller', and as observed by Anthony (2007: 65), we cannot know for certain if the original meaning was 'carriage pole' or perhaps 'plough shaft'. Consequently, the Anatolians may have separated before the development of wheeled vehicles.

have entered Proto-Indo-European after the date when wool sheep were developed. But if we are to use the wool vocabulary as a dating tool, we need to know both the exact meaning of the reconstructed roots and the date when wool sheep first appeared. Both issues are problematic."

Against this background, it seems justified to re-examine the linguistic evidence in order to evaluate what precisely we can say about the dating and original meaning of the words for 'sheep', 'wool' and a few other textile terms traditionally ascribed to the Indo-European protolanguage. In the following notes to the comprehensive studies by Barber (especially 1991) and the surveys of the Indo-European textile vocabulary, including later dialectal creations, by Mallory-Adams 1997 passim and Mallory-Adams 2006: 230-38, I shall concentrate on a few terms that must be ascribed to Proto-Indo-European proper.

1. Sheep and wool

The existence of a common Indo-European word for 'sheep' is uncontroversial. With continuations in Anatolian (Cuneiform Luwian *hāwa/i-*, Lycian *xawa*); Tocharian B. pl. *awi*; Indo-Iranian (Vedic *ávi-*); Greek *o(v)ís*; Armenian (*hoviw* 'shepherd'); Latin *ovis*; Celtic (Old Irish *oí*); Germanic (Old Norse *ær*, English *ewe*; also Gothic *awebi* 'flock of sheep'); and Balto-Slavic (Lithuanian *avìs*, Old Church Slavic (diminutive) *ovьci* 'ewe'), we arrive at a protoform $*h_2o\mu is$ or $*h_3o\mu is$,[3] which must go back to a time before Anatolian separated from the rest of the Indo-European family. While this does not tell us whether the word was originally applied to the wild sheep/Asiatic mouflon, an early type of domesticated sheep, or the later wool sheep, it is still remarkable that the designation is so uniform and so widespread, attested in nine out of the ten branches with the sole exception of Albanian, as opposed to the 'goat', where the vocabulary is characterized by a variety of apparently dialectal terms (cf. Mallory-Adams 1997: 229f).

In order to determine if the sheep of the Indo-Europeans served for wool production we have to determine the derivational pattern and the basic root of the word for 'wool'. As is the case of the 'sheep' word, the term for 'wool' is extremely well attested and widespread in the Indo-European languages. Vedic *ū́rṇā-*, Avestan *varənā-*, Latin *lāna*, Welsh *gwlan*, Gothic *wulla*, Lithuanian *vìlna* and Old Church Slavic *vlьna* unanimously point to a protoform $*(h_x)\mu lh_x-nah_2$, which may be further specified as $*(h_x)\mu lh_1-nah_2$ on the evidence of Greek *lēnos* (n) (for expected *lēnē* (f)), probably modelled after the synonymous neuters *eĩros* and *pókos* 'wool'. Significantly, a similar if not identical stem is also attested in Hittite *hulana-* 'wool' which may go back to either $*h_2ul\partial_1-nah_2$ with revocalization or $*h_2ulh_1\mathring{n}nah_2$ with a slightly different suffix variant.[4] The Anatolian evidence finally makes it possible to establish the precise reconstruction of at least the Core Indo-European derivative as $*h_2\mu lh_1-nah_2$ and the basic root for Proto-Indo-European as $*h_2\mu elh_1-$.

If we can determine the meaning of this root it becomes possible to reveal what exactly the Indo-Europeans meant by "$*h_2\mu lh_1-nah_2$". In Bill Darden's treatment (2001: 189f and 200), largely followed by Anthony (2007: 60), it is implied that the original root was shorter, "*Hwe/ol-*", and that "[v]arious suffixes, such as *-s-*, *-g-*, *-j-*, *-H-*, either form specific nouns or form verbs indicating processes applied to animal hair or wool. The stem *HwelHn-* is a tertiary derivative, indicating a particular type of animal hair, wool, which is appropriate for processing or has been processed into a textile" (Darden p. 204). It is suggested (Anthony l.c.) that meanings such as 'roll', 'beat' and 'press' may be united under the common denominator of 'felt'. The process is compatible with the short-haired annual shedding of wild or early domesticated sheep, and if this interpretation holds true, our word may thus pre-date the spinning and weaving of actual wool by a couple of millennia, the earliest attestations of felted material going as far back as 6000 BC in Anatolia. Now, the splitting up of a root into a basic root segment + "extensions" or "suffixes" will always be quite speculative, though in fact several candidates for approximately the right basic structure may be mentioned. Thus the root $*\mu elh_3-$ 'beat' is continued in Hittite *walhzi* 'beats' and probably Greek *heálōn* 'was conquered' (LIV 679); $*\mu elh_x\mu-$ 'roll, envelop, wrap' in Armenian *gelum*, Latin *volvō* (cf. LIV 675, and in particular, Rasmussen 1989: 99f for the root structure); and $*(h_2)\mu el-$, also 'roll, turn' in Sanskrit *valati* etc. (cf. note 45 and LIV 675 where $*\mu el-$ and $*\mu elh_x\mu-$ are united under one root). However, as shown by Hittite *walhzi*, $*\mu elh_3-$ 'beat' does not have the initial $*h_2-$ of the 'wool' word, which is at the same time incompatible with the root-final $*-\mu-$ of $*\mu elh_x\mu-$ 'roll'. As for the root $*\mu elh_x-$ of Lithuanian *vélti* 'full, roll, beat', adduced by Darden (2001: 202; cf. also Fraenkel 1965: 1220f, LIV 677), the primary meaning appears to be 'roll', so 'full' would be a secondary semantic development.[5]

---

[3] Cf. Wodtko, Irslinger & Schneider with references. The reconstructions $*h_1$, $*h_2$ and $*h_3$ represent the so-called "laryngeals" of which at least $*h_2$ and (partly) $*h_3$ are directly continued as consonants in Anatolian (*ḫ(ḫ)* in Hittite). A laryngeal of unknown quality is noted $*h_x$ and the "vocalic" alternants of the laryngeals (in reality prop vowels), $*\partial_1$, $*\partial_2$, $*\partial_3$, $*\partial_x$ respectively. Whether the word for 'sheep' had an $*h_2$ or $*h_3$ is immaterial to the present discussion.

[4] A derivation from $*h_2ul\partial_1-nah_2$ is possible if the laryngeal was regularly vocalized in interconsonantal position, while $*h_2ulh_1\mathring{n}nah_2$ would be a secondary derivative of $*h_2el\partial_1m\mathring{n}-$ (> $*-m\mathring{n}o-$ > $-n\mathring{n}o-$), cf. Armenian *gelmn* 'fleece, wool'. The revocalization is probably inspired by the synonymous *huliya-* < $*h_2ulh_1(i)jo-$. Kloekhorst (2008: 357f) doubts this otherwise generally accepted etymological connection altogether, pointing to ᴳᴵˢ*hulāli-* 'distaff' as a possible internal cognate instead. However, this word belongs to the same word family as *haḫliliya-* 'wind around', *hulhuliya-* 'entwine, embrace' and *hulhula-* 'wrestling', so it seems more natural to relate the Hittite forms to Sanskrit *valati* 'turn round', Greek *eiléō* 'roll, turn, wind', Armenian *glem* 'roll' (thus Puhvel 1991: 363).

[5] The root may be reconstructed as $*\mu elh_x-$ or perhaps $*h_x\mu elh_x-$, but there is no way to confirm the existence of the initial laryngeal or the quality of the final one. At any rate, the root seems to be geographically restricted to the northern European branches, Germanic and Balto-Slavic.

What is important here, since *-no-/-nah₂- is a well-known noun suffix, is whether we can point to a root with the exact structure *h_2uelh_1- combined with an appropriate meaning, and whether this meaning gives a hint to the literal interpretation of the 'wool' word.

An important testimony in this connection is that of Latin *vellus, -eris* (n) 'wool, fleece' (Varro+; cf. Ernout & Meillet 1959: 718; Walde-Hofmann 1954: 654f; de Vaan 2008: 659) and the verb *vellō* 'pluck'. The semantic connection between *vellus* and *$h_2ulh_2nah_2$ is perfect, and within Latin, it is natural to connect *vellus* with *vellō*. With the connecting link of *vellus*, we do not have to speculate with hypothetical primary meanings such as 'roll', and since the sense of *vellō* is indeed 'pluck out', of hairs etc., this is a strong argument in favour of real wool with long hairy fibres.

Previous etymological explanations of the Latin verb accounting for the geminate *-ll-*, include derivations of *vell-* from:

- *$uels$- (Walde-Hofmann 1954: 744f), allegedly an *s*-extension of *uel- 'break, tear' for which there is no external evidence
- *$ueld^h$- or perhaps *$uelHd^h$- (Schrijver 1991: 180f), again without external support
- *$ueln$- where the verb would have had an otherwise unattested nasal present *$ul-n(e)-h_3$- and an aorist stem *$uelh_3$- 'strike'; suggested cognates are South Picene **ehueli** 'tears down', Hittite *walḫ-* 'hit, strike', Greek *halískomai* 'I am caught', aorist *heálōn* 'was killed' and Tocharian A. *wälläṣtär* 'dies' (de Vaan 2008: 659; LIV 679).

None of these explanations is flawless: derivations from *$uels$- and *$ueld^h$- are ad hoc solutions, and an underlying root *$(h_x)uelh_3$- 'strike' is semantically problematic. Meiser (1998: 110) tries to overcome this difficulty by assuming a double meaning "schlagen, rupfen" which is hardly helpful, 'striking' and 'tearing (out)' being two quite diffferent concepts.

The meaning of *vellō* is unambiguously 'pluck (out, especially hairs, feathers)' as seen in the following examples:

Hor.Ep.II.45: ... *caudaeque pilos ut equinae paulatim vello et demo cum demo etiam unum* ... 'like hairs on a horse's tail, first one and then another I pluck ... little by little'

Hor.Sat.I.133f: *vellunt tibi barbam lascivi pueri* 'mischievous boys pluck at your beard'

Columella, Agr.VIII.3: *Attamen praestat ex se pullos atque plumam, quam non, ut in ovibus lanam, semel demetere, sed bis anno, ver et autumno vellere licet* 'yet it produces goslings and feathers you may gather not once a year, like wool from sheep, but you can pluck twice in spring and in summer'

Similarly in compound verbs:

Devellō 'pluck bare' (Pl+), e.g. Poen.870f: *Sine pennis volare hau faciest: meae alae pennas non habent. Nolito edepol devellisse* 'Flying without feathers is not easy: my wings have no feathers.' 'Then stop plucking them.'

E(x)vellō 'uproot' (Pl+), e.g. Tru.288f: *iam hercle ego istos fictos compositos crispos cicinnos tuos unguentatos usque ex cerebro exvellam* 'Lord, I'll grab that hair you've got fixed up so slick and fine, all frizzled and perfumed, and pull it out away down from your brains.'

Revellō 'pluck or pull away' (Enn+), but also 'tear down, remove', e.g. plants from the root, or the graves of the ancestors (*maiorum sepulchra*)

With this in mind, Weiss' objection (2002) against the derivation of *vellō* from *$uelh_3$- 'strike' is quite justified: "None of the other avatars of *$welh_3$- has the sense 'tear'. It seems to me that the traditional connection with Gothic *wilwan* 'to rob', which the LIV 616 classifies under *wel- 'drehen', is preferable. Cf. also the Hesychian gloss *géllai·tílai* 'to pluck'. It seems best to classify these forms together under a root *wel- 'pluck'." Consequently, Weiss translates South Picene **suaipis ehvelí** "if anyone tears up this (monument)" as a precise cognate of Latin *ēvellō* and a striking semantic match of *revellō + maiorum sepulchra*. However, an unextended root *uel- in the meaning 'pluck' seems to be unattested, so we still have to account for the geminate *-ll-*. Weiss' comparison with Gothic *wilwan* is hardly semantically evident, and moreover it is difficult to understand how the verbal stem would have influenced the noun *vellus*, so the Gothic verb is perhaps better connected with Latin *volvō* 'roll' etc. ('turn (to oneself)' → 'steal'? cf. LIV 675).[6] If, on the other hand, we maintain the more natural etymological connection with the root of *lāna* 'wool' etc., the simplest explanation of *vellō* is as a thematic verb *h_2uelh_1-e/o-*,[7] while *vellus* would represent a regular *s*-stem with *e*-grade in the root, i.e. *h_2uelh_1os, with the presumably regular development *$-lh_x$- > *-ll-*.

It is now possible to establish the derivational pattern of the root *h_2uelh_1- 'pluck':

- Thematic verb *h_2uelh_1-e/o- 'to pluck' > Latin *vellō*
- *s*-stem neuter *h_2uelh_1os 'what is plucked' > Latin *vellus* 'fleece'
- *-men*-stem neuter *$h_2uelə_1$-mn̥ (> Armenian *gełmn* 'fleece, wool')[8] →

---

[6] Cf. for the semantics Swedish *sno* 'turn, twist' and 'filch'.

[7] As argued by Schrijver (1991: 180f), it is unlikely that *vellō* originally had a nasal present where *-ll-* would go back to *-ln-* because of the perfect *vellī*, and moreover *vellus* would then have to be secondarily influenced by the verb. Most importantly, a protoform *$h_2uelə_1$-n- from a root ending in a laryngeal would yield *-ln-* rather than *-ll-*, cf. *volnus, vulnus* 'wound' < *$uelə_3no$- from *$uelh_3$- 'strike'.

[8] The translation "Filz" ('felt') given by Fraenkel 1964: 1254 and adduced by Darden (2001: 202) cannot be confirmed by the classical literature or the standard dictionaries of Old Armenian.

- -nah₂-stem collective/feminine (*h₂ulh₁-mn-áh₂ >) *h₂ulh₁-n-áh₂ 'what pertains to the fleece', i.e. 'wool' > Latin *lāna* etc.[9]

Summing up, the Latin verb *vellō* 'pluck' and the cognate noun *vellus* 'fleece', more or less intuitively connected with *lāna* 'wool' by several scholars despite formal difficulties,[10] may after all be considered derivatives of the same root. However, the suggested, otherwise straightforward explanation has the phonological implication that the cluster *-lh₁- yields -ll-, i.e. we seem to be dealing with a "resonant gemination" somewhat similar to the development in Hittite and, according to Lühr 1976, also Germanic.[11]

Despite his lack of a precise reconstruction, it would thus seem that Frisk (II: 117) provided the correct answer: "Das Wort [for 'wool'] gehört wahrscheinlich als Verbalnomen auf -nā („das Ausrupfen, die Ausgerupfte, Raufwolle") zu einem Verb für 'reißen, rupfen', das u. a. in lat. *vellō* 'rupfen' erhalten ist …; hierher auch *vellus* n. 'abgeschorene Wolle'". This suggests that already at the time of the proto-language, the Indo-Europeans must have not only had domesticated sheep, but the later mutation of wool sheep, so that a root meaning 'pluck' would be meaningful.

A transparent semantic parallel is found with the root *peḱ-, where the original meaning is preserved in the Lithuanian verb *pešù* 'pluck, pull out', while Greek *pékō* means 'comb, card', and the derivative *pókos*[12] 'plucking' or 'that which is plucked', i.e. 'sheep's wool, fleece' (cf. e.g. Beekes 2010: 1164); another cognate seems to be Armenian *asr* 'wool', in spite of minor formal uncertainties.[13] It is, however, not considered quite certain that the association of the verbal root with the concept of 'sheep's wool' goes back to the proto-language. Here, the decisive proof would be the widely attested *u*-stem *péḱu, cf. Vedic *páśu*, Avestan *pasu* 'livestock', Latin *pecū* 'flock, herd',[14] Gothic *faíhu* 'livestock, cattle', which is traditionally believed to have assumed the general meaning of 'livestock' from the more specific 'small cattle' or 'wool sheep', probably because sheep were the most common type of livestock, as also suggested by the predominance of sheep in sacrifices from the steppe cultures from the 5th millennium BC (Anthony 2007: 62).

This view was challenged by Benveniste (1969: 47ff) who, based on Indo-Iranian, Latin and Germanic, claimed that the original meaning of *péḱu was simply 'personal mobile wealth' (cf. e.g. Latin *pecū* : *pecūnia* 'property, money'), that the similarity to *peḱ- 'pluck' is quite accidental, and that the underlying identical root of *péḱu remains obscure. A similar opinion is expressed by Mallory-Adams (1997: 23). Still, an etymological connection between the stems of 1) *peḱe/o- 'pluck', 2) the protoform of Greek *pékos/pókos* 'fleece' and 3) *péḱu is much the easiest way to understand such peculiarities as the *u*-stem inflection of Armenian *asr* 'wool' and the formal identity between Greek *pékos* 'fleece' on the one hand, and Latin *pecus, -oris* 'livestock' on the other, both going back to an *s*-stem *péḱos.

From the existence of Hittite *ḫulana-* 'wool' as a derivative of *h₂uelh₁- 'pluck', we have deduced that wool sheep were part of Indo-European culture even before the split between Anatolian and Core Indo-European. If the relation between *peḱ- 'pluck' and *peḱu- 'livestock' holds true, the situation is a little different in so far as the stem *peḱu- is not directly attested in Anatolian. However, in Hittite the sumerogram UDU 'sheep' is commonly written with phonetic complements nom. UDU-*uš*, acc. -*um* which probably stand for *pekku-/*pikku-.[15] *U*-stem inflection is also attested in the complements of the word for 'cow', GUD-*uš*, acc. GUD-*um* (new reading GU₄) which must stand for the continuation of Indo-European *gʷṓus (Vedic *gauḥ*, Latin *bōs* etc.; cf. also Kloekhorst 2008: 507f), and as discussed in detail by Watkins 1979, the phrase NAM.RA GUD (GU₄) UDU is the equivalent of Avestan *pasu vīra* and Umbrian *u(e)iro pequo* (*uih₂ro- 'man' + *peḱu- 'livestock'),[16] with the modification that while the continuations of *péḱu in Core Indo-European may also be applied to cattle/movable wealth in general, there is an explicit distinction in Hittite between 'large cattle, Großvieh' (GU₄(-*uš*)) on the one hand, and 'small cattle, Kleinvieh' (UDU-*uš* = *pekkuš*) on the other. Note, however, that the existence of a Core Indo-European formulaic connection of *uih₂ro- + *peḱu- does not exclude a distinction between large and small cattle, i.e. cows and *peḱu, exactly as in Hittite. Thus the Romans paired *boues* indifferently with *oues* and *pecus* in the meaning 'large and small cattle/cows and sheep' (Watkins 1979: 278), and a similar situation may be argued for Vedic.[17] The natural conclusion to be drawn from this observation is that in Proto-Indo-European, *péḱu originally had the specific meaning 'small cattle', or specifically 'sheep', the 'movable wealth' par excellence, while the extended general meaning 'livestock', sometimes even including

---

[9] Another derivative seems to be the Greek *oũlos* 'woolly, fluffy, frizzy, crinkly' (in the oldest attestations, of woollen fabrics and hair) < *h₂uolh₁no- with loss of the second laryngeal after the -*o*-grade derivative (the so-called "Saussure effect"), cf. Rasmussen 1989: 202.

[10] Cf. Ernout-Meillet 1954: 718: "La caractère de la racine rend malaisé le rapprochement avec *lāna*, tentant pour lui-même"; Walde-Hofmann 1954: 745; IEW 1139.

[11] Cf. examples like *tellus* 'earth' from *telh₂- 'support, carry'; *fel, fellis* 'bile, gall' from *ǵʰelh₃-; perhaps *antecellō, praecellō* 'surpass' < *kelh_x- (Lithuanian *kélti*); *polleō* 'be strong' < *plh₁-eh₁- (root *pleh₁- 'fill'; Olsen 2014). I intend to treat this phenomenon in more detail in another article.

[12] Rarely also a neuter *s*-stem *pékos*.

[13] Cf. Olsen 1999: 202 and forthcoming, and Martirosyan 2010: 122-24, with references.

[14] Also *pecus, -udis* 'head of cattle'.

[15] Cf. Tischler 2001: 558f with references. The name of a scribe, ᴸᵁ*Pikku* (l.c., p. 280), may also belong here.

[16] See Schmitt 1967: 214-16 on this phrase as an element of Indo-European poetic language, and cf. also Weitenberg 1984: 82f and EWAia II: 108f, with references.

[17] The Rigvedic passage (8.41.1) *pasvó gá iva* is usually translated as a gen.sg. + acc.pl.: Jamison & Brereton (II: 1111) "(who guards the insights of the sons) like the cows in a herd"; Geldner (II: 353): "(bewacht) wie (der Hirt) die Herdentiere"; Renou (1959: 72): "comme (on garde) les vaches du (troupeau de) bétail", but it is equally possible to interpret *pasvó* as an acc.pl. in an asyndetic construction, i.e. "as small and large cattle/cows and sheep".

people, and the specific poetic phrase *$u̯ih_xro$- + *$peḱu$- was a Core Indo-European innovation.

Consequently, it still seems reasonable to assume that the original sense of *$peḱu$ was in fact 'plucking (animal)' or the like, and thus, we would have two independent indications for wool sheep as a vital part of Indo-European culture.[18] From a formal point of view, primary neuter u-stems are quite rare, especially as counterparts of transitive verbs such as *$peḱe/o$-. However, two of the most prominent, and at the same time most difficult examples are *h_1osu-/*h_1esu- (?) > Hittite adj. āššu- 'good', neut. subst. āššu- 'good things, goods, possessions' (cf. also Greek adj. eús 'good')[19] and *$h_1u̯osu$-/*$h_1u̯esu$- > Vedic vásu- 'good' and 'goods, wealth', Cuneiform Luvian wasu- 'good', Palaic wāsu- 'goods, wealth'.[20] As is natural in a pastoralist society, the Indo-Europeans counted their wealth in 'mobile' and 'not mobile' goods (Watkins 1979),[21] the mobile component (taken in raids) consisting of humans, and large and small cattle. As we have already seen, this was expressed in Hittite by the phrase NAM.RA GU₄ UDU. Sometimes the collected 'movable wealth' is mentioned in juxtaposition with the 'wealth that is not mobile', e.g. NAM.RA GU₄ UDU (i.e. *$pekkun$) KUR-eaš āššū arḫa ᵁᴿᵁḪattuši uwatenun "deportees, cattle, sheep, goods of the land I brought off to Hattusas" (Puhvel 1984: 200). Hence one might perhaps suggest that the stem formation of *$peḱu$, as the final and most important member of 'movable wealth', was influenced by its u-stem opposite.

2. Flax and linen
Obviously, wool is not the only material fit for spinning and weaving. Plant fibres, in particular flax, were used for the production of textiles several millennia earlier than wool, so the Indo-European vocabulary of textile production[22] does not necessarily apply to wool alone. Nevertheless, it is remarkable that the word for 'flax, linen', in opposition to the widespread and regularly derived word for 'wool', is only attested in a few European branches: Greek línon 'flax, thread; linen' (already Mycenaean ri-no-), Balto-Slavic (Lithuanian lìnas 'flax plant', pl. linaĩ 'flax, linen'), Old Church Slavic adj. lьnъ ⇒ lьněnъ 'linen') and Italic (Latin līnum 'flax, linen' and linteum 'piece of linen, cloth'). The cognates in Albanian (liri 'linen'), Celtic (Old Irish lín 'net', Welsh llin 'flax, linen') and Germanic (Gothic lein 'linen' etc.) may all be borrowed from Latin. At the same time, it is impossible to reconstruct a common Indo-European proto-form, the Greek and Balto-Slavic terms going back to a short-vocalic *$līnom$, while Latin points to either *$līnom$ with a long root vowel or *$lei̯nom$ with a diphthong, and the formation of linteum is formally isolated and unexplained. Most likely, we are dealing with a non-Indo-European cultural loan, and we may deduce that linen was not an integrated part of Proto-Indo-European culture, which is perhaps not all that surprising for a nomadic population.

3. Textile manufacture
The technology of spinning, weaving and sewing has left its trace in a quite extensive specialized vocabulary, but only a few terms go back to the earliest period. The common root for 'weave' is *$(h_1)u̯eb^h$- (or *$(h_1)u̯ebh_1$-; LIV 658), continued in Hittite wep- 'weave', wepa- 'woven fabric'; Tocharian B. wāp- 'weave'; Vedic ubhnáti 'bind';[23] Avestan vaf- 'praise' (from the poetic language), but also adj. ubdaēna- 'of woven fabric'; Greek huphaínō 'weave';[24] Albanian vej; and Germanic (e.g. OHG weban 'weave, plait').[25]

The wide distribution of this root with corresponding meanings within the Indo-European family, including Anatolian, clearly suggests that the Indo-Europeans practiced weaving, but does not tell us how advanced the technology was or whether we are originally dealing with weaving on a simple band-loom or a more advanced type of warp-weighted loom (Mallory-Adams 572f). There is no common word for 'loom', and specific words for 'warp' and 'weft', even when based on inherited elements, seem to be later dialectal formations. Thus e.g. Armenian azbn, Greek ásma 'warp' with the corresponding verb áttomai 'set the warp in the loom' may be derived from a root *h_2at-, continued in Hittite as ḫatt- 'pierce, prick' (cf. van Beek apud Beekes 2010: 167; Olsen 2017), and we may even have a further cognate in Oscan asta, probably 'that which has been carded, pricked out' (Flemestad & Olsen 2017), but still the specialization as a textile term meaning '(set the) warp' may be restricted to the common predecessor of Greek and Armenian.

Another word family related to weaving in Core Indo-European is represented by Latin texō 'weave, plait; join, fix together, build', Vedic tā́ṣṭi 'builds, fashions, makes', Avestan tāšt 'made', Old Church Slavic tesati, Lithuanian tašýti 'hew' and the n-stem noun Vedic tákṣan-, Greek téktōn 'carpenter' (Mycenaean te-to-ko-n-) and Avestan tašan- 'creator'. Usually, the double meaning of 'weaving' and 'building, doing carpentry' is explained as being derived from the concept of wattling in the construction of houses (Mallory & Adams 1997: 139). The more basic

---

[18] Another potentially interesting root is *b^herd^h-, analyzed by Janda (2000) as a collocation of *b^her- + d^hh_1- 'take booty', which may be continued in Armenian burd 'fleece' with the denominative verb brdem 'shear (sheep)', Latin forfex 'shears' (with Sabellic development of internal *-d^h- > -f-) and Umbrian furfa-, perhaps 'shear' (for a different interpretation, cf. Meiser 2013); here the semantic shift from 'harvest (wool)' to 'shear' has followed the advancing technology since shears only became common during the Iron Age. Cf. Olsen 2017 and Flemestad & Olsen 2017 with references.
[19] Cf. Wodtko, Irslinger & Schneider 2008: 239-43 for references and discussion of the paradigm; Kloekhorst 2008: 223-25 for the tentative alternative reconstruction *h_1osh_1u-/*h_1esh_1u- that would account for the Hittite geminate -šš-.
[20] Wodtko, Irslinger & Schneider 2008: 253-58, with references and discussion.
[21] Cf. also the common Hittite word for 'sheep', iyant-, lit. 'going', Greek próbata 'small cattle' (lit. 'going ahead') and Old Norse gangandi fé 'livestock'.
[22] Cf. Mallory-Adams 1997: 206.

[23] Cf. also ūrṇavā́bhi- 'spider', lit. 'wool-weaver'.
[24] The Mycenaean fut.ptc. e-we-pe-se-so-me-na justifies the reconstruction with initial *h_1-, cf. Beekes 2010: 1540.
[25] An unextended root form *$(h_1)eu̯$- is perhaps continued in Vedic váyati 'weave' < *$h_1u̯$-éi̯e- (EWAia I: 276: "*$h_2u̯$-éi̯e-"), ótu- < *$h_1éu̯$-tu- 'the woof of a web'.

meaning of the corresponding Hittite verb *takkešzi*, 3.pl. *takšanzi* 'join' is in itself an argument in favour of an early separation of the Anatolian branch, but additionally one might make the tentative suggestion that the technique of wattling would not belong in an early nomadic society.

Spinning in order to make thread for weaving or plaiting is expressed through various roots whose primary meaning seems to be either 'twist' or 'draw', thus from the root *$sneh_1i$- (LIV 571f): Greek *néō*, Latin *neō* 'spin', Middle Irish *sníid* 'twists, binds', Welsh *nyddu* 'spin', Old High German *nāen* 'sew, stich' with nominal derivatives such as *$sneh_1mn$ > Greek *nēma* 'thread, yarn', Latin *nēmen* 'tissue, fabric' and *$sneh_1$-ti- > Greek *nēsis* 'spinning', Old High German *nāt* 'seam'; similarly, the Armenian verb *niwtʰem* 'spin' is a denominative of *niwtʰ* 'stuff, material' < *$sneh_1tu$- or *$sneh_1tōi$-. From the alternative root *$(s)penh_1$- 'draw, stretch' (LIV 578) we have e.g. Armenian *henum* 'weave, sew together', Gothic *spinnan* 'spin', Lithuanian *pìnti* 'braid'. None of these formations can be traced beyond Core Indo-European.

The same goes for the otherwise well attested root for 'plait': *$plek̂$- (Mallory-Adams 1997: 570), cf. Sanskrit *praśna-* 'braiding', Greek *plékō* 'braid, plait', Latin *plectō* 'braid, interweave', Old English *flehtan* 'braid, plait', though it is of course unthinkable that the Indo-Europeans would have mastered weaving, but not plaiting.

The fact that we have an old specialized root for 'sewing', *$si̯euh_x$- (LIV 545f) whence e.g. Vedic *sīvyati*, Latin *suō*, Gothic *siujan*, Lithuanian *siū́ti* 'sew', with the derivative *$si̯uh_xmn$ > Greek *humḗn* 'membrane, sinew', Vedic *syū́man-* 'band, strap' and perhaps Hittite *šumanza(n)-* '(bul-)rush', is hardly surprising since sewing can be carried out on a wide variety of materials, including felt and skin.[26]

4. Garments

Since primitive weaving started on simple band looms and the production of broader textiles demands larger and more advanced equipment, it is probably not accidental that we are familiar with several inherited words for 'girdle' and 'gird', while other linguistic evidence for specific garments is extremely scarce and generally restricted to a few branches. Thus, Barber (1991: 254) states: "It can hardly be a coincidence ...that the only word for cloth or clothing that can be widely reconstructed for the Indo-European languages is the word for "belt" ..., despite the fact that the textile crafts were sufficiently well-known to the proto-Indo-Europeans that the difference between weaving (*webh-) and plaiting (*plek̂-) was carefully distinguished ... Although argument from silence is hardly strong, the linguistic evidence tallies well in this way with the archaeological evidence. Note, among other things, that we never see the Indo-Europeans using any kind of large loom *other* than that of the various indigenes they end in with, a fact that suggests that they did not learn to weave larger textiles until after the main dispersal of the Indo-European tribes." Barber further comments on the Scandinavian Bronze Age textiles, in that the careful band weaving is opposed to the sloppy weaving of major fabrics, suggesting that the latter was due to a recently learnt technology.

The most widespread Indo-European root for 'girding' and 'girdle' is *$i̯eh_3s$- (Mallory-Adams 223f), continued in Avestan *yāh-* 'belt', *yā̊ŋhaiieiti* 'girds'; Greek *zṓma*, *zṓnē* 'belt', *zṓnnumi* 'gird'; Albanian *n-gjesh* 'gird, fasten on'; Lithuanian *júosta* 'girdle, belt', *júosiu* 'gird, girdle, buckle on (a sword)'; Old Church Slavic *po-jašǫ* 'gird'. However, we can only claim Core Indo-European age for these terms since the root does not seem to be attested in Hittite. Here, we find derivatives of another inherited root *sh_2ei- 'bind' (cf. e.g. Vedic *sinā́ti*) in the verb *išhiya-*, *išhay-* and various nouns such as *išhiyal-* 'bond, band, belt', *išhuz(z)i-* 'band, belt, girdle' (cf. Puhvel 1984: 398ff; Kloekhorst 2008: 391-93). A remarkable piece of evidence for a common cultural feature of at least Core Indo-European, including Tocharian (presumably the second branch to separate, after Anatolian), is the so-called string skirt, famously preserved in two Danish finds, the burial dress of the Egtved girl and a bronze figurine of an acrobatic female dancer from Grevensvænge, but also, in a very similar shape, in the Tarim Basin as part of the dress of the so-called Beauty of Xiaohe: "a string skirt which is an undergarment made out of the waistband with many strings of twisted wool attached to it to cover the pubic region" (Becker 2012: 105). A third, indirect testimony may be the description of Hera's belt, intended for the seduction of Zeus and described as being "crafted with a hundred tassels" (Mallory-Adams 1997: 224).

One Indo-European textile term, however, seems to be even older than the words for 'gird, girdle', going all the way back to the protolanguage including Anatolian. As shown by Watkins (1969), Hittite *wašpa-* 'shroud for the dead' and the basic stem of Latin *vespillō* 'undertaker (for the poorest classes)' go back to an inherited stem *$u̯ospo$- 'shroud'. Watkins himself believed that the underlying root was *$(h_2)u̯es$- 'dress' with a somewhat obscure root extension, but as I have tried to demonstrate elsewhere (Olsen 2016), the derivation is more straightforward if we assume an originally denominal *s*-stem extension of the above-mentioned *$(h_1)u̯ebʰ$- 'weave', i.e. *$(h_1)u̯obʰso$- > *$(h_1)u̯opso$-, dissimilated to *$(h_1)u̯ospo$-. The secondary root *$(h_1)u̯eps$- (/*$(h_1)u̯esp$-) has the modified meaning 'wrap', as also in Greek *ósprion* 'pulse' (German 'Hülsenfrucht') (cf. Janda 2000: 84f and 208ff) and in the word for 'wasp',[27] literally a 'wrapper' (not, as traditionally assumed, a 'weaver', which is semantically unlikely), named for the multilayered construction of a typical wasp's nest. In the

---

[26] As shown by Melchert (2003; cf. also Kloekhorst 2008: 780f), the meaning of the Hittite word is '(bul)rush' rather than 'cord, binding' as previously assumed, but despite Kloekhorst's rejection, the old etymology may still be valid as bulrushes are often used for plaiting, e.g. of baskets or shoes. The contexts seem favourable to this interpretation, e.g. "rushes (or 'a rush') and red wool are braided together".

[27] With and without metathesis in Middle Persian *vaβz*, Old Prussian *wobse*, Old English *wæfs* and *wæsp* and Latin *vespa*.

Old Hittite "Song of Nesa", a dead soldier cries out for his shroud:

"Clothes of Nesa, clothes of Nesa, bind me, bind!

Bring me down (for burial) with my mother – bind me, bind!

Bring me down (for burial) with my *nurse* (?) – bind me, bind!"[28]

Now, the question arises how we are to envisage the shroud and the binding. If the basic root is indeed *$(h_1)ueb^h$-*, the shroud must be of woven material, but if, on the other hand, Barber is correct in assuming that the Indo-Europeans did not know the warp-weighted loom, it can hardly have consisted of a large piece of fabric wrapped tightly around the corpse, unless the cloth was sewn together from narrow bands.[29] Alternatively, we may be dealing with a sort of mummy cloth or swaddling band that was possible to weave on a transportable band loom. Whether the 'binding' relates to the bands themselves or perhaps a plaited cord tied around the woven material is something we can only guess at.[30] At any rate, the scenario is consistent with the bodies found in the cemeteries of the Dnieper-Donets II culture (ca. 4500 BC) where "... the skeletons were heavily contracted at the sides .... This may be indicative of the fact that prior to burial, the dead were tightly bound or swaddled" (Telegin & Potekhina 1989: 129).[31]

5. Conclusion

The present brief sketch, focusing on a selection of lexical elements that can safely be traced back to the proto-language before the separation of Anatolian, seems to be supportive of the theory of an Indo-European homeland in the steppes: the society was characterized by a pastoral economy where sheep – more precisely wool sheep – were a primary source of wealth.[32] And while the Indo-Europeans did master weaving no doubt beside other techniques such as felting and plaiting, a simple band loom was the practical limit of their nomadic lifestyle since "they could not lug a loom around as they followed their sheep through distant pastures" (Barber 2001: 3).

References

Allentoft, Morten E. et al. 2015. Population genomes of Bronze Age Europe. doi: 10.1038/*nature* 14507.

Anthony, D. 2007. *The horse, the wheel, and language: How Bronze-Age riders from the Eurasian steppes shaped the modern world*. Princeton & Oxford: Princeton University Press.

Anthony, D. 2013. Two IE Phylogenies, three PIE migrations, and four kinds of steppe pastoralism. *Journal of Language Relationship* 9, 1-21.

Barber, E.J. 1991. Prehistoric Textiles. *The Development of Cloth in the Neolithic and Bronze Ages with Special Reference to the Aegean*. Princeton University Press.

Barber, E.J. 1999. *The Mummies of Ürümchi*. London: MacMillan.

Barber, E.J. 2001. The Clues in the Clothes. Some Independent Evidence for the Movements of Families. In: Robert Drews (ed.): *Greater Anatolia and the Indo-Hittite Language Family. Papers Presented at a Colloquium Hosted by the University of Richmond, March 18-19, 2000*. Washington D.C.: Journal of Indo-European Studies Monograph Series, Number 38, 1-14.

Becker, Julia. 2012. The Tarim Basin Beauties of Xiaohe and Krorän. In: Victor H. Mair (ed.): The "Silk Roads" in Time and Space: Migrations, Motifs and Materials (= *Sino-Platonic Papers* 228, July 2012), 94-121.

Beekes, Robert S.P. 2010. *Etymological Dictionary of Greek* I-II. Leiden – Boston: Brill.

Beekes, Robert S.P. 2011. *Comparative Indo-European linguistics: An introduction*. 2nd ed. Amsterdam: John Benjamins.

Benveniste, Émile. 1969. *Le vocabulaire des institutions indo-européennes*. 1. économie, parenté, société. Paris: Minuit.

Bouckaert, R., Lemey P., Dunn M., Greenhill, S.J., Alekseyenko, A.v., Drummond, A.J., Gray, R.D., Suchard, M.A: & Aktinson, Q.D. 2012. Mapping the origins and expansion of the Indo-European language family. *Science* 337 (6097), 957-60. doi: 10.1126/science. 1219669.

Chang, W., D. Hall, C. Cathcart & A. Garret. 2015. Ancestry-constrained phylogenetic analysis supports the Indo-European steppe hypothesis. *Language* 91(1), 1-51.

Darden, Bill J. 2001. On the question of the Anatolian origin of Indo-Hittite. In: Robert Drews (ed.): *Greater Anatolia and the Indo-Hitite Language Family. Papers presented at a colloquium hosted by the University of Richmond, March 18-19, 2000*. Washington D.C.: Journal of Indo-European Studies Monographs No. 38, 184-228.

de Vaan, M. 2008. *Etymological Dictionary of Latin and the other Italic Languages*. Leiden – Boston: Brill.

Demoule, Jean-Paul. 2014. *Mais où sont passés les Indo-Européens? Aux origines du Mythe de l'Occident*. Seuil.

Eichner, Heiner. 1974. *Untersuchungen zur hethitischen Deklination*. Erlangen (dissertation).

Ernout, A. & A. Meillet. 1959. *Dictionnaire étymologique de la langue latine. Histoire des mots*. 4. éd. Paris: Klincksieck.

EWAia = Manfred Mayrhofer: *Etymologisches Wörterbuch des Altindoarischen* I-III. Heidelberg: Winter, 1986-2001.

Flemestad, Peder & Birgit Anette Olsen. 2017. Sabellic textile terminology. In: Salvatore Gaspar, Cécile Michel & Marie-Louise Nosch (eds.): Textile Terminologies from the Orient to the Mediterranean and Europe 1000. BC - 1000 AD. Zea E-Books 56. Lincoln Nebraska: University of Nebraska at Lincoln, 210-21.

Fortson, Benjamin W. 2010. *Indo-European language and culture: An introduction*. 2nd ed. Malden, MA: Blackwell.

Fraenkel, Ernst. 1962-65. *Litauisches etymologisches Wörterbuch* I-II. Heidelberg: Carl Winter/Göttingen: Vandenhoeck & Ruprecht.

Frisk, Hjalmar. 1973-79. *Griechisches etymologisches Wörterbuch* I-III. Heidelberg: Winter.

---

[28] Translation by Melchert 1998: 492. For the interpretation of the verb *tiya-* as 'bind' (: Greek *déō*), cf. Melchert (1983: 14). An internal cognate is *tiyamar-* 'cord, string' (Eichner 1974: 57).
[29] Cf. Barber 1999, photo 10 and 11. These bands, however, are plaited, not woven.
[30] Here one may recall the baby mummy found in Chechen whose shroud is tied together with a cord plaited of blue and red wool (Barber 1999, photo 8).
[31] Cf. Olsen 2016. I am grateful to David Anthony for the reference.
[32] As pointed out by Watkins (1979: 287), land tenure is significantly left out.

Geldner, Karl. 1951-57. *Der Rig-Veda aus dem Sanskrit ins Deutsche übersetzt und mit einem laufenden Kommentar versehen*, I-IV. Cambridge, Massachusets: Harvard University Press.

Gimbutas, Marija. 1973. Old Europe c. 7000-3500 BC: The earliest European civilization before the infiltration of the Indo-European peoples. *Journal of Indo-European Studies* 1, 1-21.

Gimbutas. Marija. 1997. *The Kurgan culture and the Indo-Europeanization of Europe: Selected articles from 1952 to 1993*. Washington C.D.: Institute for the Study of Man.

Gray, R.D. & Q.D. Atkinson. 2003. Language-tree divergence times supports the Anatolian theory of Indo-European Origin. *Nature* 426, 2003.

Haak, Wolfgang, I. Lazaridis, N. Patterson, N. Rohland, S. Mallick, B. Llamas, G. Brandt, S. Nordenfelt, E. Harney, K. Stewardson, Q. Fu, A. Mittnick, E. Bánffy, E. Econonmou, M. Francken, S. Friedrich, R.F. Pena, F. Hallgren, V. Khartanovich, A. Khokhlov, M. Kunst, P. Kuznetson, H. Meller, O. Mochalov, V. Moiseyev, N. Nicklisch, S.L. Pichler, R. Risch, M.A.R. Guerra, C. Roth, A. Szécsényi-Nagy, J. Wahl, M. Meyer, J. Krause, D. Brown, D. Anthony, A. Cooper, K.W. Alt & D. Reich. 2015. Massive migration from the steppe was a source for Indo-European languages in Europe. *Nature* doi:10.1038/nature 14317.

Heggarty, Paul. 2006. Interdisciplinary Indiscipline? Can Phylogenetic Methods Meaningfully be Applied to Language Data – and to Dating Language. In: *Phylogenetic Methods and the Prehistory of Languages*, 183-94.

IEW = Julius Pokorny: *Indogermanisches etymologisches Wörterbuch*. Bern: Francke, 1959.

Janda, M. (2000) *Eleusis. Das indogermanische Erbe der Mysterien*. Innsbruck: Innsbrucker Beiträge zur Sprachwissenschaft.

Kloekhorst, Alwin. 2008. *Etymological Dictionary of the Hittite Inherited Lexicon*. Leiden – Boston: Brill.

Kristiansen, Kristian. 2012. The Bronze Age expansion of Indo-European languages: an archaeological model. In: *Becoming European. The transformation of third millennium BC Northern and Western Europe*. Oxford: Oxbow, 165-81.

Kristiansen. K. & T.B. Larsson. 2005. *The Rise of Bronze Age Society. Travels, Transmission and Transformations. Cambridge*: Cambridge University Press.

LIV = *Lexikon der indogermanischen Verben. Die Wurzeln und ihre Primärstammbildungen*. Unter Leitung von Helmut Rix und der Mitarbeit vieler anderer bearbeitet von Martin Kümmel, Thomas Zehnder, Reiner Lipp, Brigitte Schirmer. Zweite, erweiterte und verbesserte Auflage bearbeitet von Martin Kümmel und Helmut Rix. Wiesbaden 2001: Dr. Ludwig Reichert Verlag.

Lühr, Rosemarie. 1976. Germanische Resonantengemination durch Laryngal. *Münchener Studien zur Sprachwissenschaft* 35, 73-92.

Mallory, J.P. 1989. *In search of the Indo-Europeans: Language, archaeology, and myth*. London: Thames and Hudson.

Mallory, J.P. & D.Q. Adams (eds.). 1997. *Encyclopedia of Indo-European Culture*. London & Chicago: Fitzroy Dearborn.

Mallory, J.P. & D.Q. Adams (eds.). 2006. *The Oxford introduction to Proto-Indo-European and the Proto-Indo-European World*. Oxford: Oxford University Press.

Meiser, Gerhard. 1998. *Lateinische Laut- und Formenlehre*. München: C.H. Beck.

Meiser, Gerhard. 2013. Umbrisch *furfant* und *efurfatu*. *Linguarum Varietas* 2, 157-63.

Melchert, H. Craig. 1993. A "New" PIE *men Suffix. *Die Sprache* 29, 1-26.

Melchert, H. Craig. 1998. Poetic Meter and Phrasal Stress in Hittite. In: Jay Jasanoff, H. Craig Melchert & Lisi Oliver (eds.): *Mír Curad. Studies in honor of Calvert Watkins*. Innsbruck: Innsbrucker Beiträge zur Sprachwissenschaft, 483-94.

Melchert, H. Craig. 2003. Hittite nominal stems in *-anzan-*. In: Eva Tichy et al. (eds.): *Indogermanisches Nomen. Akten der Arbeitstagung der Indogermanischen Gesellschaft / Society for IE Studies / Société des Études Indo-Européennes. Freiburg 19. Bis 21. September 2001*. Bremen: Hempen Verlag, 129-39.

Nicholls, Geoff & Russel D. Gray. 2008. Dated ancestral trees from binary traitdata and their application to the diversification of languages. *Journal of the Royal Statistical Society*, Series B 70.545-66.

Olsen, Birgit Anette. 1999. *The Noun in Biblical Armenian. Origin and Word-Formation – with special emphasis on the Indo-European heritage*. Berlin – New York: Mouton de Gruyter.

Olsen, Birgit Anette. 2014. Latin *-ll-* and potential gemination by laryngeal. Handout from *Sound of Indo-European 3*, Opava.

Olsen, Birgit Anette. 2016. Latin *vespillō* 'undertaker' – Calvert Watkins in memoriam. *Journal of Indo-European Studies* 44, 1/2, 92-110.

Olsen, Birgit Anette. 2017. Armenian textile terminology. In: Salvatore Gaspar, Cécile Michel & Marie-Louise Nosch (eds.): *Textile Terminologies from the Orient to the Mediterranean and Europe 1000. BC - 1000 AD*. Zea E-Books 56. Lincoln Nebraska: University of Nebraska at Lincoln, 188-201.

Pereltsvaig, Aysa & Martin W. Lewis. 2015. *The Indo-European Controversy: Facts and Fallacies in Historical Linguistics*. Cambridge: Cambridge University Press.

Puhvel, Jaan. 1984-. *Hittite Etymological Dictionary*. Berlin – New York – Amsterdam: Mouton.

Rasmussen, Jens Elmegård. 1989. *Studien zur Morphophonemik der indogermanischen Grundsprache*. Innsbruck: Innsbrucker Beiträge zur Sprachwissenschaft.

Renfrew, Colin. 1987. *Archaeology and Language. The Puzzle of Indo-European Origins*. London: J. Cape.

Renfrew, Colin. 1999. Time depth, convergence theory and innovation in Proto-Indo-European. *Journal of Indo-European Studies* 27, 257-93.

Renfrew, Colin. 2003. Time depth, convergence theory and innovation in Proto-Indo-European: 'Old Europe' as a PIE linguistic area. In: Alfred Bammesberger and Theo Vennemann (eds.): *Languages in prehistoric Europe*. Heidelberg: Winter, 17-48.

Renou, Louis. 1959. *Études védiques et pāṇinéennes*, V. Paris: E. de Bocard.

The Rigveda. The Earliest Religious Poetry of India I-III. Translated by Stephanie W. Jamison and Joel P. Brereton. Oxford: Oxford University Press, 2014.

Schmitt, Rüdiger. 1967. *Dichtung und Dichtersprache in indogermanischer Zeit*. Wiesbaden: Harrassowitz.

Schrijver, P. 1991. *The Reflexes of the Proto-Indo-European Laryngeals in Latin*. Amsterdam – Atlanta: Rodopi.

Telegin, D.Y. & I.D. Potekhina. 1987. Neolithic Cemeteries and Population in the Dnieper Basin. In J.P. Mallory (ed.): *British Archaeological Reports International Series* 383. Oxford.

Tischler, Johann. 2001. *Hethitisches etymologisches Glossar*. Mit Beiträgen von Günter Neumann und Erich Neu. Teil II, Lieferung 11/12, P. Innsbruck: Innsbrucker Beiträge zur Sprachwissenschaft.

Walde, A. & J.B. Hofmann. 1938-54. *Lateinisches etymologisches Wörterbuch* I-II. 3. Neubearbeitete Auflage. Heidelberg: Winter.

Watkins, Calvert. 1969. A Latin-Hittite Etymology. *Language* 45, 235-47.

Watkins, Calvert. 1979. NAM.RA GUD UDU in Hittite: Indo-European poetic language and the folk taxonomy of wealth. In: Neu, Erich & Wolfgang Meid (eds.): *Hethitisch und Indogermanisch. Vergleichende Studien zur historischen Grammatik und zur dialektgeographischen Stellung der indogermanischen Sprachgruppen Altkleinasiens*. Innsbruck: Innsbrucker Beiträge zur Sprachwissenschaft, 269-87.

Weiss, Michael. 2002. Observations on the South Picene Inscription TE 1 (S. Omero). In: M. Southern (ed.): *Indo-European Perspectives*. Washington D.C.: Journal of Indo-European Studies Monograph No. 43, 351-66.

Weitenberg, J.J.S. 1984. *Die hethitischen u-Stämme*. Amsterdam: Rodopi.

Wodtko, Dagmar, Britta Irslinger & Carolin Schneider. 2008. *Nomina im Indogermanischen Lexikon*. Heidelberg: Winter.

Ancient Witches and Modern Folktales in the Archaeological Records of Northern Italy

Debora Moretti, University of Bristol

Introduction

In Italian witch trial records, there seem to be differences in the nature and perception of the crime of *maleficium*, and also a fundamental distinction in the characterization of the witch. These differences seem to follow a geographical pattern, the witches of the Alps having a more demoniac character. The accusations are filled with references to the use of magic ointments before flying to the sabbat, the sabbat being located on top of a mountain, honouring the devil with the infamous 'kiss', copulation with the devil, and cannibalism, but most importantly, the sin of apostasy. The witch *stricto sensu* (in a strict sense), as we know it, with elements typical of the witchcraft phenomenon in Central Europe, is almost totally absent in the Italian areas south of the Alps where the demoniac character of the witch is almost non-existent.[1] Here, we are dealing more with the witch *lato sensu* (in a broad sense).[2]

This hypothetical dichotomy seems to have survived within the modern Italian language, and especially so in the regional dialects. In the Italian language, there are various words used to denote a woman who practices magic and witchcraft.[3] The three main terms denoting a woman endowed with magical and/or supernatural powers are *fata* (fairy), *maga* (sorceress/female mage) and *strega* (witch). The difference between these three words lies in the levels of benevolence or malevolence with which these powers are used. The majority of regional terms derive from *fata*, *strega* or *maga*, but some are strictly tied to a specific dialect, like the Sardinian *bruixa* (witch), clearly influenced by the Spanish word for witch, *bruja*, and the *Valdostano* (the dialect of Val D'Aosta) *sorché* (witch) from French *sorciére* (sorcerer, sorceress, witch). It is perhaps legitimate to believe that the great variety of regional terms synonymous to *fata*, *maga*, but mostly *strega* in Italy is an indication of the survival of different historical folk traditions connected to the witch.

One of the most historically and ethnographically documented regional terms for a witch, and specifically a witch *stricto sensu*, is the Piedmontese *masca*.[4] The modern *masca* seems to be a relic of not only a linguistic archaism but also an ancient folk tradition, and this paper aims to examine the history of this word and the changes in its meaning through time. The goal of this paper is also to explain the origins of the tradition behind the *masca* and its survival into modern times with a study of the available linguistic, folkloric and archaeological data.[5]

The *masca*

In the dialect of the Piedmont region (North-West Italy), and occasionally in the dialect of Liguria, a *masca* is a witch and a spirit, and also a soul of the dead.

This figure was already attested before and during the Great European Witch-Hunt between 1450 and 1750, and most importantly, is still well documented today in the folk tradition of Piedmont.[6] It is a popular figure, featuring in thousands of early modern and modern folktales, and is nowadays also a tourist attraction presented as the most unique characteristic of the Piedmont region.[7]

It is therefore quite safe to say that this figure has survived unaltered in the collective imaginations of the people of Piedmont for almost six hundred years.

So, who is a *masca*?

At the same time, a *masca* has the character of the witch, both *stricto sensu* and *lato sensu*, and the character of a ghost in the sense of a spirit or soul of a dead person or spirit of a living person, a concept very similar to the Scandinavian (ON) concept of *hug*.[8] More strictly speaking, in the Piedmontese dialect, *masca* means: *strega* (witch), *maliarda* (bewitcher), *maga* (female mage), *saga* (female sage) and *fata* (fairy). The plural form, *masche*,

---

[1] This paper is part of the PhD dissertation 'The Witch and the Shaman: Elements of Paganism and Regional Differences in Italian Witch Trials' defended by the author at the Faculty of Arts of the University of Bristol in the year 2017.
[2] For the concept of *stricto sensu* and *lato sensu*, see B. Beccaria, Inquisizione episcopale e Inquisizione romano-domenicana di fronte alla stregoneria nella Novara post-tridentina (1570-1615), *Novarien* 34 (2005), 170-171.
[3] The regional dialects have many different variations.
[4] M. Centini, *Streghe in Piemonte. Pagine di storia e di mistero* (Turin: Priuli & Verlucca, 2010).
[5] M.Centini, *I segni delle Alpi: Simboli credenze religiosita' miti e Luoghi della Montagna,* (Turin: Priuli & Verlucca, 2014); D. Bosca, *Masche: Voci Luoghi personaggi di un "Piemonte Altro" attarverso ricerche racconti testimonianze autentiche* (Turin: Priuli & Verlucca, 2012); M. Centini, *La Masca. Donna e magia nella tradizione Piemontese,* (Turin: Neos Edizioni, 2012); M. Centini, *Streghe in Piemonte. Pagine di Storia e di mistero* (Turin: Priuli & Verlucca, 2010); M. Andreis: *Le Masche. Il sabba, il Diavolo e le streghe nella tradizione alpina* (Turin: Ananke, 2009); D. Bosca, *Masca ghigna faussa. Il mistero delle streghe Piemontesi dalla Veglia Contadina alla'analisi sociologica* (Turin: Priuli & Verlucca, 2005); M. Centini, *Nascere, vivere e Morire. Magia, medicina, superstizioni e credenze nella tradizione popolare Piemontese* (Turin: Priuli e Verlucca, 2001); M. Centini, *Magia, medicina, superstizioni e credenze nella tradizione popolare Piemontese* (Turin: Priuli e Verlucca, 2001).
[6] 'Furono Spesi cinque fiorini per il rogo che, il 29 gennaio 1462, avvolse un'anonima donna di Vercelli, condannata a morte poiche' riconosciuta colpevole di Stregoneria: "Giovanni Sapino, massarolium (sic) della suddetta comunita' di Vercelli per il rogo di una masca, che fu bruciati da pochi giorni, spese riguardo alle quali chiese (il rimborso) in una lista da lui stesso preparata, il Consiglio approva che se ne paghi l'importo di 5 fiorini"' (Five florins were spent on the fire which, on the 29th of January 1462, burnt a woman from Vercelli, condemned to death because she was found guilty of witchcraft. She was burnt for being a *masca*) Centini, *Magia*, 21; Centini, *Streghe*, 61, 62, 63, 67, 68, 73, 75, 77, 78 and 79.
[7] Bosca, *Masca*, 41.
[8] S. Beneduce, S. De Benedetti and G.R. Morteo, *Spettacolo e spettacolarita' tra Langhe e Roero,* (Cuneo: L'Arciere, 1981), 22; C. Tolley, *Shamanism in Norse Myth and Magic,* Vol. 1 and 2, (Helsinki: Academia Scientiarum Fennica, 2009), 177.

can also have the meaning of *spiriti* (spirits) and *ombre dei morti* (souls of the dead).[9]

In folk tales, there are two types of *masche*: the *masca brava* or *faja*, the good *masca* or fairy, and the *masca putasca*, the bad *masca*.[10] References to the good *masca* are extremely rare.

The *masche* (pl.) have a dual nature, referred to both as real living people and as evil spirits. When depicted as real people, they are presented as next-door neighbour figures (usually people less fortunate than others with physical defects, a bizarre temperament and lacking in social skills), but skilled in spells and incantations.[11]

In their human form, they would acquire powers enabling them to perform black magic by receiving the 'book of command' from the devil himself and learning to use the magic formulae in this book. Having learnt the magic from the book, they would gain the ability to become spirits. Owning the 'book of command' is a privilege, but also a burden. A *masca* would own the book for her entire life and she would not be able to die peacefully unless she had passed it on to another person, who would automatically become a *masca* as well.[12]

There are male *masche* in the folklore tradition, but they are extremely rare. The majority are women, usually old women able to use metamorphosis to transform themselves into animals or beautiful young humans, and with the ability to leave their body while asleep through their mouths in the form of an insect to commit their evil deeds in spirit form.

The reality of the belief in *masche* in everyday rural life in the Piedmont region in the early modern and modern period is proven by very real physical attacks carried out on people known as *masche* by villagers and locals.

The last *masca* (we now know of) to be killed in Piedmont was a woman called Margherita Degaudenzi, known by the nickname of *gattina* (female kitten), from the village of Cervarolo in Valsesia. She was beaten to death by fellow villagers in 1828. She was accused by the entire village of being the cause of the illness of two men and the subsequent death of one of them. The villagers asked her to cease the *maleficium* and save the surviving man, but she refused. After a meeting, the villagers decided that the only way to stop her *maleficium* was to kill her. Two young men carried out the murder and despite a police investigation, the two murderers escaped not only a prison sentence but a criminal charge altogether, because the entire village lied to protect them. In 1946, Don Giuseppe Flori. a priest and then secretary to the Bishop of Alba Luigi Grassi affirmed on national television to

have examined and read a real 'book of command' – a nineteenth-century manuscript written in Latin and belonging to a family known to have had a *masca* among its members.[13]

The reality of the belief in *masche* and the survival of these beliefs into modern times have led to great interest in the academic world, particularly in the study of folklore and social anthropology, from the 1950s onwards.

The *masca* in folklore

The bulk of the legends and tales collected over decades of field surveys represent the rural oral traditions and folk beliefs of pre-industrial Piedmont, and the majority have been collected from oral sources. The majority of the collected testimonies are memorats: personal stories about a supernatural experience told by either the individual or by a third person quoting them. According to Reimund Kvideland and Henning Sehmsdorf:

> Memorats are our most important source for the study of folk belief. They tell about socially accepted supranormal experiences. Wherever we find memorats, we can assume that legends describing the same experience represent actual folk belief in that geographical area.[14]

The main characteristic of the *masca* identified in the memorats of Piedmont, and also of Liguria, are consistent and uniform:

1. In the majority of the tales, the masca is a woman.
2. She is part of the community/village, but lives on the margins of the village and of society. Sometimes, she is a foreigner.
3. She possesses the 'book of command'.
4. She practices black magic, known as *fisica*, and only in extremely rare cases does she help people.
5. She performs her magic at night.
6. She meets other *masche* in isolated places to feast and dance.
7. She can use metamorphosis to change herself into animals or different human beings.
8. She can leave her body and practice her magic in spirit form.
9. She can therefore fly.
10. She is extremely knowledgeable in the use of healing herbs and stones.
11. She fears everything that is holy, but goes to church every Sunday.
12. She is always connected to the spirits of the dead.[15]

Of all the characteristics listed above, those most feared by the people (until very recently) were the use of metamorphosis and the ability of the *masca* to exit her own body in spirit form and harass people as a ghost. These are exactly (minus the sin of apostasy and – strictly

---

[9] Vittorio Sant' Albino, *Gran Dizionario Piemontese-Italiano*, 3rd edition (Turin: L'Artistica Editrice, 2009); GianLuigi Beccaria, *I nomi del mondo. Santi, demoni, folletti e le parole perdute* (Turin: Einaudi 1995), 219-220.
[10] Centini, *Magia*, 26.
[11] Called *fisica*.
[12] Bosca, *Masche*, 76; Centini, *Magia*, 27.

[13] Bosca, *Masche*, 51.
[14] R. Kvideland and H.K. Sehmsdorf, (eds.), *Scandinavian Folk Belief and Legend*, (Oslo: Norwegian University Press, 1988), 20.
[15] Bosca, *Masche*; Basca, *Masca gigna*; Andreis, *Masche*; Centini, *Magia*.

speaking – the pact with the devil) the same characteristics a so-called 'witch' would have been accused of during witches' trials five or six hundred years earlier.[16] The witches tried in Piedmont in the early modern period were in fact women believed to fly across the night sky to join the devil up on a mountain.[17]

Although there are many theories regarding the myth of flying – from an archaic cult of the sun to transcendence from reality and rite of passage – Carlo Ginzburg and Éva Pócs have interpreted these elements and these tales as the remnants of an ancient folkloric substratum characterized by the shamanic elements of pre-Christian Europe.[18]

One of the recurring themes in the folktales of Piedmont is people witnessing the *masche* flying across the sky. Indeed, during ethnographical field research carried out between 1982 and 2007 by researcher Alessandro Norsa, surveying modern folk beliefs in witches, an interviewee from Turin (Piedmont), Mr Arciso Corzetto (born 1924), recalled the local common belief during his youth of how the *masche* would acquire the ability to fly: to be able to move fast and fly, the *masche* would anoint themselves with a serum (called *self* in dialect) which they would preserve in a terracotta jar (called a *tupin*). To be able to keep up a good provision of the ointment, the *masca* in charge would periodically order a junior *masca* to kidnap an infant from its cradle during the night without alerting the parents. The masche would keep the infant alive during the day and then, the following evening, they would take the infant to an isolated place high in the mountains, prepare a fire, and would extract the *self* from the infant with a syringe.[19] Once the infant was 'emptied' of the serum, the *masche* would dump the infant in the fire where it would be burnt to ashes. This was apparently a ritual transmitted for generations from mother to daughter until one day, one of the junior *masche*, perhaps more sensitive than the others, decided to stop this tradition by smashing the *tupin* against a rock. After that day, the *masche*, having nothing to 'feed' on, decided to leave the village.[20]

Another recurring theme described in the ethnographic study is people witnessing an insect, a mouse or other small creature coming out of the *masca*'s mouth while she is fast asleep on a chair, indicating that the spirit of the *masca* is coming out of her body. According to the folk material collected during Norse's survey, an interviewee from Cuneo (Piedmont), Mr Pietro Giusiano (born 1950), recalled a tale of the *masca farfalla* (butterfly) he learned when he was a child. In the village of Melle (Cuneo-Piedmont), it was believed that the local mid-wife was a *masca* who would often travel to her place of birth in France and would change herself into a butterfly to make her journeys quicker.[21]

These type of metamorphoses are quite well known all across the Germanic speaking world (they are also present in the Scandinavian folk tradition as a migratory legend) and seem to be related to the original legend of king Guntram, as told by the Lombard historian Paulus Diaconus in his *Historia Langobardorum* (AD787-796):

> One day, while he was sleeping, watched over by a squire, an animal, a sort of tiny serpent, suddenly came out of the mouth of the Burgundian King Guntram (561-590 – but identified by Diaconus as king of the Franks). It moved towards a nearby brook which it in vain tried to cross. The squire then placed his sword across its banks. The serpent crossed to the other side and disappeared behind a small hill; after a while it retraced its route, slipping back into the mouth of the sleeping man. The King awoke and said that he had dreamt that he had crossed an iron bridge, and then had gone into a mountain where a treasure was kept, and which was in fact found.[22]

This ancient and recurring belief that the soul can abandon the body of a sleeping person in the form of an insect or small animal is considered by modern academics, among them historians Mircea Eliade, Carlo Ginzburg and Éva Pócs, a clear remnant of shamanistic practices based on trance, following the original interpretation of the legend given by Jakob Grimm in his *Deutsche Mythologie* (1835). Carlo Ginzburg in his book - *Ecstasies: Deciphering the Witches Sabbath* – affirms that this belief has to be connected 'to the presence of shamanistic themes in Celtic literary texts'.[23] Considering that the remnants of these shamanistic practices seem to be present all across Europe and that 'Celtic literary texts' is a rather loose and generic interpretation, perhaps it is worth having a closer look at the etymology of our *masca* to see if it is possible to pin-point a more specific geographical or cultural background.

Masca - etymology

Despite its antiquity, the etymology of this word is still quite a mystery. Many are the theories behind its origins: from pre-Roman/Italic *marsicus*, in its feminine form *marsica*, derived from the Marsi tribe of Abruzzo (central

---

[16] Historic Diocesan Archive of Novara (ASDN), XII, 2, 5, *Libri Constitutorum in causis fidei*, Vol 2: 1610-1611, fol. 19r-30r.

[17] B. Beccaria, "Credenze, superstizioni, ritualità nelle valli della Diocesi di Novara fino al XVI e XVII secolo. Dalla Persistenza del paganesimo nell'alto Medioevo alle superstizioni come Relitti dello stesso nel basso Medioevo e nell'epoca moderna." *Società Valsesiana di Cultura*, no. 1 (2004), 125.

[18] W. K. Mahony, "Volo."in *Enciclopedia delle religioni*, Vol. 4, ed. M. Eliade, 666-670. Milan: Marzorati Jaca Book, 1995; B. Malinowski, *Argonauti del pacifico Occidentale. Riti magici e vita quotidiana nella societa' primitiva*, Vol. 1, (Turin : Bollati Boringhieri, 2004), 79, 81 and 83; C. Ginzburg, *Ecstasies: Deciphering the Witches Sabbath*, (Chicago: The University of Chicago Press, 1991); É. Pócs, Between the Living and the Dead, (Budapest: CEU Press, 1999).

[19] From the ethnographical data it is not clear what this serum actually was.

[20] A. Norsa, *Nell'antro della strega: La magia in Italia tra Racconti popolari e ricerca etnografica*, e-book edition: (Pessano: Editrice Liberamente, 2014), loc. 2155.

[21] Norsa, *Antro*, loc. 7707.

[22] Paulus Diaconus Book III: 34 - translated from Italian to English by DM.

[23] Ginzburg, Ecstasies, 139.

Italy) famous for practicing magic;[24] Arabic *masakha* and its substantive *maskh* denoting metamorphosis,[25] to the more probable Germanic origins including Köbler's Indo-European (IE) theory starting from an original **mozgo-* "net", with an evolution of net into mask, and the Proto-Indo-European (PIE) theory advanced by Johannes Hubschmid, which sees the PIE **mask-* with the meaning of "black, sooty" as an easy way to yield the meaning mask.[26]

The earliest account of the word *masca* dates to AD 643. It appears in fact in the edict of the Lombard king Rothari. This was the first written codification of Lombard laws, originally 388 chapters, written in Latin with frequent Lombard words. It is clear that the compilers knew Roman law but drew upon it only for methodology and terminology as 'the document presents Germanic law in its purity derived from oral tradition'.[27]

In clause 197 of the edict we read:

> De criminem nefandum. Si quis mundium de puella libera aut muliere habens eamque strigam, quod est mascam, clamaverit, excepto pater aut frater, ammittat mundium ipsius, ut supra, et illa potestatem habeat vult ad parentes, vult ad curtem regis cum rebus suis propriis se commendare, qui mundium eius in potestatem debeat habere. Et si vir ille negaverit, hoc crimen non dixissit, liceat eum se pureficare et mundium, sicut habuit, habere, si se pureficaverit.[28]

> Of the wicked crime.[29] If he who possesses the *mundium* (guardianship/protection) of a free girl or a woman accuses her of being a witch, that is a *masca*, unless he is her father or her brother, he shall lose her *mundium*, as above (clause 198), and she shall have the right to choose whether she wishes to return to her relatives or to commend herself with her own property to the court of the king, who will then have her *mundium* in his control. If the man denies that he accused her of the crime, let him have the opportunity to clear himself, and if he succeeds he shall have her *mundium* as before.[30]

In clause 376 of the edict we read:

> Nullus presumat aldiam alienam aut ancillam quasi strigam, quem dicunt mascam, occidere, quod christianis mentibus nullatenus credendum est nec possibilem, ut mulier hominem vivum intrinsecus possit comedere. Si quis de cetero talem inlecitam et nefandam rem penetrare presumpserit: si aldiam occiderit, conponat pro statum eius solidos LX, et insuper addat pro culpa solidos centum, medietatem regi et medietatem cuius aldia fuerit. Si autem ancilla fuerit, conponat pro statum eius, ut supra constitutum est, si ministiriales aut rusticana fuerit; et insuper pro culpa solidos LX, medietatem regi et medietatem cuius ancilla fuerit. Si vero iudex huic opus malum penetrare iusserit, ipse de suo proprio pena suprascripta conponat.[31]

> No-one may presume to kill another man's *aldia* or female slave as if she were a witch,[32] which the people call *masca*, because for the Christian mind it is neither credible nor possible that a woman can eat a living man from within. If in the future anyone presumes to perpetrate such an illegal and wicked act, if he kills an *aldia*, he shall pay sixty solidi as compensation according to her status and, in addition, he shall add a hundred solidi for the guilt, half to the king and half to him whose aldia she was; if he kills a female slave instead, he shall pay composition for her status as is provided above according to whether she is a household slave or a field slave (130-136). In addition, he shall pay sixty solidi as compensation for the guilt, half to the king and half to him whose slave she was. If a judge has ordered him to perpetrate this evil act, then the judge shall pay compensation according to the above written penalty from his own property.[33]

From these two clauses, it is perhaps legitimate to assume the existence of a past belief in evil supernatural magic among the Lombard people, a belief which, by the seventh century and after the conversion to Christianity, was no longer credible and acceptable for the governing class. It is obvious that, although Lombard legislators did not believe in witches, the populace did, and accused women of being witches: hence the need for laws and punishments to prevent this. It was therefore a great offence to call a woman a witch, a *masca*, and most of all, it was illegal to kill her based on this accusation.

---

[24] R. Caprini and M. Alinei, QI 503: Sorcière, Witch, Hexe, Bruja, Strega. Carte de motivations, in *ALE*, eds. R. Caprini and M. Alinei, Vol. V, (Rome: Instituto Poligrafico e Zecca dello Stato, 1997), 206, 208; Bosca, *Masca*, 43.

[25] Caprini and Alinei, QI 503, 207.

[26] P. Toschi, *Le origini del teatro Italiano*, Vol. 1, (Turin: Universale Bollati Boringhieri, 1955), 169-170: G. Bonomo, *Caccia alle Streghe: La Credenza nelle Streghe dal sec. XIII al XIX con Particolare Riferimento all'Italia*, Palermo: Palumbo, 1971), 480; G. Köbler, Wörterbuch des althochdeutschen Sprachschatzes, (Paderborn, Munich: Scöning, 1993), 765; Caprini and Alinei, QI 503, 207-208.

[27] Azzara, C. and Gasparri S., *Le Leggi dei Longobardi. Storia, memoria e diritto di un popolo germanico*, (Milan: Editrice la Storia, 1992), 95; S. Gasparri, *La cultura tradizionale dei Longobardi. Struttura tribale e Resistenze pagane*, (Spoleto: Panetto&Petrelli, 1983), 95.

[28] Azzara and Gasparri, *Leggi dei Longobardi*, 56.

[29] Translated by Katherine Fisher Drew as 'On Witchcraft' (1973: 90).

[30] This translation is based on Katherine Fisher Drew's translation (1973, 90) with adjustments made by the author of this paper based on the translation from Latin to Italian done by Gasparri (1992, 57).

[31] Azzara and Gasparri, *Leggi dei Longobardi*, 100.

[32] Katherine Fisher Drew traduced the Latin *strigam* with vampire without giving an explanation (1973, 126). As the Latin word is obviously clear, the translation 'witch' seems to be the most appropriate.

[33] This translation is based on Katherine Fisher Drew's translation (1973, 126-7) with adjustments made by the author of this paper based on the translation from Latin to Italian done by Gasparri (1992, 101).

Another important element clear in the edict is the association of witchcraft with adultery. This strong connection is evident in clause 198:

> De crimen in puella iniectum, qui in alterious mundium est. Si quis puellam aut mulierem, qui in alterious mundium est fornecariam aut histrigam clamaverit et pulsates penitens manefestaverit, per furorem dixissit, tunc praeveat sacramentum cum duodecim sacramentalis suos, quod per furorem ipso nefando crimen dixissit, nam non de certa causa cognavissit. Tunc pro ipso vanum inproperii sermonem, quod non convenerat loqui, conponat solidos vigenti, et amplius non calumnietur, nam si perseveraverit et dixerit, se posse probare, tunc per camphionem causa ipsa, id est per pugnam, ad dei iudicium decernatur. Et si provatum fuerit, illa sit culpabilis, sicut in hoc edictum legitur. Et si ille, qui crimen misit, provare non puoterit wergild ipsius mulieres secundum nationem suam conponere conpellatur.[34]

> Concerning him who accuses the girl in the *mundium* of someone else of having committed an offence. If anyone accuses the girl or free woman in someone else's *mundium* of being a harlot or a witch, and if it is clear that he spoke against her uncontrolled wrath, he may then offer oath with twelve oath-helpers to the effect that he accused her of the offence of witchcraft in wrath and not with any certain knowledge. For making such an unfounded accusation, he shall pay twenty solidi as composition and he shall not be held further liable. But if he perseveres in his charge and says that he can prove it, the case shall be determined by *camfio*, that is, by duel, according to the judgement of God. If he proves his charge by combat, then she shall be guilty and punished as provided in this code [Rothari 189 and 376]. But if he who accused her of the offense is not able to prove it, he shall be compelled to pay as composition an amount equal to the wergild of that woman as determined by the status to which she was born.[35]

In this edict, the word *masca* has the same meaning of the Latin word *striga*. Therefore, like the Latin *strigae*, the *masca* is an evil spirit and devourer of men, with an overall dark sexual connotation.

This connection between adulterous women and witches is present in other Barbaric law codes. In the Burgundian laws (*ca* AD 500), there is a reference to witchcraft in chapter XXXIV/3 – Of divorces:

> Si quis uxorem suam forte dimittere voluerit, et ei pouerit vel unum de his tribas criminibus adprobire, id est, adulteram, maleficam, vel sepulchrorum violaticem (?), dimittendim eam habeat libera potestatem: et judex in eam, sicut (?) debet in criminosam, proferat ex lege sententiam.[36]

> If by chance a man wishes to put away his wife, and is able to prove one of these three crimes against her, that is, adultery, witchcraft, or violation of graves, let him have full right to put her away: and let the judge pronounce the sentence of the law against her, just as should be done against criminal.[37]

In the Burgundian laws, the punishment for adulterous women is also clearly stated:

> Si qua mulier maritum suum, cui legitime juncta est, dimiserit, necetur in luto.[38]

> If any woman leaves (puts aside) her husband to whom she is legally married, let her be smothered in mire.[39]

In the *Lex Salica* (after AD 500), in clause XXXVII, concerning sorcerers, we read:

> He who calls a free woman a witch (*striam* or *meretricem*) and is not able to prove it (*faras* in the Malberg gloss) shall be liable to pay three times twenty-five hundred denarii…[40]

In the later *Lex Salica Karolina* (*ca* AD800) in clause XXXVIII [LXVII] we read:

> If anyone calls a free woman a witch (*striam*) or a harlot (*meretricem*) and cannot prove it, he shall be liable to pay seven thousand denarii…[41]

In the 100-title version of the *Lex Salica*,[42] containing the Malberg glosses, this connection between a prostitute and a witch is even stronger. Here the word *faras* (see above) seems to have the double meaning of night traveller/witch and female vagabond/prostitute, almost seeming to indicate a whore with supernatural or magical connotations.[43]

Moving to England and almost fifty years after Rothari's edict, the word *masca* – with the meaning of spirit/spectre – is used by Aldhelm, Abbot of Malmesbury Abbey and bishop of Sherborne in probably his most famous work, *De Laude Virginitatis*. This treatise on virginity was

---

[34] Azzara and Gasparri, *Leggi dei Longobardi*, 57-58.
[35] K. Fisher Drew, *The Lombard Laws*, (Philadelphia: University of Pennsylvania Press, 1976), 90.
[36] P. Canciani P., 1789, *Barbarum Leges Antiquae Cum Notis et Glossariis*, digital edition (Venice 1789), XXXIV.IV, 22.
[37] K. Fisher Drew, *The Burgundian Code*, (Philadelphia: University of Pennsylvania Press, 1976), 45.
[38] Canciani, *Barbarum*, XXXIV.I., 22.
[39] Fisher Drew *op. cit.*
[40] K. Fisher Drew, *The Laws of the Salian Franks*, (Philadelphia: University of Pennsylvania Press, 1991), 125.
[41] Fisher Drew, Salian Franks, 199.
[42] Generally speaking, the most important versions of *Lex Salica* are the 65-title version (closer to Clovis' issue), the 100-title version (containing the Malberg glosses and also incorporating the Merovingian capitularies of Childebert I, Chlotar I, and Chilperic I), and the 70-title version of Charlemagne (*Lex Salica Karolina*).
[43] H. Tiefenbach, "Malbergisch Faras" in *Historische Sprachforschung/Historical Linguistics* 110.bd, 2H, (1997), 272-280.

written between AD 700 and AD 706 and was later adapted into a shorter poetic version.[44]

The word *masca* - meaning witch and *lamia* - is also used in later documents. Of particular interest is Gervasius of Tilbury's work *Otia Imperalia* - a sort of encyclopaedic assemblage written in 1212 to amuse the Holy Roman emperor Otto IV - in which, among other wonderful things, he describes the behaviour of *lamias*:

> ...ex quibus lamie dicuntur esse mulieres, que noctu domos momentaneo discursu penetrant: dolia relent, cophinos, catinos, et olas perscrutantur, infants a cunis extrahunt, luminaria accendunt, et nonnumquam dormientes affligunt. (Otia Imperialia. III. 85)

> ...Of these, lamias are said to be women who steal into houses by night for a brief raid: they unseal barrels, pry into baskets, pots, and pans, snatch babies from their cradles, light the lamps, and sometimes molest people in their sleep.[45]

It is in Book III. 86 that he explains what *lamias* are:

> Lamias, quas uulgo mascas aut, in Gallica lingua, strias nominant, fisici dicunt nocturnas esse ymaginationes, que ex grossitie humorum animas dormientium turban et pondus faciunt. (Otia Imperialia. III. 88)

> Physicians maintain that lamias, which are popularly known as masks or, in the French language, strias, are simply nocturnal hallucinations which, as a result of a thickening of the humours, disturb people's spirits in their sleep and cause heaviness.[46]

Among other things he tells us that *Lamias* fly great distances at night, have feasts in people's houses, sometimes extract people's bones while dismembering them and put them back in the wrong order that they drink human blood.

Much has been written on Gervasius' marvels, their authenticity and in his belief in them, but as stated by Banks and Binns, it suffices to say that 'like Herodotus, he applied himself to report what was said, whether or not he believed it: hence the immense value of his collection to folklorists'.[47]

So, what we can say about *masca* after reading Rothari's edict and Gervasius' marvels is that the word was not a Latin or French/Gallic term, it was used by the people the edict was written for, was known in a geographical area stretching from south-eastern France to north-western Italy and was in use for at least five hundred and sixty-nine years.

Cardini affirms that the word *masca* comes from low Latin and is related to the spirits of the dead with a similarity to the concept of *lamia*,[48] but in the *Thesaurus Linguae Latinae* we find:

> **Masca-ae**: *faciem habere cristatam* (person with a crested helm, mask), synonymous to Anglo-Saxon *grima* = mask

Masca with the meaning of mask is therefore already attested in Classic Latin, and maybe we could use this as a hypothetical *terminus post quem* for the assimilation of *masca* and *striga*, although the assimilation of *masca*, *lamia* and *larva* had already occurred.[49]

In his studies on the etymology of the Italian *maschera* 'mask', the eminent scholar Paolo Toschi affirms that it derives from the Lombard *masca*, which first and foremost had the meaning of 'evil spirit', similar to the Roman *strigae*, and therefore devourer of men. Toschi affirms that, originally, the Lombard *masca* had the meaning 'a corpse wrapped in a net/mesh, to prevent its coming back', a practice apparently present in some ancient cultures. Later on, *masca* acquired also the meaning of "evil spirit, dark shadow" similar to *lamia* and *larvas*. As proof that the Italian *maschera* derives from *masca*, he refers to *talamasca*, a term attested in Old High German glosses – for instance in the *Capitula presbyteris*, XIV – and in Latin as *thalamasca/dalamasca*, and derived from a combination of *masca* and *thala/dala*, which seems to be connected to the Germanic verbs meaning 'muttering' and 'stammering'. The general broad meaning of *talamasca* seems to be 'a masked person'.[50]

Generally speaking, judging from the Du Cange Glossarium, the Dutch etymological dictionaries from 1923 to 2009, the Germanic etymological dictionaries and the Französisches Etymologisches Wörterbuch,[51] *masca* is translated as *stria*, *larva*, *hexe*, *sorcière*, and derived either from a pre-Gallo/pre-Romance etymon *mask* meaning 'black, to soil, to blacken': hence the Old Occitan *masco*, meaning witch, and surviving in the modern dialects; or from a Germanic etymon related to 'mesh'.[52]

---

[44] Michael Lapidge, James L. Rosier and Neil Wright, *Aldhelm: the poetic work* (Cambridge: Brewer, 1985), 166.
[45] S.E. Banks and J.W. Binns J.W.,(eds. and transl.), *Gervase of Tilbury: Otia Imperialia – Recreation for an Emperor*, (Oxford: Claredon Press, 2002), 719.
[46] Banks and Binns, Otia, 723.
[47] Banks and Binns, Otia, lxii.

[48] F. Cardini, *Radici della Stregoneria: dalla protostoria alla cristianizzazione dell'Europa*, Rimini: Il Cerchio, 2000), 51.
[49] Charles Du Fresne Du Cange, *Glossarium Ad Scriptores Mediae Et Infimae Latinitatis*, Vol. 6, (Osmont, 1762).
[50] Toschi, *Origini del teatro*, 169.
[51] https://apps.atilf.fr/lecteurFEW/index.php/page/view.
[52] F.A. Stoett, *Nederlandsche Spreekwoorden, Spreekwijzen, Uitdrukkingen en Gezegden*, (Zutphen : Thieme, 1991); J. Vercoullie, *Beknopt etymologisch woordenboek der Nederlandsche taal*, ('s-Gravenhage, M. Nijhoff; Gent, Van Rysselberghe & Rombaut,1925); J. Franck, *Etymologisch woordenboek der Nederlandsche taal*, 2nd ed. (The Hague, 1930. Supplemented by C. B. van Haeringen, 1936.); N. van Wijk, *Franck's Etymologisch woordenboek der Nederlandsche taal*, ('s-Gravenhage : M. Nijhoff, 1936); J. de Vries J. de, *Nederlands Etymologisch Woordenboek*, (Leiden : Brill, 1971); P.A.F. van Veen and N. van der Sijs, *Etymologisch Woordenboek*, (Amsterdam : Van Dale 1997/2004); N. van der Sijs, *Chronologisch Woordenboek : de ouderdom en herkomst van onze woorden en betekenissen,*(Amsterdam, Antwerp: Veen, 2002); G.J. van Wyk, *Etimologiewoordeboek van Afrikaans*,

Considering the intriguing Lombard meaning for the word *masca*, 'a dead body wrapped in a net/mesh to prevent its coming back', a look at the etymology of 'mesh' is probably a must.

Mesh seems to derive from the Proto-Indo-European root

1. **mezg-* 'to knit, plait, twist'

Which is reflected in:

2. Proto-Germanic **mask-*

With cognates in:

3. Old High German (*ca* 6th-9th c.) *macs*
4. Old Low German/Old Saxon (*ca* 8th-12th c.) *masca*
5. German (*ca* from 16th c.) *masche*
6. Old English (*ca* 7th – 11th c.) *max* = net
7. Late 14th c. English *masche* = open space in a net
8. Old Norse (*ca* 9th c.) *möskvi*
9. Danish *maske*
10. Swedish *maska*
11. Middle Dutch (1150-1500) *maessce*
12. Dutch (from 1500) *maas*

Obviously, the etymon is rather widespread but is still rather far from the meaning 'dead body wrapped in a net/mesh to prevent its coming back'. Could it be possible that an original word meaning 'mesh', passing through a funeral rite or tradition where certain dead bodies are wrapped in a net, acquired a more sinister connotation of a dark spirit, and subsequently that of a witch? Can this be supported by the historical and archaeological evidence in the specific case of Italy and the Lombard culture?

History and archaeology
In view of the 'Germanic' theory for the etymology of *masca*, a possibility discussed in the previous paragraph, it is perhaps useful to provide an overview of the historical period during which the term may have come to be located culturally and geographically in the northern Alpine regions of Italy for the first time.[53]

In AD 568, led by king Alboin, the Lombards left Pannonia and settled in Italy, which was severely depopulated and devastated after the long Gothic War (535–554) between the Byzantine Empire and the Ostrogothic Kingdom. The Lombards were joined by other peoples – Germanic or otherwise – and their invasion of Italy was almost unopposed.[54]

By AD 572, the entire north of the peninsula except for the Ligurian and Venetian coastal areas belonged to the Lombards. They also formed the Duchies of Tuscany, Spoleto and Benevento.

The Byzantine empire retained control of the Exarchate of Ravenna and the so-called 'Byzantine Corridor' that linked Ravenna to Rome and divided the Lombard Kingdom into two parts: the northern *Langobardia Major* and southern *Langobardia Minor*. The capital of the Kingdom was established in Pavia.

The entire Lombard territory was divided into thirty-six duchies, whose leaders settled in the main cities. The king ruled over them and administered the land through emissaries known as *gastaldi*. This form of subdivision, however, along with the independent instincts of the duchies, deprived the kingdom of unity, and made it weak. It was eventually defeated by the Franks in AD 774, when the papacy called on them for help. Only Benevento, raised to the rank of principality, retained its autonomy until the Norman Conquest in 1076.[55]

When they arrived in Italy, the Lombards were a people in arms led by an aristocracy of knights and a warrior king elected from the ranks of the army. The social structure was based on *farae*, aristocratic military clans. At the head of each was a duke who commanded the *arimanni*, free-men belonging to the aristocratic class and bound to him by ties of kinship. Below them were the semi-free men (the *aldii*), and at the bottom of society were the slaves.

In Italy, the *farae* settled on the land, refusing any intermixing with the extant population, and the characteristics that set them apart from both the Byzantine and the Romans remained unaltered (language, religion – pagan and Arian – militarized social structure). This is well documented by the grave goods of early cemeteries, and also the location – separate but side by side – of the Lombard cemeteries and the Romans.

It is perhaps legitimate to believe that to be able to maintain power over all the Germanic and non-Germanic groups joining them in their descent to Italy, the Lombards gave a special importance to their group identity, which gave validity to their tribal traditions, therefore avoiding any 'mixing' with the locals.[56]

The relationship with the natives was initially difficult and violent, but with time, signs of change manifested themselves, especially after the Lombards converted to Catholicism. They began to integrate with the old Roman elites who gradually accepted their presence. This is also manifest in the archaeological records, with more mixed cemeteries and grave goods.[57]

Stellenbosch [South Africa] : WAT, Buro van die Woordeboek van die Afrikaanse, 2003); M. Philippa, *Etymologisch Woordenboek van het Nederlands*, (Amsterdam: Amsterdam University Press, 2003-2009).
[53] See above.
[54] C. Wickham, *Early Medieval Italy: Central Power and Local Society 400-1000*, (Ann Arbor: The University of Michigan Press, 1989).

[55] Wickham, *Medieval Italy*, 28-63; G. Menis, (ed.), *I Longobardi*, (Milan: Electa, 1990).
[56] A. Melucco Vaccari, *I Longobardi in Italia*, 2nd edition, (Milan: Longanesi, 1988); J.C. Barret, A.P. Fitzpatrick and L. Macinnes, (eds.), *Barbarians and Romans in North-West Europe*, BAR International Series 471 (Oxford: British Archaeological Reports, 1989).
[57] Melucco Vaccaro, *Longobardi*, 96-154.

Indeed, the majority of archaeological data comes from the cemeteries. The Lombard way of settling within ancient Roman villages and towns, and the fact that later Lombard architecture was altered and destroyed over time or has not been explored archaeologically because it is underneath later medieval structures, have caused a paucity of urban archaeological data.

Even the monumental architecture has been lost, destroyed or swallowed up by later rebuilds. The only few surviving examples are mostly churches.

The principal Italian cemeteries contained hundreds of burials laid out in parallel lines. They were generally located on the plains at some distance from the towns, near roads or ancient Roman settlements. In Alpine foothills and other hilly areas, cemeteries consisted of small groups of a few burials, while in towns, isolated tombs were found near houses. As Christianity spread, it became more common to bury the dead in or near churches, which were often founded by the Lombards as funerary chapels.

Although data from the excavation of Lombard settlements and cemeteries in Italy is fragmented and poor, it presents a certain coherence and unity in the typologies of the grave goods (well identified metalworking in the weapons of male burials, precious metalwork in the female burials, and pottery) in the typologies of the burials, domestic structures and settlements in general, almost indicating a well-defined Germanic *koine* separated from the indigenous late Roman one. The two cultures tend to mix towards the end of the Lombard kingdom and this is once again visible in the grave goods.

This Germanic *koine*, although visible in the archaeological data, is not visible enough to allow us to identify specific Germanic or Lombard funerary traditions and rituals.

Paulus Diaconus tells the story of at least one Lombard funerary tradition: as in Pannonia, in Italy too, the grave of one who died far from home was often marked by a pole (*pertica*) surmounted by a dove (Book V: 35), and this custom is immortalized in several place names such as Santo Stefano in Pertica (Cividale del Friuli) and Santa Maria alle Pertiche (Pavia), but there is so far no archaeological evidence of this custom.Going back to the original question: can the archaeological and historical data support the theory that the modern word *masca* is a survival of a Germanic-Lombard linguistic archaism and that it is a folk tradition derived from a specific funerary custom of wrapping the dead, or certain dead, in a net or mesh with the intent of 'pinning them down, keeping them in place'?

In their innovative work on the relationship between wrapping materials, wrapping practices, objects and bodies, Susan Harris and Laurence Douny present a new approach to the concept of wrapping, especially so in archaeological contexts. Starting from the presupposition that wrappings '…may also be perceived as boundaries to create interfaces between objects, subjects and the world … wrapping may make the contents clearer or conceal them to the extent that they cease to exist. To unwrap may reverse these outcomes or create an entirely new state of existence', it is easy to understand the importance of wrapping in funerary contexts.[58]

Wrapping of the dead is a practice well attested in literary sources around the world and archaeologically attested in those countries where favourable weather conditions have permitted the survival of ancient organic materials, like in Egypt, for example.[59] In Europe, because of the fragile nature of the organic materials used for wrapping (textile, leather, wood), and the extremely unfavourable weather conditions, 'archaeological evidence for wrapping is often complex, partial and fragmentary'.[60] The survival of organic material in Europe takes place in very specific conditions: anaerobic conditions – usually when the archaeological context is waterlogged – or when the organic material is in contact with metals.

The importance of 'wrapping' in European funerary traditions has been reevaluated in the light of more recent advancement in the study of textiles in archaeological contexts.[61] The extensive archaeological data gathered, and currently being gathered at the European level from burials dating as far back as the Bronze Age, shows that wrapping of the deceased – either inhumed or cremated – and of some funerary goods belongs to a pan-European funerary tradition chronologically spanning thousands of years. The most remarkable examples come from the Bronze Age barrows of Northern Europe and the Iron Age princely burials of central Europe.[62]

These data give archaeologists and historians the evidence to advance hypotheses on the reasons behind the use of funerary wrappings. If we consider 'the many terms used to describe the act of wrapping … such as to cover; preserve; conserve; to veil; camouflage; transform; to hide; to conceal; to mask; to disguise; and to reveal, highlight, exhibit',[63] what significance can we give to wrapping in funerary contexts? Is the purpose of wrapping to offer the dead or conceal them? Were all these

---

[58] S. Harris and L. Douny, (eds.), *Wrapping and Unwrapping material Culture: Archaeological and Anthropological Perspectives*, Institute of Archaeology Publications (Walnut Creek, California: Left Coast Press, 2014), 16.
[59] Harris and Douny, Wrapping, 21,-23, 36, 79 and 163.
[60] Harris and Douny, Wrapping, 20.
[61] M. Gleba and U. Mannering, (eds.), *Textile and Textile Production in Europe from Pre-history to AD 400*, Oxford: Oxbow Books, 2007); M. Gleba, *Textile Production in Pre-Roman Italy*, (Oxford: Oxbow Books, 2008); K. Randsborg, *Bronze Age Texztiles: Men, Women and Wealth*, (London: Bristol Classical Press, 2011); M. Carroll and J.P Wild (eds.), *Dressing the Dead in Classical Antiquity*, (Stroud: Amberley Publishing, 2012).
[62] Denmark – Muldbjern Man (1365BC) and Germany – Hochdorf Duke (540BC).
[63] J. Banck-Burgess, "Wrapping as an Element of Early Celtic Burial Customs: The Princely Grave from Hochdorf and its Cultural Context." in *Wrapping and Unwrapping material Culture: Archaeological and Anthropological Perspectives*, eds. S. Harris and L. Douny, Institute of Archaeology Publications, (Walnut Creek, California: Left Coast Press, 2014), 147.

layers just there to bury the dead? Did they have a spiritual meaning? Did they represent a conceptual boundary between the living, the dead and the spiritual world? Did they protect the dead or were they meant to protect the living from the dead? Were they supposed to hide the dead away or to make them more visible? Could 'pinning down the body to prevent its coming back' be one aspect of this funerary tradition of wrapping?[64] Despite the advancement in the scientific disciplines related to archaeology, these questions remain unanswered.

Very recently in Italy, there has been an active interest in the natural preservation of organic materials (textile, leather, wood) in contact with metallic objects found in graves, especially so in Lombard graves. The quantity and richness of Lombard grave-goods, in particular metal objects, are the reasons why this very specific type of research is tightly connected – at least in Italy – to Lombard artefacts. Due to the crystallisation and corrosion of metals and the specific conditions inside graves, organic materials in contact with such metals are preserved and visible during the various phases of restorations of metal objects. In the specific case of textiles (animal and vegetable), fragments varying between a few millimetres and few centimetres in length are found attached to belt buckles, shoe buckles, weapons and jewellery. Despite such small dimensions, these have specific characteristics which can identify them as textiles, such as clothing, blankets or funerary shrouds.[65]

A survey of the excavations of the major Italian Lombard cemeteries in connection with the grave goods and organic materials identified carried out for the regions of Lombardy, Piedmont, Friuli Venezia Giulia, Tuscany, Umbria and Puglia, and a survey of the Lombard funerary tradition in Italy, resulted in no data related to a specific funerary ritual involving the use of a net, mesh or any other material to wrap up or pin down – to prevent 'a coming back' – in the Lombard culture of Italy.[66] At present, there is no clear evidence of such a tradition in Italy, or conversely, no evidence has been found yet.[67]

This paucity of archaeological data and the etymological survival of the word *masca* in only a small north-western corner of what was the Lombard kingdom in Italy – while other Lombard words have not only survived in dialects, but have been absorbed into the Italian language – could be an indication that *masca* was after all not a Lombard word, but a loan word from a more ancient language and culture, maybe an earlier Germanic substratum already existing in the area of the northern west Alpine regions by the time the Lombards arrived in Italy.

Generally speaking, the only Germanic or otherwise funerary tradition in Europe featuring the intentional 'pinning down' of the dead present in literary sources and also archaeological data is the tradition of the bog bodies.

---

[64] Toschi, *Origini del teatro*, 169-170.

[65] M. Rottoli and E. Castglioni, "I resti organici dalle sepolture (legni, tessuti e cuoi)", in *Archeologia Medievale a Trezzo sull'Adda*, eds. S. Lusuardi and C. Giostra (Milan: Vita & Pensiero, 2012), 516.

[66] For Lombardy see: E. Roffia, (ed.), La Necropoli Longobarda di Trezzo sull'Adda, *Ricerche di Archeologia Altomedievale e Medievale* 12/13 (1986), 265-274; A. Maspero, "Analisi di reperti tessili." in *Testimonianze archeologiche a S. Stefano di Garlate* (2002), 215-222; A. Mazzucchi, A. Dal Pass and C. Cattaneo, "Bolgare (BG),Via S. Chierico: Necropoli altomedievali." *Soprintendenza per I Beni Archeologici della Lombardia Notiziario* 2003-2005 (2006), 64-72; P.M. De Marchi, "Il mondo funerario: Le necropolis Longobarde in Lombardia." ed. G.P. Brogiolo and A. Chavarria Arnau, *I Longobardi: dalla caduta dell'Impero all'alba dell'Italia*, (Cinisello Balsamico (MI): Silvana Editoriale: 2007), 235-241; P. Chiarini, "Montichiari (BS): Localita' Breda dei Morti." in *Soprintendenza per I Beni Archeologici della Lombardia Notiziario* 2007 (2009), 68-78; C. Giostra, "La fisionomia culturale dei Longobardi in Italia settentrionale: la necropolis di Leno Campo Marchione (Brescia)." in *Archeologia e Storia delle Migrazioni : Europa, Italia, Mediterraneo fra tarda eta' romana e alto medioevo*, ed. C. Ebanista & M. Rotili, (Campobasso: Universita' degli studi del Molise, 2010); M. Rottoli, "Resti tessili e di cuoio dalle guarnizioni di cintura della tomba 1." in Archeologia e storia della Chiesa di San Pietro di Tignale, ed. G.P. Brogiolo, *Documenti di Archeologia* 39 (2012), 65-76; M. Fortunati and E. Garatti, "Fara Olivana (BG): Lotto 2, Necropoli Longobarda." in *Soprintendenza per I Beni Archeologici della Lombardia Notiziario* 2010-2011 (2013), 98-150; G. Bellandi, "Nuove sepolture tardoantiche-altomedievali dall'area del Capitolium." in *Un luogo per gli dei: L'area del Capitolium a Brescia*, ed. F. Rossi (Firenze: All'Insegna de Giglio, 2014), 467-468; For Piedmont see: P. Comba,"Dal tessuto all'abito: moda e acconciature in eta' longobarda." in Presenze Longobarde: Collegno nell'alto medievo, ed. L. Perjrani Baricco, *Ministero per I Beni e le Attivita' Culturali, Soprintendenza per I Beni Archeologici del Piemonte* (2004)128-205; L. Pejrani Baricco, "Il Piemonte tra Ostrogoti e Longobardi." in *I Longobardi: dalla caduta dell'Impero all'alba dell'Italia*, ed. G.P. Brogiolo and A. Chavarria Arnau (Cinisello Balsamico (MI): Silvana Editoriale, 2007), 255-275.; for Friuli Venezia Giulia see: C. Giostra, "Luoghi e segni della morte in eta' Longobarda: Tradizione e transazione nelle pratiche dell'aristocrazia." in Archeologia e societa' tra Tardo Antico e Alto Medioevo, XII Seminario sul tardo antico e l'alto medievo, Padova 2005, *Documenti di Archeologia* 44 (2007), 311-344; For Tuscany see: E. Vaccaro, "Il sepolcreto di eta' longobarda presso la Pescaia nel quadro delle evidenze insediative e funerary tardoantiche e altomedievali nella valle del Bruna." in *Roccastrada e il suo Territorio. Insediamenti, Arte, Storia, Economia*, ed. R. Farinelli and G. Marruchi, (Empoli: Editori dell'Acero, 2005) 21-26; E. Vaccaro, "L'occupazione tardoantica delle grotte di Scoglietto e Spaccasasso nei Monti dell'Uccellina (GR)." in La preistoria nelle grotte del Parco Naturale della Maremma, ed. C. Cavanna, *Atti del Museo di Storia Naturale della Maremma* 22 (2007), 227-242; for Umbria see: C. Rupp., "La necropolis longobarda di Nocera Umbra (loc. Il Portone)." in *Umbria Longobarda: La necropolis di Nocera Umbra nel centenario della scoperta*, ed. Catalogo Mostra,(Comune di Nocera Umbra: Edizioni De Luca,1996), 23-40; for Puglia see: Campese Simone 2003 and for Italian Lombard funerary traditions see: L. Paroli, "Mondo Funerario." in *I Longobardi: dalla caduta dell'Impero all'alba dell'Italia*, ed. G.P. Brogiolo and A. Chavarria Arnau, 203-209. (Cinisello Balsamico (MI): Silvana Editoriale, 2007); C. Giostra, "Goths and Lombards in Italy: the potential of archaeology with respect to ethnocultural identification." in *Post-Classical Archaeologies*, 1 (2011), 7-36; E. Passenti, (ed.), *Necropoli Longobarde in Italia: Indirizzi delle ricerche e nuovi dati*, Atti del Convegno internazionale tenuto presso il Castello del Buonconsiglio di Trento il 26-27-28 settembre 2011 (Trento: Università degli Studi di Trento, 2014).

[67] There are however examples from Northern European Bronze Age and Iron Age burials.

In his *Germania*, Tacitus tells us:

> Licet apud concilium accusare quoque et discrimen captious intendere. Proditores et transfugas arboribus suspendunt, ignavos et imbelles et corpore infames caeno ac palude, iniecta insuper crate, mergunt. Diversitas supplicii illuc respicit, tamquam scelera ostendi oporteat, dum puniuntur, flagitia abscondi (XII)
>
> In the assembly it is allowed to present accusations, and to prosecute capital offences. Punishments vary according to the quality of the crime. Traitors and deserters they hung upon trees. Cowards, and sluggers, and unnatural prostitutes they smother in mud and bogs under a heap of hurdles. Such diversity in their executions has this view, that in punishing of glaring iniquities, it behoves likewise to display them to sight: but effeminacy and pollution must be buried and concealed.[68]

This is of course 'no new theory'. Already in the 1980s a lively discussion raised the possibility that the bog bodies could have been the real archaeological example of the Germanic practice described by Tacitus in the first century AD, but the majority of the academics involved in the discussion dismissed it, dismissing evidence that the same practice is not only mentioned but also incorporated in laws nearly four hundred years later.[69]

We have seen above how this tradition not only continued, but was also recognised as an 'official' type of punishment for adulterous women in Burgundian laws a few centuries after Tacitus. Archaeologically, there is no doubt that some of the bog bodies found in the marshes of Northern Europe were intentionally kept 'in place' by hurdles which survived with the bodies thanks to the preserving agents of the bogs themselves, and there is no doubt that chronologically, this tradition dates back to the Iron Age period, centuries before the writing of the Barbarian law codes.[70]

Considering that the Barbarian laws were the first written codification of ancient tribal laws transmitted orally, it is probably reasonable to think that the tradition of the punishment by drowning in marshes of deviants and 'unnatural prostitutes' survived through time and space, carried to the south of Europe by the Germanic people who settled there.[71]

Conclusions
From the ethnographical, philological, archaeological and historical evidence summarised in this paper, it seems quite clear that the modern Italian *masca* with the meaning of 'witch, dark spirit' is indeed the survival of a linguistic archaism. It also represents the survival of a folk magic tradition belonging to a cultural background developed outside the cultural boundaries of early medieval Italy.

Clearly, more work needs to be done to explain the etymology of *masca*, and this work has to be based on a collaboration between linguists, archaeologists and historians, but despite the lack of certainty regarding the etymon of *masca*, the connection between Tacitus' reference to the punishment of 'unnatural prostitutes', the punishment of adulterous women 'smothered in mire' in the Burgundian laws, and the way of dealing of adultery and witchcraft in the same clauses and sections of the Barbarian laws; the equivalence of witch/whore in the Barbarian laws – well represented for example by the word *faras* – and the implied reference to cannibalism in the Lombard laws, cannot be ignored or dismissed without further study.

Maybe, the ritualised killing of adulterous women could be related to the social significance of funerals in Late Antiquity. In his article regarding the burial evidence of female status and power in the early Merovingian period, Halsall affirms that '…the funeral was thus part of a continuum of public ritual in which the families redefined or confirmed the relationships of power between them…', that is, the funerary ritual was a display of the status of the family and its importance within a specific social group.[72] The ritual killing of an adulterous woman, on the other hand, might have been something to be hushed away. Although the proposition of Professor Morris that 'a burial is part of a funeral, and a funeral is part of a set of rituals by which the living deal with death' stands correct, it is perhaps important to extend it to include the ritual killing of 'anti-social' or 'uncomfortable' people.[73] Perhaps we should consider intentional death as a regulator of social structure and social balance. It is quite obvious that the ritual killing of criminals and adulterous women in bogs or mud and the intentional pinning down of the bodies can be read in a symbolic way: nothing so shameful should be visible! Let us not forget that even in later Medieval and early modern Europe, the attitude of society towards shameful women was quite strong and the association between adulterous women, prostitutes and witches was quite the norm:

> In most traditional studies of medieval history, the image of a woman is confined to the cult of the virgin or the ladies of courtly love, both of which placed women on a pedestal. The witch is, of course, the other extreme of this culture that demonized women and female sexuality. She is the antithetical archetype of the virgin.[74]

---

[68] Tacitus, *A Treatise of the Situation, Customs, and People of Germany*, e-book (M&J Publishing, 2015), loc. 201.
[69] I. Morris, *Death-Ritual and Social Structure in Classical Antiquity*, (Cambridge: Cambridge University Press, 1992), 71.
[70] M. Aldhouse-Green, *Dying for the Gods: Human Sacrifice in Iron Age and Roman Europe*, 2nd edition (Stroud: Tempus, 2002); M. Aldhouse-Green, *Bog Bodies Uncovered: Solving Europe's Ancient Mystery*, digital edition (London: Thames & Hudson, 2015); S. Sanders, *Bodies in the Bog and the Archaeological Imagination*, (Chicago: The University of Chicago Press, 2009).
[71] Gasparri, *Cultura tradizionale*, XXIII.

[72] G. Halsall G., 1996, Female Status and Power in Early Merovingian Central Austrasia: The Burial Evidence, in *Early Medieval Europe* 5:1 (1996), 12.
[73] Morris, *Death-Ritual*, 1.
[74] K. Morris, *Sorceress or Witch? The Image of Gender in Medieval Iceland and Northern Europe*, (Lanham: University Press of America, 1991), 6.

Both the whore and the witch are the symbol of a woman 'out of place', and therefore condemned by society.[75]

Professor Aldhouse-Green concludes the last chapter of one of her books on bog bodies with the affirmation that although not all the bog bodies were victims of human sacrifices, 'sacrificial rites were the main reason for the Iron Age European bog killings'.[76] Could it be that in later times, what originally started as a religious human sacrifice became a social and judicial purging which, hundreds of years later, survived as a confused memory and became the base of legends regarding dark evil spirits devouring men, which were eventually transformed into witch figures like the Italian *masca*? Or does this require a leap of faith a little too wide?

References

Primary sources

Azzara, C. and Gasparri S., Le Leggi dei Longobardi. Storia, memoria e diritto di un popolo germanico, Milan: Editrice la Storia, 1992.

Banks S.E. & Binns J.W., (eds. and transl.), Gervase of Tilbury: Otia Imperialia – Recreation for an Emperor, Oxford: Claredon Press, 2002.

Canciani P., Barbarum Leges Antiquae Cum Notis et Glossariis, digitised edition. Venice, 1789.

Du Fresne Du Cange, C., Glossarium Ad Scriptores Mediae Et Infimae Latinitatis, Vol. 6. Osmont, 1762.

Fisher Drew K., The Lombard Laws, Philadelphia: University of Pennsylvania Press, 1973.

Fisher Drew K., The Burgundian Code, Philadelphia: University of Pennsylvania Press, 1976.

Fisher Drew K., The Laws of the Salian Franks, Philadelphia: University of Pennsylvania Press, 1991.

Französisches Etymologisches Wörterbuch (https://apps.atilf.fr/lecteurFEW/index.php/page/view).

Haeringen C.B. van, Etymologisch woordenboek der Nederlandsche taal, Martinus Nijhoff, Den Haag, 1936.

Historic Diocesan Archive of Novara (ASDN), XII, 2, 5, Libri Constitutorum in causis fidei, Vol 2: 1610-1611, fol. 19r-30r.

Philippa M., Etymologisch Woordenboek van het Nederlands, Amsterdam: Amsterdam University Press, 2003-2009.

Sijs N. van der, Chronologisch Woordenboek : de ouderdom en herkomst van onze woorden en betekenissen, Amsterdam, Antwerp: Veen, 2002.

Stoett F.A., Nederlandsche Spreekwoorden, Spreekwijzen, Uitdrukkingen en Gezegden, Zutphen : Thieme, 1991.

Tacitus, A Treatise of the Situation, Customs, and People of Germany, e-book. M&J Publishing, 2015.

Thesaurus Linguae Latinae, vol. 8, Lipsiae 1936-1966.

Veen P.A.F. van & Sijs N. van der, Etymologisch Woordenboek, Amsterdam : Van Dale 1997/2004.

Vercoullie J., Beknopt etymologisch woordenboek der Nederlandsche taal, 's-Gravenhage, M. Nijhoff; Gent, Van Rysselberghe & Rombaut, 1925.

Vries J. de, Nederlands Etymologisch Woordenboek, Leiden : Brill, 1971.

Zanella A. (ed. and transl.), Paolo Diacono: Storia dei Longobardi, Milan: BUR Rizzoli, 1997.

Wijk N. van, Franck's Etymologisch woordenboek der Nederlandsche taal, 's-Gravenhage : M. Nijhoff, 1936.

Wyk G.J. van, Etimologiewoordeboek van Afrikaans, Stellenbosch [South Africa] : WAT, Buro van die Woordeboek van die Afrikaanse, 2003.

http://etymonline.com

http://etymologiebank.nl

http://www.koeblergerhard.de

www.treccani.it

Secondary sources

Aldhouse-Green M., Dying for the Gods: Human Sacrifice in Iron Age and Roman Europe, Stroud: Tempus, 2001.

Aldhouse-Green M., Bog Bodies Uncovered: Solving Europe's Ancient Mystery, e-book edition. London: Thames & Hudson, 2015.

Andreis, M., Le Masche: I Sabba, il Diavolo e le Streghe nella Tradizione Alpina, Turin: Ananke, 2009.

Banck-Burgess, J., "Wrapping as an Element of Early Celtic Burial Customs: The Princely Grave from Hochdorf and its Cultural Context." in Wrapping and Unwrapping material Culture: Archaeological and Anthropological Perspectives, edited by S. Harris and L. Douny, 147-156, Institute of Archaeology Publications, Walnut Creek, California, Left Coast Press, 2014.

Barbiera I., "Affari di famiglia in eta' longobarda: Aree sepolcrali e corredi nella necropolis di Santo Stefano a Cividale del Friuli." in I Longobardi: dalla caduta dell'Impero all'alba dell'Italia, edited by G.P. Brogiolo and A. Chavarria Arnau, 243-254, Cinisello Balsamico (MI): Silvana Editoriale, 2007.

Barbiera I., "Le trasformazioni dei rituali funerari tra età romana e alto Medioevo." Reti Medievali Rivista 14: 1 (2013), 291-314.

J.C. . Barret, A.P. Fitzpatrick and L. Macinnes, (eds.), Barbarians and Romans in North-West Europe, BAR International Series 471. Oxford: British Archaeological Reports, 1989.

Beccaria, B., "Credenze, superstizioni, ritualità nelle valli della Diocesi di Novara fino al XVI e XVII secolo. Dalla Persistenza del paganesimo nell'alto Medioevo alle superstizioni come Relitti dello stesso nel basso Medievo e nell'epoca moderna." Società Valsesiana di Cultura, no. 1 (2004), 93-140.

Beccaria, B., „Inquisizione episcopale e Inquisizione romano-domenicana di fronte alla stregoneria nella Novara post-tridentina (1570-1615). "Novarien 34 (2005), 165-221.

Beccaria B., "Le leggende walser fonti per un'interpretazione del fenomeno stregonico documentato sulla catena alpina centrale e nordoccidentale in età moderna." Augusta (2010), 66-74.

Beccaria, G.L., I nomi del mondo. Santi, demoni, folletti e le parole perdute, Turin: Einaudi 1995.

Bellandi G., "Nuove sepolture tardoantiche-altomedievali dall'area del Capitolium." in Un luogo per gli dei: L'area del Capitolium a Brescia, edited by F. Rossi, 467-468. Firenze: All'Insegna de Giglio, 2014.

Beneduce, S., S. De Benedetti and G.R. Morteo, Spettacolo e spettacolarita' tra Langhe e Roero, Cuneo: L'Arciere, 1981.

---

[75] P. Skinner, *Women in Medieval Italian Society 500-1200*, (Harlow: Pearson Education, 2001), 62.
[76] Aldhouse-Green, *Bog Bodies*, 3213.

Breda, A., "Montichiari (BS), Monte San Zeno: Necropoli Longobarda e Insediamenti medievali." Soprintendenza per I Beni Archeologici della Lombardia Notiziario 2005 (2007), 74-77.

Breda A., (ed.), Longobardi nel Bresciano: gli Insediamenti di Montichiari, Brescia: Fondazione della citta' di Brescia, 2007.

Bonomo G., Caccia alle Streghe: La Credenza nelle Streghe dal sec. XIII al XIX con Particolare Riferimento all'Italia, Palermo: Palumbo, 1971.

Bosca, D., Masca Ghigna Faussa: Il Mistero delle Streghe Piemontesi dalla Veglia Contadina all'Analisi Sociologica, Turin: Priuli & Verlucca, 2005.

Bosca, D., Masche: Voci Luoghi Personaggi di un "Piemonte Altro" Attraverso Ricerche di Racconti e Testimonianze Autentiche, Turin: Priuli & Verlucca, 2012.

Campese Simone A., "I cimiteri tardoantichi e altomedievali nella Puglia settentrionale. Valle del Basso Ofanto, Tavoliere, Gargano." Archeologia Medievale 35 (2003), 377-381.

Campana S., Francovich R., Vaccaro E., "Il popolamento tardo romano e l'alto medievale nella bassa valle dell'Ombrone: Progetto Carta Archeologica della Provincia di Grosseto." Archeologia Medievale 32 (2005), 463-476.

Caprini, R. and M. Alinei, QI 503: Sorcière, Witch, Hexe, Bruja, Strega. Carte de motivations, in ALE, edited by R. Caprini and M. Alinei, Vol. V, 169-225. Rome: Instituto Poligrafico e Zecca dello Stato, 1997.

Cardini F., Radici della Stregoneria: dalla protostoria alla cristianizzazione dell'Europa, Rimini: Il Cerchio, 2000.

Carroll, M., and J.P Wild (eds.), Dressing the Dead in Classical Antiquity, Stroud: Amberley Publishing, 2012.

Centini, M., Nascere, Vivere, Morire: Magia, medicina, superstizione e credenze nella tradizione popolare Piemontese, Turin: Priuli & Verlucca, 2001.

Centini, M., Magia, medicina, superstizioni e credenze nella tradizione popolare Piemontese, Turin: Priuli e Verlucca, 2001.

Centini, M., Streghe in Piemonte. Pagine di storia e di mistero, Turin: Priuli & Verlucca, 2010.

Centini, M., La Masca. Donna e magia nella tradizione Piemontese, Turin: Neos Edizioni, 2012.

Centini, M. I segni delle Alpi: Simboli credenze religiosita' miti e Luoghi della Montagna, Turin: Priuli & Verlucca, 2014.

Chiarini, P., "Montichiari (BS): Localita' Breda dei Morti." Soprintendenza per I Beni Archeologici della Lombardia Notiziario 2007 (2009), 68-78.

Comba P., "Dal tessuto all'abito: moda e acconciature in eta' longobarda." in Presenze Longobarde: Collegno nell'alto medievo, edited by L. Perjrani Baricco, Ministero per I Beni e le Attivita' Culturali, Soprintendenza per I Beni Archeologici del Piemonte, (2004)128-205.

De Marchi P.M., "Il mondo funerario: Le necropolis Longobarde in Lombardia. " edited by G.P. Brogiolo and A. Chavarria Arnau, I Longobardi: dalla caduta dell'Impero all'alba dell'Italia, 235-241, Cinisello Balsamico (MI): Silvana Editoriale: 2007.

Eliade, M., Miti, sogni e misteri, Milan: Rusconi, 1976.

Everett, N., Literacy and the Law in Lombard Government, Early Medieval Europe 9:1 (2000), 93-127.

Fortunati M. and Garatti E., "Fara Olivana (BG): Lotto 2, Necropoli Longobarda." in Soprintendenza per I Beni Archeologici della Lombardia Notiziario 2010-2011 (2013), 98-150.

Gasparri S., La cultura tradizionale dei Longobardi: Struttura tribale e Resistenze pagane, Spoleto: Panetto&Petrelli, 1983.

Ginzburg C., Ecstasies: Deciphering the Witches Sabbath, Chicago: The University of Chicago Press, 1991.

Giostra C., "Luoghi e segni della morte in eta' Longobarda: Tradizione e transazione nelle pratiche dell'aristocrazia." in Archeologia e societa' tra Tardo Antico e Alto Medievo, XII Seminario sul tardo antico e l'alto medievo, Padova 2005, Documenti di Archeologia 44 (2007), 311-344.

Giostra C., "La fisionomia culturale dei Longobardi in Italia settentrionale: la necropolis di Leno Campo Marchione (Brescia)." in Archeologia e Storia delle Migrazioni: Europa, Italia, Mediterraneo fra tarda eta' romana e alto medievo, edited by C. Ebanista & M. Rotili, Campobasso: Universita' degli studi del Molise, 2010.

Giostra C., Goths and Lombards in Italy: the potential of archaeology with respect to ethnocultural identification, in Post-Classical Archaeologies, 1 (2011), 7-36.

Gleba M. and Mannering U. (eds.), Textile and Textile Production in Europe from Pre-history to AD 400, Oxford: Oxbow Books, 2007.

Gleba M., Textile Production in Pre-Roman Italy, Oxford: Oxbow Books, 2008.

Halsall G., 1996, Female Status and Power in Early Merovingian Central Austrasia: The Burial Evidence, in Early Medieval Europe 5:1 (1996), 1-24.

Harris, S. and L. Douny, (eds.), Wrapping and Unwrapping material Culture: Archaeological and Anthropological Perspectives, Institute of Archaeology Publications. Walnut Creek, California: Left Coast Press, 2014.

Köbler, G., Wörterbuch des althochdeutschen Sprachschatzes, Paderborn, Munich: Scöning, 1993.

Kvideland R. & Sehmsdorf H.K., (eds.), Scandinavian Folk Belief and Legend, Oslo: Norwegian University Press, 1988.

Lapidge, M., James L. Rosier and Neil Wright, Aldhelm: the poetic work, Cambridge: Brewer, 1985.

Mahony, W. K., "Volo." in Enciclopedia delle religioni, edited by M. Eliade, Vol. 4. Milan: Marzorati Jaca Book, 1997.

Malinowski, B., Argonauti del pacifico Occidentale. Riti magici e vita quotidiana nella societa' primitiva, Vol. 1, Turin: Bollati Boringhieri, 2004.

Maspero, A., "Analisi di reperti tessili." in Testimonianze archeologiche a S. Stefano di Garlate (2002), 215-222

Mazzucchi A., A. Dal Passo and C. Cattaneo, "Bolgare (BG), Via S. Chierico: Necropoli altomedievali." Soprintendenza per I Beni Archeologici della Lombardia Notiziario 2003-2005 (2006), 64-72.

Melucco Vaccari A., I Longobardi in Italia, Milan: Longanesi, 1988.

Menis G., (ed.), I Longobardi, Milan: Electa, 1990.

Morris I., Death-Ritual and Social Structure in Classical Antiquity, Cambridge: Cambridge University Press, 1992.

Morris K., Sorceress or Witch? The Image of Gender in Medieval Iceland and Northern Europe, Lanham: University Press of America, 1991.

Norsa A., Nell'antro della strega: La magia in Italia tra Racconti popolari e ricerca etnografica, e-book edition. Pessano: Editrice Liberamente, 2014.

Paroli L., "Mondo Funerario." in I Longobardi: dalla caduta dell'Impero all'alba dell'Italia, edeted by G.P. Brogiolo and A. Chavarria Arnau, 203-209. Cinisello Balsamico (MI): Silvana Editoriale, 2007.

Passenti E., (ed.), Necropoli Longobarde in Italia: Indirizzi delle ricerche e nuovi dati, Atti del Convegno internazionale tenuto presso il Castello del Buonconsiglio di Trento il 26-27-28 settembre 2011. Trento: Università degli Studi di Trento, 2014.

Pejrani Baricco L., "Il Piemonte tra Ostrogoti e Longobardi." in I Longobardi: dalla caduta dell'Impero all'alba dell'Italia, ededed by G.P. Brogiolo and A. Chavarria Arnau, 255-275. Cinisello Balsamico (MI): Silvana Editoriale, 2007.

Pócs, E., Between the Living and the Dead, Budapest: CEU Press, 1999.

Randsborg, K., Bronze Age Texztiles: Men, Women and Wealth, London: Bristol Classical Press, 2011.

Roffia, E. (ed.), La Necropoli Longobarda di Trezzo sull'Adda, Ricerche di Archeologia Altomedievale e Medievale 12/13 (1986), 265-274.

Rottoli M., "Resti tessili e di cuoio dalle guarnizioni di cintura della tomba 1." in Archeologia e storia della Chiesa di San Pietro di Tignale, edited by G.P. Brogiolo, Documenti di Archeologia 39 (2012), 65-76.

Rottoli M., Castglioni E., "I resti organici dalle sepolture (legni, tessuti e cuoi)." in Archeologia Medievale a Trezzo sull'Adda, ededed by S. Lusuardi and C. Giostra, 308-320. Milan: Vita & Pensiero, 2012.

Rupp C., "La necropolis longobarda di Nocera Umbra (loc. Il Portone)." in Umbria Longobarda: La necropolis di Nocera Umbra nel centenario della scoperta, edited by Catalogo Mostra, 23-40. Comune di Nocera Umbra: Edizioni De Luca, 1996.

Sanders K., Bodies in the Bog and the Archaeological Imagination, Chicago: The University of Chicago Press, 2009.

Sant' Albino, V., Gran Dizionario Piemontese-Italiano, 3rd edition. Turin: L'Artistica Editrice, 2009.

Skinner P., Women in Medieval Italian Society 500-1200, Harlow: Pearson Education, 2001.

Tiefenbach H., Malbergisch Faras, in Historische Sprachforschung/Historical Linguistics 110.bd, 2H (1997), 272-280.

Tolley C., Shamanism in Norse Myth and Magic, Vol. 1 and 2. Helsinki: Academia Scientiarum Fennica, 2009.

Toschi P., Le origini del teatro Italiano, Vol. 1, Turin: Universale Bollati Boringhieri, 1955.

Vaccaro E., "Il sepolcreto di eta' longobarda presso la Pescaia nel quadro delle evidence insediative e funerary tardoantiche e altomedievali nella valle del Bruna." in Roccastrada e il suo Territorio. Insediamenti, Arte, Storia, Economia, edited by R. Farinelli and G. Marruchi, 21-26. Empoli: Editori dell'Acero, 2005.

Vaccaro, E., "L'occupazione tardoantica delle grotte di Scoglietto e Spaccasasso nei Monti dell'Uccellina (GR)." in La preistoria nelle grotte del Parco Naturale della Maremma, edited by C. Cavanna, Atti del Museo di Storia Naturale della Maremma 22 (2007), 227-242.

Wickham C., Early Medieval Italy: Central Power and Local Society 400-1000, Ann Arbor: University of Michigan Press, 1989.

Related Titles

N-TAG TEN
Proceedings of the 10th Nordic TAG conference at Stiklestad, Norway 2009
Edited by Ragnhild Berge, Marek E. Jasinski and Kalle Sognnes

Oxford, BAR Publishing, 2012   BAR International Series **2399**

**II Jornadas Predoctorales en Estudios de la Antigüedad y de la Edad Media.
Κτῆμα ἐς αἰεὶ: el texto como herramienta común para estudiar el pasado**
*Proceedings of the Second Postgraduate Conference in Studies of Antiquity and Middle Ages,
Universitat Autònoma de Barcelona, 19–21st November 2014*
Edited by N. Olaya Montero, M. Montoza Coca, A. Aguilera Felipe and R. Gómez Guiu

Oxford, BAR Publishing, 2015   BAR International Series **2775**

For more information, or to purchase these titles, please visit **www.barpublishing.com**

www.ingramcontent.com/pod-product-compliance
Lightning Source LLC
Chambersburg PA
CBHW061547010526
44114CB00027B/2956